H

No Five Fingers Are Alike

No Five Fingers Are Alike

Cognitive Amplifiers in Social Context

Joseph C. Berland

Harvard University Press
Cambridge, Massachusetts, and London, England   1982

Library of Congress Cataloging in Publication Data

Berland, Joseph C.
  No five fingers are alike.

    Bibliography: p.
    Includes index.
      1. Qalandar (Pakistani people)—Psychology.
2. Cognition and culture—Pakistan.   I. Title.
DS380.Q35B47   305.8′914   81-7154
ISBN 0-674-62540-4   AACR2

To my ancestors
with respect

To Virginia, Kelsay, and John
with love

To the Qalandar
with gratitude

Foreword
by Michael Cole

It has been roughly a hundred years since scholars concerned with the nature of human nature began to fashion the elaborate division of labor that has resulted in the modern social sciences. E. B. Tylor, "the father of anthropology," believed that the cultures of the world were "apt subject" for the study of human thinking. Yet little of enduring value is to be found on this topic in his writings. Wilhelm Wundt, who was also interested in culture and thought, wrote volumes on the language, folklore, and beliefs of primitive peoples in what he called *Volkerpsychologie* (roughly, the psychology of folk). However, this work has fallen into almost total obscurity. Instead Wundt is remembered for founding one of the first experimental psychology laboratories in 1879. Wundt's "new psychology" sought to eliminate from the laboratory all influence of cultural experience as an essential step toward isolating the basic contents of consciousness produced by highly controlled, precisely measured, meaningless stimuli.

In later generations the methods and concepts elaborated by these two men produced a set of contrasting categories that still dominates scholarly efforts to understand culture and cognition. In lists headed by the disciplinary labels we find:

Anthropology	*Psychology*
study of humankind	study of the mind
content of thought	process of thinking
field studies	laboratory studies
observational techniques	experimental techniques

At the end of the nineteenth century there was more than enough justification for the division of labor that generated this set of contrasts. Anthropologists were racing to describe the basic features of as many as possible of the world's societies before they disappeared under the onslaught of industrialized development. Psychologists, on the other hand, were seeking to resolve the important disputes about human thought processes that had grown out of Darwin's revolutionary claims about human phylogeny, long-standing philosophical debates about the sources of human knowledge, and the data from accounts of the behavior of primitive peoples. Their desire to build a scientific basis for the study of the human mind is certainly understandable, even if their hopes were unduly optimistic.

Whatever the justifications, the separation between studies of culture and of mind has been a continuing source of dissatisfaction among some social scientists. For one thing, there have always been grave doubts that totally *individual* psychological processes, except perhaps in the area of psychophysics, could ever be isolated in the laboratory; it may be easier to ignore culture in the laboratory than to exclude it. There has also been an enduring interest in the apparently wide variety of cognitive skills manifested in people growing up under widely different cultural circumstances. This line of inquiry took on special urgency following World War II, when fundamental education was declared a human right, and modern education was viewed as the only road to economic and political salvation for people of the Third World.

Whether out of intellectual curiosity or applied concern, a relatively small number of psychologists and anthropologists, some working as early as the turn of the century, have borrowed each other's concepts and methods in attempts to carry out cross-disciplinary, cross-cultural studies of human thinking. This line of work has always been a risky intellectual business. Having struggled to construct rules of evidence and plausible inference to define their areas of expertise, social scientists look with suspicion upon those who cross their carefully constructed frontiers. In the no-man's land between disciplines, the all-other-things-equal assumptions upon which psychological methods are based lose their plausibility. In constructing analyzable task environments, the psychologist violates the anthropological dictum that the observer must report on native activities in terms consistent with the natives' own categories of understanding. It requires special circumstances and exceptional knowledge of another culture to warrant importing psychological tasks from one culture to another.

It is precisely in these ways that Joseph Berland's study of South

Asian nomads and entertainers is unique among cross-cultural studies of cognition. Berland, an anthropologist by training, has spent several years living among the people he describes. This familiarity already sets him apart from most psychologists, like myself, who have limited time to spend among the people they study. Even more remarkable is the appropriateness of the people chosen for this research. The Qalandar offer a special opportunity to overcome obstacles posed by alien test procedures, because their cultural traditions and world view encompass the very theory and methods that Berland wanted to use! In fact, as we quickly discover, the Qalandar sophistication in testing people and in being tested to determine intellectual competence is sufficient to tax the researcher's ingenuity. Like the people who won his admiration in this research, Berland knows how to live by his wits. He judiciously mixes anthropological observation and psychological experimentation. He permits the setting to guide his choice of method and his knowledge of the overall cultural context to constrain his interpretation. His work will provide an important model for those of us who, like Tylor long ago, believe that the study of culture can shed light on the nature of human thinking.

Acknowledgments

This book is based on field research in Pakistan between January 1971 and May 1973, and follow-up studies in 1979 and 1980. The initial study was funded by the United States National Institute of Mental Health in support of my dissertation research at the University of Hawaii at Manoa, Honolulu. The subsequent field trips were made possible through Fulbright-Hays (C.I.E.S.) awards.

This volume would not have been possible without the support of many people. John Zubek and George von Bekesy, having patiently trained me in sensory psychology, encouraged my interest in the influence of experience in naturalistic environments on patterns of human sensorimotor and perceptual performance. In organizing my material, I received sound counsel and guidance from Stephan Boggs, Alice Dewey, Thomas Maretzki, Katherine Luomala, Ronald Johnson, and Jagdish Sharma at the University of Hawaii. I also received encouragement from several of my former colleagues at Northwestern University, notably Ethel Albert, Edward T. Hall, Francis L. K. Hsu, Robert Launay, and Stuart Struever. I would not have been able to complete the statistical analyses without the generous assistance of Timothy Liston and Donald T. Campbell. Two of my former students at Northwestern, Emet Schneiderman and Elizabeth Addison, contributed the map and the drawings. Laura Distelheim and Mary B. Fulcher edited original drafts of the chapters dealing with peripatetic social organization. I am also indebted to Andrea Dubnick and Neil Steinberg for typing several drafts of the manuscript.

I am particularly grateful to Herman Witkin and Michael Cole for their generous counsel and advice on writing the book. I am especially obliged and honored that Michael Cole has contributed the foreword to this volume. I also appreciate Professor Piaget's sending me his 1964 paper explicating his position on the role of experience in cognitive development and John Berry's drawing my attention to the correspondence between his notion of cultural aids and my cognitive amplifier construct. At Harvard University Press I am grateful to Eric Wanner and Elyse Topalian for their patient encouragement and guidance through several revisions of the manuscript, and to Peg Anderson for her herculean patience and perceptive editing skills. In the day-to-day contexts in which this book was written, I owe the most gratitude to my dear friend and wife, Virginia Sawyer Priest Berland.

I am indebted to many people in Pakistan. The project would not have been possible without the cooperation of the Ministry of Education and the Ministry for Home and Kashmir Affairs. I am especially grateful to Dr. Mahammad Ajmal for sponsoring the original research. During subsequent visits I received generous encouragement and support from Dr. Mohammad Rauf, Dr. A. H. Dani, and Dr. S. H. Hashmi at Quaid-I-Azam University, as well as Robert d'Arcy Shaw, director of Ford Foundation in Pakistan. The United States Education Foundation in Islamabad was instrumental in helping my family settle in and adjust to life in Pakistan. My travels with peripatetic artisans and entertainers throughout Pakistan were made possible by the cooperation of the Pakistan Armed Forces and Provincial Police. My special thanks to D. S. P. Turner in Lahore for his spirit of understanding and cooperation.

In conducting the field research, I am greatly indebted to my research assistants and translators. Mahmud Ahmad (deceased), A. B. Shabana, and Shaida Haq risked their lives, health, and reputations in rendering invaluable assistance. My appreciation is monumental, and my debt to them is lifelong. To those villagers and Lahoria who participated in the study, I extend my sincerest thanks.

Certainly my greatest debt is to the khānābādōsh in Pakistan, especially the Qalandar and Kanjar. My special thanks to Hussain Buksh (deceased), Baba Surf Din, Padja, Korshada, and Allah Ditta for opening their tents to me. Without their initial gesture and subsequent adoption of this investigator into their *biradari,* survival in the world of peripatetic artisans and entertainers might not have been possible. Indeed, without the trust and acceptance of the Qalandar, my presence and endless questions would have resulted in my demise some night when I was sleeping soundly. My debt to them can never be repaid; my appreciation, like my hookah, will always be open to them.

Contents

You cannot step twice into the same river, for other waters
are constantly flowing on.
—Heraclitus

Panjun unglian baraber nahee handyan.
No five fingers are alike.
—Qalandar maxim

Introduction

Snake charmers, bards, acrobats, magicians, trainers of performing animals, tinkers, smiths, and other nomadic artisans and entertainers have long been colorful elements of complex societies. Their structurally flexible and organizationally fluid social systems are based on highly specialized individual skills and spatial mobility. The milieu of these peripatetic craftsmen and entertainers sharply contrasts with the more rigid social systems of sedentary peasants and traditional urban dwellers. This study is concerned with cognitive socialization among peripatetic artisans and entertainers and, in contrast, among sedentary rural and urban dwellers in Pakistan and how experience in each ecocultural setting contributes to basic perceptual habits and skills.

Zeitgeist

My purpose in this book, drawing on four years' (1971–1973 and 1979–1980) participant observation of cognitive socialization among peripatetic and sedentary groups in Pakistan, is threefold. My primary purpose is to demonstrate that intensive ethnographic description of perceptual-cognitive activities in naturalistic contexts can greatly contribute to our understanding of how socially organized experience shapes the ontogeny of psychological functions. Secondly, I present a detailed ethnography of cognitive experience and skills in order to interpret patterns of variabilty in levels of psychological performance both within and between these groups from the perspective of ordinary, day-to-day subsistence-related activities. Finally, I examine the role of context and experience in Piaget's and Witkin's developmental theories of cognitive ontogeny in contrasting milieus.

The past three decades have witnessed a growing concern in the social and behavioral sciences for greater "ecological" or "cultural" validity of claims about the role of experience and context in determining patterns of psychological functioning. An increasing number of investigators in cross-cultural perception and cognitive development research have echoed Cole and Scribner's call for "more precise characterizations of the cognitive demands of nonexperimental situations" (1977:367). By focusing attention on context and experience, such studies have served to sharpen distinctions between competing paradigms in perceptual and cognitive development. At the theoretical level, ecocultural validity emphasizes the contrast between *constructivist, cognitive mapping,* or *central processor* orientations characteristic of investigators such as Piaget and Witkin and the *ecological* or *situational-deterministic* approaches championed by J. J. Gibson (1966, 1979), Neisser (1979), and Cole and his collaborators at the Laboratory of Comparative Human Cognition (1979, 1981). In keeping with a methodological tradition which may be traced to Brunswik's (1943) and Lewin's (1943) early discussions regarding ecological validity and representative design in experimental cognitive research, contemporary investigators are increasingly concerned with the relationship between experience in natural, day-to-day activities and patterns of psychological performance in laboratory contexts (see, for example, Bronfenbrenner 1977; Cole, Hood, and McDermott 1978; and Neisser 1976). Whether we are interested in "situating the experiment" (Scribner 1976) in "naturalistic settings" or in making the laboratory more like everyday contexts of psychological performance, our knowledge of the material and social composition of these ecocultural milieus must be enhanced.

This study is presented as a logical next step for experimental as well as naturalistic investigations of psychological functioning. In an effort to bridge these traditionally disparate domains, my methodological orientation is in the direction established by W. H. R. Rivers (1905), Meyer Fortes (1938), Egon Brunswik (1956), Roger G. Barker (1968), Thomas Gladwin (1970), and Michael Cole (Cole et al. 1971). Consequently, the format of this volume may be disconcerting for "tough-minded" as well as "tender-minded" readers, in that extensive psychological test data are combined with intensive, often anecdotal, ethnographic descriptions of the social and ecocultural contexts of psychological performance. This type of analysis is necessary, especially if we keep in mind Earl Count's (1958) reminder that "organism-environment interactions are biosocially mediated." We must also remain sensitive to J. J. Gibson's more recent admonition: "It is not true 'that the laboratory can never be like life.' The laboratory *must* be like life" (1979:3). Going a step further, we should remember that the laboratory, as a performance context, is inextricably embedded within the larger social system and represents only one of many ecocultural settings of psychological functioning—as such, it is life.

Ortgeist

In the daily routine of my three years with the Qalandar, nomadic entertainers in Pakistan, I found the hours in the evening between supper and sleep to be the most interesting and enjoyable. During this period the nomads would frequently gather about a fire in front of a tent, discuss daily events, and reminisce. Sitting shoulder to shoulder, with infants on laps and small children sitting in front, they would smoke, sharing hookahs and cigarettes, while relating individual or group activities. Poking in the fire or dust with sticks to add color or emphasis, some would recount their search for grass for their donkeys; others would describe their encounters while begging door to door or in the marketplace. Adults and children who had performed well would often recount their strategy for the benefit and pleasure of the listeners. Specific markets, streets, neighborhoods, even specific households would be analyzed as contexts for begging activities, and each strategy assessed in terms of actual performance and success in extracting cash or other payment. There would be reports of forthcoming weddings and other special celebrations at which they might perform and admonitions about garrulous guards or police. Some would describe an audience's response to their performing bears, monkeys, and goats. More experienced animal handlers would discuss experiences and skills related to particular routines and how "old" or "forgotten" activities might be revived, modified, and incorporated into current activities. Specific animals would be evaluated in terms of their level of training and experience, and new ideas and recommendations would be critically assessed. New routines or innovations would be tried in actual practice sessions the next morning when animal handlers took advantage of the cool hours following dawn to sharpen their performance routines.

Discussions of animal training frequently generated evaluations of children's learning skills as jugglers, acrobats, and magicians. A child would be called upon to perform a particular routine before the group, with more experienced members offering support and criticism of the child's manipulations. Frequently, to add levity, those who worked as impersonators would take special pleasure in recounting the response of the individual being fooled. Disguises would be discussed, accents evaluated, and the gait, posture, and other characteristics of the social group being impersonated assessed. This would often lead to lengthy accounts of how the response of individuals from different cultural groups varied, depending on their economic status, marital status, and age, as well as on the season, social context, and other conditions the Qalandar recognized as important in determining how and why people behave as they do.

Such discussions would often lead older members of the group to recall experiences from other places and other times. The British were nostalgically remembered, their affluence and generosity praised, their compassion and gullibility regarding hungry children and animals marveled about. The British would then be compared with other foreigners, and these in turn compared with Punjabis, Sindhis, Pathans, or Multanis. Villagers would be compared with urban dwellers, and rich compared with poor. Individual performance, material culture, and other characteristics would be discussed in accounts which were both humorous and serious.

Although I had anticipated their intercultural awareness to some degree, I was impressed early in my fieldwork with the fact that the subjects of my investigation were extremely curious and knowledgeable about the very phenomena I was there to investigate among them—the nature of individual and group differences in behavior. From experience in my own culture and in previous research among sedentary populations in the Pacific and Asia, I had observed stereotyped humor, knowledge, and curiosity about other people, but never to the extent that I found expressed among these nomadic entertainers. In preparing my research, I had intellectually assumed a relationship between intercultural awareness and the success of nomads before I fully comprehended that diversity and skillfulness in interpersonal as well as intercultural perception are basic behavioral skills characteristic of this type of subsistence strategy. Where groups such as hunters and some seafaring peoples must be skilled in identifying and organizing a wide range of perceptual cues, such as the horizon, clouds, wind, stars, sounds, and tracks, the professional entertainer must be particularly sensitive to perceptual and social cues from an audience. Certainly these peripatetic performers recognized that flexible social skills across a wide range of ecocultural contexts were as

vital to their survival as individual mastery of the numerous perceptual-motor activities associated with their entertainment routines.

A brief summary of an observation sequence from my field notes illustrates the variable sociocultural milieu within which an individual
Qalandar entertainer acquires and utilizes experience and skills on a
daily basis. Early in my fieldwork I observed from a distance a five-
year-old boy, Raja, working alone in a public market as a beggar. His
strategy of impersonating a poor, hungry orphan who was totally dependent on his target's generosity was reasonably successful. During
the two hours he circulated throughout the market, he approached
numerous individuals and started his well-rehearsed litany of desper-
ate need.The majority brushed past him, many verbally abusing him
as a "dirty animal" and telling him to get away. Several struck or
kicked him; a teenage boy accompanying an older female spit on him
after giving a single coin. A fruit vendor gave a bunch of bananas, and
a well-dressed, middle-aged male propositioned him for fellatio. Only a
half dozen people—five older females and an old man—gave him
cash.

Later in the morning, but before the heat of the day, Raja abandoned his begging activities and started back toward camp, stopping at
a roadside vendor's stall to purchase a bottle of 7-Up and a cigarette,
which he enjoyed in the shade at the side of the road. I joined Raja at
this point and, as the two of us walked the seven kilometers back to
camp, he patiently helped me with the difficult phonetic characteristics of his language. Inside the camp he tossed the hand of bananas to
his mother, then went over to a group of adults and children observing
a goat being trained to perform a balancing routine. That afternoon I
observed Raja curled up in his mother's sister's lap nursing at her
breast and being comforted during a bout of high fever associated with
his chronic malaria. He slept through supper that evening but later
aggressively participated in obscene, sexual joking with adults and
children gathered in front of a tent. Later, after checking to see if the
family animals were securely tied for the night, he gathered up his
restless infant sister and gently rocked her to sleep in his cradled arms
while singing lullabies. The following morning he worked steadily
with his father practicing a dangerous routine with a 300-pound Asian
brown bear. After the wind was knocked out of him from an unex-
pected swipe of the bear's paw, Raja, with tears in his eyes, gathered
himself up out of the dust and, gasping for breath, returned to his father and the bear. They successfully completed the performance then
secured the animal inside their tent to protect him from the sun. Raja,
his father, and two older women who had been watching the training

session sat together, sharing a cigarette while all participated in a critique of the performance routine. When the conversation turned to other matters, Raja, knowing that his tent was moving to another region the next morning, excused himself and briefly searched the camp for a companion with whom to renew his begging activities. Finding none, Raja shuffled off toward the city, conscious that the tear stains on his dust-covered cheeks would enhance his credibility as a "poor, hungry orphan" dependent on the generosity of strangers for his survival.

Participating in the day-to-day activities of these peripatetic entertainers, I became increasingly sensitized to the diverse contexts in which people acquired, practiced, and analyzed the experiences and skills associated with survival within the larger social system of Pakistan. In contrast to the more reflective, analytical atmosphere of the evening campfire, the daily round of activities is a busy stream of energy related to their subsistence strategies. Individuals flow through camp while groups of adults and children engage in instructional activities associated with their performances. Evening sessions around the fire serve numerous social functions; it is an expression of group solidarity of the tents traveling together as well as an opportunity for amusement. Equally important, however, is that these intergenerational groups provide supportive contexts for analysis of the socioecological niches in which each person acquires and utilizes psychological experience and skills.

For my study, the ecocultural milieu of the Qalandar emphasized a range of socially situated opportunities, experiences, and skills which contrasted with those of the more sedentary populations in Pakistan. Indeed, the very fact of their historical survival as peripatetic specialists *within* a larger social system indicated differences in the psychological experiences and skills available in each cultural domain.

Cognitive Amplifiers in Psychological Performance

In shifting from observation of psychological performance in the daily round of naturally occurring activities to comparative analysis and interpretation of the data, I found that traditional anthropological and psychological constructs seemed inadequate. For example, Western-oriented classifications of enculturation domains into discrete areas, such as "work," "school," "play," "family," and the like, tend to be ethnocentric, especially insensitive to the *interpersonal* nature of the cultural milieu. This is particularly the case in the highly fluid social milieu of peripatetic groups. Equally confusing, if not cross-culturally invalid, to me and my Qalandar informants were popular Western notions like "independence," "dependence," "nurturant," and "aggressive," as relatively static characterizations of "individual" psychological functioning across contexts. When examined against the ethnographic record of an individual's day-to-day activities, such "personality attributes" are situationally sensitive and variable throughout the lifespan. Similarly, explanatory constructs such as "culture," "environment," or "biology"—as macro-independent variables—are coarse and incomplete for interpreting the role of environmental or experience factors per se in patterns of individual psychological performance. In this study quantitative as well as qualitative variation in the everyday milieu of intellectual activities called for a new construct. Diverse contexts of psychological functioning demand a broad theoretical concept which is flexible yet sensitive to the relationship among ecology, social structure, interpersonal experience, and individual patterns of perceptual-cognitive performance through a broad spectrum of socially embedded settings—hence the term, *cognitive amplifiers*.

Outside the laboratory and other structured contexts of psychological assessment, the ethnographic record should serve to remind us that all societies are composed of individuals, embedded within larger ecocultural systems. Each of these groups may be viewed as having a relatively "unique" *curriculum* of interpersonal, perceptual-motor, and cognitive activities provided by a variety of lifelong socialization processes through participation in numerous socially embedded contexts. These experiences and skills, as cognitive amplifiers, are expressed as individual patterns of psychological performance. As such, they amplify or promote continuity and variability in psychological functioning both within and across groups.

By emphasizing the role of socially situated experience and skills in perceptual-cognitive performance, the notion of cognitive amplifiers begs the question of intellectual capacities as either inherent or exclusive attributes of individual psychological functioning per se. As used throughout this volume, the term *cognitive amplifiers* includes the consideration of ecocultural variables in psychological activities. More importantly, the construct stresses that *individual patterns of experience and skills are temporally embedded and manifested in social mediated contexts*. The reader is asked to keep in mind that my major purpose in this book is not to present the notion of cognitive amplifiers as a *cause célèbre* for future cross-cultural psychological research. Rather, as an ethnographer in the less familiar psychologist's camp, my overall objective is to explicate cognitive amplifiers as they are manifested in day-to-day activities in natural settings. I hope that this record will promote further understanding of the role of interpersonal processes and experience in determining patterns of psychological functioning.

The book is organized in three parts. Part One establishes the research problem in terms of previous intercultural research that links patterns of psychological performance to experiences in particular ecocultural settings. This part begins with a brief historical and theoretical overview of previous investigations concerned with the influence of culture on perception from Rivers's (1905) early efforts through the contemporary experimental anthropology approach of Cole and his collaborators (Cole et al. 1971). The emphasis in Chapter 1 is on research pertinent to interpretation of Piaget's and Witkin's theories of cognitive development in other cultures. Here the focus is on the role of ecology and cultural experience in perceptual inference habits. Chapter 2 establishes the notion of cognitive amplifiers by stressing the socially mediated and contextually embedded nature of individual experience and skills, and the construct is examined in terms of the interrelationship between ecological and cultural factors in determining patterns of psychological functioning. The basic theoretical assumptions guiding the research are summarized in formal hypotheses at the beginning of Chapter 3. This chapter introduces the various ecocultural settings in Pakistan where I conducted my research as well as the groups selected for study. Included also is a detailed description of the research methods and materials used to assess patterns of perceptual inference habits.

Part Two is a behavioral ethnography of the nomadic Qalandar. Most of the ethnographic research on perceptual-cognitive activities and skills was conducted within this group. Chapter 7 includes a brief description and rationale for the comparison groups, which include the Kanjar (peripatetic artisans), rural villagers (agriculturists), and Lahoria (traditional shopkeepers and small merchants living in Lahore).

Part Three presents the results obtained from each of the four sample groups on systematic measures of psychological functioning, which are interpreted in terms of everyday experience and skills in the diverse ecocultural systems. Chapter 8 is a relatively conservative and straightforward presentation of the results on tasks of perceptual inference habits and Piagetian measures of conservation of continuous quantities. In a departure from tradition, I interpret the results through an emic–etic model derived from Qalandar assumptions and predictions about experience, skills, and context in determining patterns of psychological performance. Chapter 9 reassesses the concept of cognitive amplifiers within the perspective of the total study, with implications for current investigations emphasizing contextual relativism and perceptual skills approaches to psychological functioning. Analyses of variance, correlation matrices, and test descriptions are included in Appendixes 1, 2, and 3, respectively.

I used several languages in this study, primarily Urdu, Punjabi, and Qalandari. I have tried not to burden the reader with innumerable non-English terms; however, where appropriate some have been included. Unless otherwise indicated, I have used Roman Urdu, following Platts' (1884) classic *Dictionary of Urdu, Classical Hindi and English*.

A word on my general use of the term culture is in order. Throughout, I have tried to follow Raymond Firth's distinction between society and culture: "If society is taken to be an aggregate of social relations, then culture is the content of those relations. Society emphasizes the human component, the aggregate of people and the relations between them. Culture emphasizes the component of accumulated resources, immaterial as well as material, which the people inherit, employ, transmute, add to, and transmit" (1951:27). Because this study emphasized the interrelationship among people, resources, and larger social and bioenvironmental systems, I have frequently linked the culture, society and ecology concepts into a relational construct, *ecoculture*. Throughout, it should be kept in mind that each society is composed of numerous ecocultural settings which are socially organized. At the same time, each ecocultural system, or society, is embedded within the wider social and ecological systems of a particular culture area such as South and Southwest Asia.

In trying to arrive at a compromise among the leading theories of perception and cognition, I have emphasized perception as an ongoing activity involving experience and skills by which individuals are aware of their internal as well as external environments. By focusing on psychological activities in diverse ecocultural settings, our attention should be directed toward interpretations of individual performance in terms of organism–environment interactions. Thus, where previous cross-cultural studies of cognitive development have tempered their generalizations through a cultural relativism paradigm, my approach directs attention toward a contextually relativistic theory of psychological performance.

I

The Problem in Context

1

Theoretical Setting

The nature of the relationship among environment, experience, and behavioral variation is one of the oldest and most enduring issues in man's efforts to understand human behavior. Apocryphal, supernatural, and religious explanations must be as old as our species, and they continue in the ethnophilosophical systems of the majority of mankind. Although naturalistic and phenomenalistic explanations of the relationship predominate, systematic and empirical investigations relating behavioral variation to differences in environment and experience predate modern experimental psychology. Well over a thousand years before the founding of the Leipzig Laboratory or publication of Wundt's *Volkerpsychologie* (1916), Plutarch recounted the experiments of Licurges: "a Spartan, demonstrating the importance of environment by raising two puppies from the same litter so that one became a good hunter while the other preferred food from a plate" (Skinner 1966:1209). However, it was not until late in the nineteenth century that investigations into the influence of culture on basic perceptual processes began in earnest.[1]

Historical Antecedents

In response to Darwin's theory of evolution, investigators in Great Britain turned their attentions toward the evolution of "mental" abilities in animals and humans. The founder of this new experimental psychology was Sir Francis Galton, whose *Hereditary Genius* (1869) and *Inquiries into Human Faculty and its Development* (1883) represent the beginning of a systematic study of individual psychology and the nature of human differences. Galton's investigations pioneered the mental-testing movement that is so popular today, and his efforts in measuring human mental resources in Great Britain generated the first impetus for cross-cultural assessment of basic sensory and perceptual processes. Following Galton's lead in *English Men of Science* (1887) that measures of sensory and perceptual discrimination were indicative of judgment and intelligence, the Cambridge anthropologist A. C. Haddon asked the St. John's psychologists Rivers, Myers, and McDougall to join his 1898 expedition to the Torres Straits to assess Melanesian sensory and perceptual capacities. A result of this first cooperative effort between psychology and anthropology was the discovery that Melanesians did not markedly differ from Victorian Britons in basic perceptual skills (Boring 1950).

Following a visit to India in 1902 to collect further comparative data on visual acuity, Rivers concluded that "there is no great difference in visual acuity between savage or barbarous and civilized races, though the balance may be slightly on the side of the former" (1905:325). In accounting for this variation, Rivers concluded that the cultural and environmental milieu of "primitives" emphasizes or reinforces for attention to minute details. This sensory emphasis, Rivers hypothesized, was due to primitives being more concrete in their cognitive skills than Europeans:

> Minute distinctions of this sort are only possible if the attention is predominantly devoted to objects of sense, and I think there can be little doubt that such exclusive attention is a distinct hindrance to higher mental development. We know that the growth of intellect depends on material which is furnished by the senses, and it therefore at first sight may appear strange that elaboration of the sensory side of mental life should be a hindrance to intellectual development. But on further consideration I think there is nothing unnatural in such a fact. If too much energy is expended on the sensory foundations, it is natural that the intellectual superstructure should suffer. It seems possible also that the over-development of the sensory side of mental life may help to account for another characteristic of the savage mind. There is, I think, little doubt that the uncivilized man does not take the same aesthetic interest in nature which is found among civilized peoples ... Experience is strongly in favour of the view that the predominant attention of

the savage to concrete things around him may act as an obstacle to higher mental development. (Rivers 1905:44–45)

Rivers' hypothesized concrete–abstract continuum in cognitive functioning between primitive man and civilized man set the *Zeitgeist* for cross-cultural research on human perceptual and cognitive variation. Where Rivers concentrated on basic sensory and perceptual variation across cultures, Franz Boas picked up the concrete–abstract theme and addressed this psychological variation between primitive and civilized people as a function of the specific cultural milieu in which it develops. Boas argued that the major characteristics differentiating man from other species is "the possession of language . . . use of tools, and the power of reasoning" (1911:96–97). Human variations in "reasoning" or cognitive processes, he concluded, are products of different cultural content in the culture-learning process:

> The first impression gained from a study of the beliefs of primitive man is that while the perceptions of his senses are excellent, his power of logical interpretation seems to be deficient. I think it can be shown that the reason for this fact is not founded on any fundamental peculiarity of the mind of primitive man, but lies, rather in the character of the traditional ideas with which each new perception associates itself. The difference in the mode of thought of primitive man and that of civilized man seems to consist largely in *the difference of character of the traditional material with which the new perception associates itself.* When a new experience enters the mind of primitive man, the same process which we observe among civilized man brings about an entirely different series of associations, and therefore results in a different type of explanation. (Boas 1911:202–203, emphasis added)

For Boas, human variation in perceptual and cognitive skills was a matter of cultural content rather than of a basic difference in process. Like Rivers, Boas attributed differences between primitive and civilized man to the primitives' greater emphasis on concrete as opposed to abstract and intellectual thought.

Wundt in 1916 approached cross-cultural variation from a different perspective, but he concurred with Boas that "the intellectual endowment of primitive man is in itself approximately equal to that of civilized man. Primitive man merely exercises his ability in a more restricted field; his horizon is essentially narrower because of his contentment under these limitations" (quoted by Berry and Dasen 1974:10). Boas and Wundt echo Rivers' earlier contention that perceptual and cognitive processes may be attributed to environmental and cultural contexts.

In the half century following Rivers' early work, the cross-cultural study of perceptual-cognitive activities was neglected by behaviorist and dynamic or psychologically oriented investigators. From the 1930s through the early 1960s, the laboratory descriptive-experimental approach of Rivers and Wundt in psychology gave way to two distinct traditions in perceptual-cognitive research. In psychology as well as anthropology, the *tender-minded*, clinically oriented "culture and personality" school was characterized by the work of Dubois (1944), Kardiner (1939), Benedict (1934), and their collaborators.[2] Although Margaret Mead attempted to test Piagetian theory against the cross-cultural enculturation record as early as 1932, and Ruth Benedict (1938) examined the influence of variable experiences associated with discontinuous childrearing activities across cultures, these comparative studies were couched in terms of character or personality theories.

The more *tough-minded* approaches of the behaviorists became entrenched in experimental-laboratory investigations emphasizing single-variable designs. Until the past two decades, behavioral approaches have tenaciously adhered to Mill's Canons of Inference in a research orientation reminiscent of Dashiell's (1931) and Underwood's (1957) admonitions for experimental manipulation in stimulus-oriented research: "The essence of a scientific experiment on any phenomena is to control all the conditions (so far as possible) keeping all constant but one. Then to vary that one to observe what other phenomena change with it (as cause of effect or co-effect). This logic will underlie all your experiments" (Dashiell 1931:1).

Environment and Perception

Despite calls for "environmental relevance" in psychological research in the mid-1930s (Tolman and Brunswik 1935), studies concerned with the socioecological validity of experimental results were neglected until the early 1960s. Following Brunswik's (1955, 1956) call for representative design emphasizing the "mutual interrelationship" of organisms and environments, a few studies began to focus on what Brunswik termed the "texture of the environment" and the "ecological validity" of experimental findings. Thus, in a period dominated by laboratory-experimental investigations of nativistic versus empiricistic theories regarding perception, Allport and Pettigrew's (1957) pioneering efforts to explain optical illusions among the Zulus may be seen as a turning point in intercultural research. A decade later this trend toward comparative cross-cultural investigation of cultural experiences in visual perception was firmly established by Segall, Campbell, and Herskovitz (1963, 1966).

Since Rivers' (1901, 1905) pioneering observation that Englishmen were more susceptible to the Muller-Lyer visual illusion than Todas or Murray Islanders, there have been scattered reports supporting his empirical-functionalist interpretation relating visual inference habits to experience in different settings. Noting that Europeans live in more "carpentered" environments, Rivers interpreted levels of susceptibility to visual illusion as "differences in direction of attention" related to variable experience in visual ecology. Following Rivers and acknowledging the influence of Brunswik's emphasis on the "mutual interrelationship between organisms and environments," Segall, Campbell, and Herskovitz (1963, 1966), in an extensive cross-cultural study of perceptual inference habits, demonstrated that subjects in carpentered settings were indeed more susceptible to visual illusions than individuals in less carpentered environments. Like Rivers, in interpreting their findings regarding the role of cultural experience in perception, these investigators posited the "carpentered world hypothesis," a model explaining variability in visual inference habits in terms of the relative frequency of carpentered features in the visual environment.

Reflecting the greater influence of the two psychologists, Campbell and Segall, compared to anthropologist Herskovitz, the carpentered world hypothesis emphasized the interaction between organisms and the physical environment rather than the mutual interrelationships of individuals in the total social ecology of psychological functioning and performance. During this period, behaviorally oriented ethnographers continued to be preoccupied with personality theory, ignoring the broad theoretical and methodological implications of the carpentered world hypothesis for bridging the psychologist's and anthropologist's common concern with the influence of cultural experiences on psychological functioning. Segall, Campbell, and Herskovitz (1966) suggested that a variety of cultural experiences, including those relating to technological activities, might contribute to visual inference habits. However, subsequent cross-cultural studies by psychologists slavishly focused on assessing physical attributes such as frequency measures of horizontal, vertical, or orthogonal dimensionality in the macro-psychophysical environment. Through cross-cultural sampling of visual ecologies, studies with results comparable to those reported by Segall, Campbell, and Herskovitz have been interpreted as support for the carpentered world hypothesis. Excellent reviews of cross-environmental investigations linking experience in visual ecologies to optical illusion susceptibility are available in Stewart (1973), Dawson et al. (1974), Bornstein (1975), Serpell (1976), and Deregowski (1980).

Although most previous studies have contributed to the validity of ecological explanations for perceptual inference habits, several studies, notably those of Pollack (1970), Berry (1971c), and Jahoda (1971, 1975), have related optical illusion susceptibility (Muller-Lyer) to physiological factors associated with retinal pigmentation, which are in turn correlated with skin pigmentation and human adaptations to variable bioecological environments. Both the biological and ecocultural evidence have been submitted as single-factor explanations of optical illusion susceptibility. However, it should be noted that these variables are interrelated, and both factors are influenced by ecological, social, cultural, and historical processes within and across the intercultural milieu. By limiting "contexts of variable experiences" to biophysical settings of sensory-perceptual activities, these studies ignore socioecological factors which quantitatively and qualitatively contribute to variable patterns of individual access to, as well as levels of experience with, the total ecocultural contexts of psychological activities.

Socioecological Perspectives

Implicit in Brunswik's notion of "representative design" and explicit in Count's (1958) explication of the vertebrate biogram is the recognition that the relationship between an individual and its environment is socially mediated. Although social, organizational, and enculturation processes have figured largely in cross-cultural investigations of personality, these factors, as well as such cognitive activities as memory and attention, have been essentially ignored as mediating processes in patterns of perceptual or cognitive performance. Until recently studies of cognitive activities have largely been confined to laboratory settings or computer-simulated models of intellectual activities in which psychological phenomena such as information processing were treated as internal representations practically independent of the eco-cultural context of performance.[3]

Ecocultural Contexts of Sensorimotor Activities

Where previous investigations documented the presence or absence of quantitative differences in perceptual functioning, current re-search had begun to focus on the temporal nature of intellective activi-ties and how the ontogeny of psychological performance corresponds with enculturation processes and variability in ecocultural domains of behavior acquisition. National as well as intercultural studies of per-ceptual development continue to focus on the visual system. While the majority of studies have concentrated on measurements of optical illu-sions, investigations of three-dimensional and pictorial depth percep-tion (Hudson 1967; Deregowski 1971, 1972a; Jahoda and McGurk 1974) as well as cross-cultural studies of spatial orientation have begun to expand the experiential base of perceptual habits (Dere-gowski 1968, 1972b; Serpell 1971a; Goodnow et al. 1976). The role of experience in the ontogeny of attention as a mediating process in vis-ual inference habits has been examined by Kagan (1970) and his col-laborators, notably Sellers et al. (1972) and Finley, Kagan, and Layne (1972). These studies indicate that experience with the elements composing the contexts of psychological functioning as well as famil-iarity with the materials (naturally occurring or introduced) related to perceptual-cognitive activities and skills influence perceptual perform-ance.

Intercultural investigations of experience in the development and manifestation of other sensory modalities and their accompanying per-ceptual processes have received much less comparative ethnographic attention. A promising line of multimodality perceptual development research involving biological, social, and ecocultural factors in the on-togeny of attention has been generated by Klein (1972; Klein et al. 1975). Using comparative studies of infants and children in Cen-tral America, Klein and his collaborators have substantively linked bioecological, especially nutritional, factors and cultural experiences to attentional processes which influence sensorimotor as well as perceptual-cognitive performance. Such bioecological approaches to perceptual development are important because they clearly link cross-cultural cognitive psychological approaches to an abundant and rap-idly growing body of research in intercultural child development. In turn, these interrelated processes contribute to variability in individ-ual experience and in the manifestation of perceptual-cognitive functioning. Although too extensive to review for this volume, the growing evidence from cross-cultural comparative studies of psychomotor development indicates that biological, ecocultural, and social factors both within and across populations interact to influence the ontogeny and the performance pattern of psychological functions. Of the numerous reviews of bioecological approaches to comparative child development, those by Konner (1977a,b, 1981), Werner (1972, 1979), Whiting (1981), and Super (1981a,b) are particularly recommended to students of cross-cultural perceptual-cognitive research.

Cross-cultural studies of child development have contributed to our understanding of perceptual functioning by identifying and broadening the base of contextual as well as processual factors included in the "interrelationship between an organism and its environment." In recent years, this ecocultural perspective has emerged in traditional areas of cognitive psychology. Here a few investigators have had the courage to abandon experimental paradigms and try to bridge the gap between laboratory and ethnographic field strategies to examine cognitive development and functioning "as it occurs in the ordinary environment and in the context of natural purposeful activity" (Neisser 1976). In contrast, the perceptual domain had received less attention from investigators interested in psychological performance in naturally occurring contexts. While the perceptual and cognitive domains overlap, much of our current knowledge regarding the influence of biological, ecocultural, and social interactive experiences and their manifestation in perceptual functioning remains embedded in larger comparative studies of psychological development. Most of these studies have evolved out of cross-cultural elaboration of two theoretical traditions in contemporary psychology: Piaget's (1951) genetic epistemology of child development and Witkin's (Witkin et al. 1962) individual psychology based on the theory of psychological differentiation.

Piaget's Genetic Epistemology

The importance of continuous interaction between an organism and its biological, physical, and social environment lies at the core of Piaget's (1951, 1970) structuralist hierarchical-stage theory of psychological development.[4] His theory has focused on qualitative variation in cognitive structures which are manifested in the temporal unfolding of psychological activities from infancy through adolescence. The sequence and qualitative changes associated with the historical manifestation of cognitive structure, characterized by four major periods of intellectual development, are considered to be universal and invariant patterns in human maturation. While the structural parameters of cognitive development may be relatively static, the qualitative processes of intellectual functioning are based on behavioral flexibility derived from assimilation and accommodation activities associated with variability in the total milieu of psychological activities. Temporally sensitive, Piaget's notion of *assimilation* involves an individual's ability to relate ongoing activities to previous experience, knowledge, and skills. *Accommodation* is the process by which traditional intellectual information is modified to accommodate psychological experiences. More implicit than explicit in Piaget's early contributions, the importance of *assimilative-accommodative* elements in the growth of intellective activities emphasizes experience and interactive processes in contexts of cognitive functioning. These social and cultural factors contribute to both quantitative and qualitative characteristics of psychological performance.

The Problem of Experience

Piaget (1964) explicitly discusses the role of experience by showing how active manipulation of the elements in a particular environment contributes to greater familiarity with and knowledge of the characteristics of materials and the properties of the manipulative processes. For example, by manipulating physical objects, the child learns that the properties of his actions are not necessarily the properties of the materials being manipulated. This enables the child to compensate when there is a discrepancy between the apparent properties of elements based on intellective actions and the actual properties of materials; that is, there is *equilibration* or compensation among the experience, actions, and elements composing the intellective milieu of psychological operations. In a more familiar paper dealing with cross-cultural extensions of his theory, Piaget (1966) summarizes four major factors that influence psychological development:

1. Biological factors involve a continuation of embryogenesis in the epigenetic system (maturation of the nervous system, for example) which "implies . . . the occurrence of sequential stages."
2. "Equilibration" or "autoregulation" factors which determine behavior and thought in various activities, that is, the sequential forms in general coordination of the actions of individuals interacting with their physical environment.
3. "General socialization" factors may be identical for all societies, Piaget suggests. These include cooperation, discus-

sion, opposition, and exchange, both within and between child and adult groups.

4. "Social" factors relate to educational and cultural transmission; Piaget feels that these differ from one culture to the next.

For Piaget, these interactive factors influence the rate of psychological development, but the sequence of stages remains invariant and universal. In subsequent writings, Piaget has emphasized the importance of experience with diverse physical environments (1966) as well as sociocultural factors (1972) in determining the rate but not the sequence of psychological development. For example, he points out that "the average age at which children go through each stage can vary considerably from one social environment to another, or from one country or even region within a country to another" (Piaget 1972:7).

Two interrelated lines of cross-cultural investigation have addressed the generalizability of Piaget's theory: (1) comparative studies of the temporal-hierarchical unfolding of intellective structures across world populations and (2) attempts to determine varieties of ecocultural experiences associated with the manifestation of particular patterns of perceptual-cognitive functioning.

Cross-Cultural Contexts of Piagetian Theory

In the past two decades studies of regional populations have explored the cross-cultural validity of Piaget's theory throughout the world. Studies from North, Central, and South America; Africa; the Middle East; Asia; and the Pacific have generated data which, to a large extent, have been used to demonstrate how the course of psychological development of non-Western children corresponds with that of Western counterparts, especially the Swiss population constituting Piaget's samples. The four stages of intellective development postulated by Piaget for Western children have received uneven treatment in the intercultural research record; the *sensorimotor* and *formal operations* stages have been studied less than the two transitional phases delineated by the shift from *preoperational* to *concrete operational* thought. Because cross-cultural research has focused on the two intermediate stages, we will briefly examine the poles of Piaget's developmental continuum first.

Contexts of Sensorimotor Development

An increasing number of intercultural studies of humans as well as of nonhuman primates (Parker 1977; Gibson 1977; Chevalier-Skolnikoff

1977) indicate that biological, social, contextual, and ecological factors influence psychological performance associated with the ontogeny of sensorimotor activities in Piaget's scheme. Particularly noteworthy are recent contributions by Dasen (1977a,b), Kopp, Khokha, and Sigman (1977), Goldberg (1977), Konner (1977b), Werner (1979), Dasen and Heron (1981), and Super (1981). The majority of these studies are based on culture areas within Africa, but reports from North America, Asia, and the Middle East clearly indicate that specific socialization activities such as caretaker stimulation and social and ecocultural skills and experience are related to patterns of performance on measures of sensorimotor activities. For example, Konner (1977b) has shown how infant handling among the Kalahari Desert !Kung appears to promote more rapid neuromotor development relative to that of North American infants. This he attributes to the fact that !Kung infants receive an unusually high degree of social and cognitive stimulation. In turn, the !Kung practice of holding infants in a vertical posture during most of the waking hours produces greater vestibular stimulation, which facilitates alertness and sensorimotor exercise (Devore and Konner 1974; Konner 1976, 1977b).

The evidence from those investigations, combined with an increasing number of studies relating oculomotor activities to perceptual selectivity habits among humans as well as nonhuman primates, indicates that a pattern of sensorimotor and training experience focuses attention on the "distinctive features" of each performance setting (see, for example, Gibson 1969; Fantz, Fagan, and Miranda 1975). Recently, Altmann (1980) has demonstrated how bioecological factors contribute to baboon social organization and infant socialization activities. Particularly noteworthy is her observation that organizational features of a baboon troop, such as the social rank of females or their male cohorts, influences parenting strategies. These diverse mothering activities influence levels of experience and patterns of sensorimotor activities among baboon infants. Altmann's ethological approach to primate socialization should serve as a model for future studies of human development in naturalistic settings.

The Formal Operational Stage

The stage of formal operational thought has received less attention than the sensorimotor domain in Piagetian theory. Despite studies in the Western world (see, for example, Lovell 1961; Kohlberg and Gilligan 1971) indicating that large proportions of the population fail to perform in a formal operational manner, Piaget (1970) has held to his assumption that most (75 percent) "normal" individuals achieve this stage. However, in a further elaboration of this assumption, Piaget (1972) notes that individuals will "reach this stage in different areas according to their aptitudes and their professional specializations." There are several excellent reviews of intercultural research on formal operational thinking in Greenfield (1976), Serpell (1976), Dasen (1977a), and Werner (1979). These and other studies indicate that Piaget's notion of a stage of propositional thinking is extremely culture bound, to the extent that performance indicative of formal logical processes must be interpreted in terms of the skills, materials, and contexts of psychological functioning. In fact, Piaget (1972) has adopted an almost cultural-relativistic position on the occurrence of propositional thinking by stressing that experience may promote logical performance in one context but not in other domains of psychological functioning. In other words, patterns of psychological performance which correspond to formal logical operations appear to be contextually bound within diverse sociocultural settings (see, for example, Goodnow and Bethon 1966; Kelly 1977).

Culture, Context, and Conservation

Since Piaget's (1966) call for cross-cultural validation of his theory, the largest number of comparative investigations have focused on the intellective shift from preoperational to concrete-operational thought, the majority focusing on conservation. Part of the appeal of comparative research on conservation is the flexibility of Piagetian methodology and the availability of materials in diverse cultural settings for measuring such property constructs as weight, volume, length, number, and area. However, like any task transported across performance contexts, problems such as semantic equivalence, experience, and "demand characteristics" in each setting make comparative analysis extremely difficult. Excellent overviews of the cross-cultural difficulties involved in utilizing Piagetian tasks are available; see, for example, Furby (1971), Dasen (1977a,b,c), Cole and Scribner (1977), Greenfield (1976), and Price-Williams (1981).[5] These methodological discussions focus on the role of experience and context in psychological performance, which is interpreted as evidence of concrete-operational functioning.

Bruner (1964, 1966) and his collaborators (Greenfield and Bruner 1966; Bruner, Olver, and Greenfield 1966) used Piagetian concepts to demonstrate how socially transmitted technologies correspond with concept formation and information processing in sensorimotor, perceptual, and cognitive development. Since these initial cross-cultural studies, Piagetian investigators, notably Dasen (1972a, 1975,

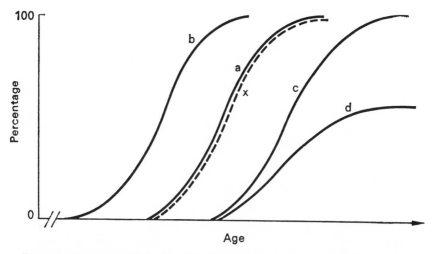

Figure 1. Percentage of subjects attaining the concrete operational stage as a function of age. (From Dasen 1972a:413; reprinted by permission of Sage Publications.)

1977a,b,c) and others, have examined performance on conservation throughout the world. Perhaps the best summary of intercultural Piagetian research during the 1960s has been Dasen's (1972a) review of conservation studies. Dasen plotted a set of ideal ogives representing possible patterns of cognitive performance based on proportions of children demonstrating operational thought as a function of age. Dasen's representative model of possible outcomes is reproduced in Figure 1.

Curve *x* is based on measures of Western European children, all of whom are expected to perform eventually in an operational manner. However, the age at which conservation performance is achieved varies with the difficulty of the concept as well as familiarity with the test materials. Curve *a* demonstrates that conservation appears at the same time as in European and North American children. See, for example, Goodnow (1962) and Goodnow and Bethon (1966), Hong Kong; Mohseni (1966), Iran; Delacey (1970, 1971), Australian Aborigines; Price-Williams (1961), Nigeria; and Okonji (1971), Zambia.

Curve *b* indicates precocity on operational measures compared to curve *x*. See Berland (1977), Pakistan; Tuddenham (1968, 1969), Oriental Americans; Bovet (1968, 1973), Algeria and Switzerland; Salkind (1977), Japan; Werner, Simonian, and Smith (1968), Hawaii; Price-Williams et al. (1969), Mexico; Goodnow (1962), Hong kong; and Adjei (1977), Ghana.

On curve *c* the concept develops later or more slowly. All children, however, eventually demonstrate concrete-operational thought. See Price-Williams (1962), Africa; Greenfield and Bruner (1966), Senegal; Vernon (1965a, 1966, 1967a,b, 1969), West Indies, Eskimo; and Peluffo (1962, 1967), Wei (1966), Mermelstein and Shulman (1967), Sigel and Hooper (1968), for European and American samples.

Curve *d* indicates that conservation appears to develop at about the same time or later than Western children; however, this curve is asymptotic: some children, and even adults, do not demonstrate concrete-operational performance. See, for example, Boonsong (1968), Thailand; Prince (1968, 1969) and Kelly (1971, 1977), New Guinea; Greenfield and Bruner (1966), Senegal; Cowley and Murray (1962), Zulu; Dasen (1970, 1972b, 1973) and DeLemos (1974), Australian Aborigines; and Dart and Pradhan (1967), Nepal.

Cursory examination of the patterns of concrete-operational performance indicated by these studies suggests qualified support for the cross-cultural validity of Piaget's notion of underlying structures in cognitive operation. On the other hand, the *rate* of their manifestations within and between populations is not invariant. This is nicely illustrated in Dasen's (1973) examination of variability in the rate of cognitive development through analysis of twenty-six studies on conservation of continuous quantities (liquids). The results of Dasen's comparative analysis are reproduced in Figure 2, which clearly indicates great variability in the proportion of individuals who perform in a concrete-operational manner. Results of other studies conducted since 1973 indicate comparable variability within and across populations (Dasen 1977a). This intellective diversity, as well as the fact that many individuals never perform in a concrete-operational manner, must generate serious doubt about the universality of an operational stage. Rather, as with Piaget's other three stages, the evidence suggests that intellective functioning characteristic of a particular level of operation in Piagetian terms may be related exclusively to individual patterns of experience, skill, and context.

While some of Piaget's collaborators remain preoccupied with verifying his theory, most investigators have turned to studies of the quantitative and qualitative aspects of cultural experience that may account for particular patterns of intellective functioning (Heron and Simonsson 1969; Cole 1975; Dasen 1975; Adjei 1977; Dasen and Heron 1981). The emphasis has shifted from simple correlation between age and stage explications of cognitive operations to systematic analysis of the role of experience and contexts; these studies are dis-

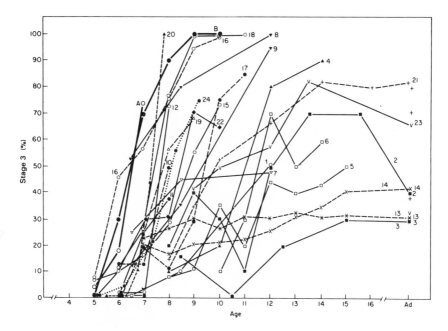

Figure 2. Variability in the rate of cognitive development: analysis of 26 studies on conservation of continuous quantities. (From Dasen 1973: reprinted by permission of the Société Canadienne de Psychologie.)

cussed in the next chapter. However, the trend toward greater ecological and cultural validity of developmental theories binds Piagetian research to other models of intellective functioning, especially Witkin's theory of psychological differentiation.

Psychological Differentiation

Like Piaget's structural approach to cognitive operations, Witkin's view is of progression along a continuum of behavioral organization from relatively undifferentiated processes through highly differentiated and increasingly specialized patterns. As developed by Witkin, psychological differentiation is a theory of *individual* differences. An individual's psychological development is postulated to proceed from less to more differentiated patterns of functioning; "a less differentiated system is in a relatively homogeneous structural state; a more differentiated system in a relatively heterogeneous state" (Witkin et al. 1962:9). The characteristic feature of greater differentiation is specialization. Following Witkin: "Subsystems emerge within the general system which are capable of mediating specific functions. This implies a measure of separation of psychological functions—perceiving separated from feeling, thinking from action; it implies as well specificity in the manner of functioning within an area" (Witkin and Berry 1975:5). Greater differentiation also has implications for how the system is integrated and how the individual relates to the environment. According to Witkin and Berry, "a more differentiated individual is characterized by separation of what is identified as belonging to the self from what is identified as external to the self" (1975:5). Like Piaget's developmental scheme, the argument emphasizes the developmental nature of integration. "Development toward differentiation involves progress from an initial, relatively unstructured state, which has only limited segregation from the environment, to a more structured state, which has definite boundaries, and which is capable of greater specificity of function" (Witkin et al. 1962:22). As Berry (1975) has pointed out, this concept of integration is analogous to that in biology, where organismic differentiation is considered to increase in complexity both phylogenetically and ontogenetically.

In investigating the relationship between differentiation and self-consistency, Witkin and his collaborators identify specific manifestations of lesser or greater differentiation. According to Berry, there are four interrelated areas of behavior—cognitive, social, affective, and perceptual—which have been empirically investigated as behavioral indicators of differentiation. In the cognitive domain an "analytical approach to problem solving (requiring a restructuring of the situation) ... is indicative of a high degree of psychological differentiation." High differentiation in the social domain is characterized by "a sense of separate identity" (involving social independence) and in the affective domain by the use of "structured controls and defenses" (Berry 1975:208). Greater differentiation in the perceptual domain is characterized by an individual's tendency to experience the parts of a perceptual field as discrete from the field as a whole. Individuals with less differentiation tend to perceive the parts of the field as fused with the whole. These characteristic patterns are contrasted as *field-dependent* and *field-independent* styles of psychological functioning.

Differentiation and Perceptual Style

In a series of comprehensive reviews of research on psychological differentiation, Witkin and his collaborators have reported over 3,000 studies through 1978 (Witkin et al. 1973, 1974b; Witkin, Cox, and

Friedman 1976; Cox and Witkin 1978). The majority deal with field dependence and independence. Tested originally on Western populations, particularly Americans, systematic measures of psychological differentiation (such as the Rod and Frame Test and the Embedded Figures Test) indicated consistent patterns of intellective performance or "perceptual styles" indicative of relative levels of field dependence/independence.[6] These characteristic patterns of styles of perceptual functioning are related to differentiation in the following manner:

> Perception is dominated by the organization of the field in which it is contained, so that the item cannot easily be disembedded from its context, this mode of perception has been labeled "field-dependent." The contrasting mode of perception, in which the organization of the prevailing field is less influential in determining the way in which part of the field is experienced, so that an item can easily be disembedded from the surrounding field, has been labeled "field-independent." Scores from any test of field dependence form a continuous distribution. The designations, "field-dependent" or "field-independent," thus reflect tendencies, or varying strengths, toward one mode of perceiving or the other, rather than distinct types. Relatively field-dependent and relatively field-independent perceptual styles may be taken as indicators of greater or lesser differentiation in the perceptual domain. (Witkin and Berry 1975:8)

Thus, field independence is a function of greater differentiation, characterized by an individual's tendency to experience items in the perceptual field as separate from their context. Relative to field-independent subjects, field-dependent individuals experience more difficulty in separating an item from its contextual whole. Most important, in relating analytical and structural abilities to development, Witkin and colleagues demonstrate that:

> In visual perception, early in development, the geometric relationship among parts of a stimulus field is a dominant determinant of perceptual organization. Stimulus fields in which parts have little systematic geometrical relationship to each other are perceived as relatively unorganized. During development, stimulus objects gain function and meaning as a consequence of continued, varied dealings with them. This acquired functional

significance may contribute to the developing discreteness of objects, and may serve as the basis for nongeometrical integrations of the field.

They go on to point out how increasing articulation in perception may profitably be extended to thinking:

> For example, pieces of furniture in a room may come to form a perceptual grouping as a result of learning through experience about their shared functional meaning. We may refer to the increasing discreteness of objects and the use of more varied and complex principles of field integration as an increase in articulation of experience. One who experiences in articulated fashion can perceive items as discrete from their backgrounds; or reorganize a field when the field is disorganized; or impose structure on a field, and so perceive it as organized, when the field has little inherent structure. Thus, the ability to analyze experience and the ability to structure experience are both aspects of increasing articulation. Just as the concept of increasing articulation has been applied to experience of an immediately present stimulus configuration (perception) so may it be applied to experience of symbolic material (thinking). (Witkin et al. 1962:7)

In recent years evidence has accumulated in support of Witkin's early hypothesis (Witkin et al. 1962) that intellective activities associated with "global" versus "articulated" cognitive styles also correspond with perceptual field independence/dependence in psychological differentiation (Witkin and Berry 1975; Witkin, Goodenough, and Oltman 1977; Berry 1981).

Outside the perceptual domain, individual differences in differentiation have been widely studied. In the area of social or interpersonal activities, the articulated cognitive style is characteristic of individuals with a sense of separate identity, an "awareness of a structured network of attributes identified as one's own . . . distinct from the attributes of others" (Witkin and Berry 1975:9).Thus, individuals with a strong sense of separate identity develop "inner frames of reference available as guides to thinking, feeling, action . . . and . . . will look less to external referents for guidance." Lesser differentiation is characteristic of individuals who rely on external referents for guidance. The research in this area has clearly demonstrated that relatively field-dependent individuals rely more on the frame of reference provided by the social field than do field-independent individuals. The articulated person characteristically takes a more impersonal approach, attending to the objective and abstract aspects of the social field. These social as well as psychological domains are highly interrelated and tend to be consistently associated through time with measures of field dependence and independence. As Berry has stated: "Cognitive style is defined by a dimension which runs between two poles: at one end, the field-dependent style (global) includes limited analytic and structuring skills in perception and cognition ... The field-independent (articulated) cognitive style includes structuring and analytical approach to perceptual and cognitive materials" (Berry 1976:31)

Ontogeny of Differentiation

In agreement with Piaget's theory of cognitive development, numerous studies in the Western world have indicated that levels of individual performance on measures of perceptual field dependence/independence are related to the ontogeny of differentiation and are relatively stable over time. Witkin, Goodenough, and Karp (1967) and Faterson and Witkin (1970) have demonstrated a definite progression in perceptual development. From early childhood through adolescence, the sequence shows a high degree of relative stability within age periods; that is, "children tend to hold the same position relative to their ages on the field-dependence dimension as they grow up, while as a group they show movement toward greater field-independence" (Witkin et al. 1971:5). After adolescence, field dependence tends toward stability through the late thirties, although women tend to be relatively more field-dependent than men. With middle age there is a change toward greater field dependence, with a marked return to field dependence reported among geriatric groups (Comalli 1965, cited in Witkin et al. 1971; Schwartz and Karp 1967).

Socialization and Perceptual Style

Early investigations in North America as well as more recent reports of longitudinal and cross-sectional studies of American children indicate that relative levels of differentiation correspond with enculturation activities (Witkin et al. 1954, 1962, 1974a; Seder 1957).[7] In their initial investigations of socialization and child-rearing practices in New York, Witkin et al. (1962) as well as Dyk and Witkin (1965) found a number of closely interrelated factors, or a socialization cluster, which influenced the child's autonomous functioning and development of a particular cognitive style. Three interrelated factors were distinguished: (1) the extent of opportunity for and encouragement of separation—primarily from the mother; (2) the nature of control over the child's aggressive, impulsive, or assertive behavior; and (3) the characteristics of the parents which influence their role in the separation process and in emotional and behavioral control. Field-independent subjects displayed an articulated body concept, a sense of separate identity, and the use of specialized, structured defenses.

The profiles of mother–child interactions with field-dependent subjects indicated:

1. The mother's physical care was not appropriate to the child's age.
2. The child's activity and movements were restricted.
3. The child was perceived as delicate—in need of special attention or protection.
4. The mother limited the child's curiosity and stressed conformity.
5. The child was not encouraged to achieve mature goals and was discouraged in self-assertion.
6. Discipline was arbitrarily administered, with irrational threats to control aggression and vacillation between submissive, indulgent, and coercive behavior.
7. The mother lacked self-assurance in child care.
8. The mother lacked self-realization, discouraging individual achievement in the child.

These characteristics were significantly related to less differentiation and the development of a more global cognitive style. As Dyk and Witkin have pointed out: "Those practices which emphasize the achievement of separation from the mother and autonomous functioning of the child tend to foster differentiation, as does a climate of warm, supportive socialization. On the other hand, practices emphasizing obedience and conformity (especially in coercive, physically controlled situations) tend to foster low levels of differentiation" (Dyk and Witkin 1965:52). Subsequent studies among diverse ethnic groups in the United States are consistent with Witkin's original formulation (Witkin 1969).

Sensorimotor Training and Perceptual Style

While interpersonal processes are significant aspects of socialization strategies, the content of these activities in terms of material as well as social manipulations may be equally important in determining relative patterns of field independence. Since Price-Williams and colleagues

(1969) demonstrated that pottery making corresponds with improved performance on Piagetian conservation tasks, several studies have shown comparable effects of training on perceptual inference habits in North American populations. For example, training in art and music has been associated with greater field independence, as have specific physical acitivities, such as gymnastic training (Meek and Skubie 1971; Ramirez and Price-Williams 1974; Gaines 1975; Parente and O'Malley 1975). Goodenough and Witkin (1977) have summarized the Western literature on training effects and levels of psychological differentiation. Such studies have recognized that although general socialization strategies, including formal education, may be important, the nature of the activities and skills as well as the contexts in which they are performed may be equally, if not more, important in determining relative levels of psychological differentiation. Cross-cultural extensions of differentiation theory illustrate how perceptual functioning is embedded within diverse ecocultural contexts.

Perceptual Style in Cross-Cultural Perspective

The extension of differentiation theory and the concept of cognitive or perceptual style across cultural and ecological settings has followed two lines of development. The first has sought out known cultural universals which provide for continuity across cultures; the second has emphasized those cultural variables which are considered to be unique. While socialization strategies figure predominantly in the cross-cultural literature dealing with cognitive style, other, complementary antecedent and interrelated variables have been implicated—namely, societal complexity and biosocial and ecological adaptations.

Societal Organization

Two sets of studies have set the framework for cross-cultural investigations of psychological variation: the hologeistic contributions by Barry, Bacon, and Child (1957), Barry, Child, and Bacon (1959), Barry and Paxon (1971), and Whiting (1981), and the controlled comparison reports of the Six Cultures Study, especially the contributions by Minturn and Lambert (1964) and Whiting and Whiting (1975).

Using the Human Relations Area Files, Barry and colleagues rated socialization practices described in the ethnographic record on six separate dimensions: obedience training, responsibility training, nurturance training, achievement training, self-reliance training, and general independence training. Two clusters of factors emerged from their survey which relate socialization practices to the ecological-cultural domain: namely, *economic factors related to socialization* and *sex differences in socialization* (Barry, Bacon, and Child 1957). In the economic sphere, these authors demonstrate a significant relationship between the economic base of a society and its particular socialization strategy: low food accumulating societies (gatherers and hunters) emphasized individual assertion or high achievement—self-reliance. High food accumulating societies (agriculturalists and pastoralists), on the other hand, reinforced compliant behavior—obedience and responsibility.

Using a controlled-comparison technique based on field studies of twenty-four families from six different cultures, Minturn and Lambert (1961) suggested that socialization practices vary as much within cultures as between cultures. This study found a number of socialization factors with pancultural meaning that are useful for analysis of the socialization process and the development of individual differences. The factor clusters reported by Minturn and Lambert were: (1) responsibility demands on the child; (2) the use of positive affect by the mother; (3) control of the child's peer aggression; (4) severity or laxity of obedience training; (5) extent of mother's caretaking; (6) control of mother-directed aggression and disobedience; and (7) mother's emotional stability or instability. These emphases in socialization are very similar to the practices associated with the development of greater or lesser psychological differentiation reported by Witkin et al. (1962), Dyk (1969), and others mentioned earlier. These early studies emphasized societal organization and socialization strategies with macro comparisons between ideal polar types of "loose" and "tight" societies.

The social tightness variable (social conformity, social stratification) refers to the degree of hierarchical structure in a society. According to Pelto (1968), a tight society has an elaborate structural organization for many different roles, whereas a loose society has a less elaborated structure with minimal role differences. Tight societies are characterized by pressure on the individual to conform: social control plays an important part in this pressure. In loose societies social control is replaced by an emphasis on self-control. This variable has been extended and investigated recently under the concepts of "social traditionalism" and "social conformity" in psychological differentiation (Witkin et al. 1974a; Nedd and Gruenfeld 1976). Emphasizing patterns of social organization and socialization strategies, cross-cultural studies have been undertaken with the assumption that high levels of perceptual field independence are associated with the greater individual autonomy characteristic of loose societies. Conversely, in tight societies, individuals are more field-dependent. In a review of cultural influence on perceptual field independence, Goodenough and Witkin presented an excellent summary of the social tightness factors:

> Societies at the tight end of the tight–loose dimension are characterized by an elaborate social structure, considerable role diversity, and pressure on the individual to conform with social, religious, and political authorities. Societies at the loose end have a less elaborate social structure, fewer roles, and individuals are allowed to "go their own way" to a greater extent . . . Socialization (in tight societies) is characterized by stress on conformity to parental authority . . . and . . . use of *strict and even harsh socialization practices.* (Goodenough and Witkin 1977:35–36, emphasis added)

In the past decade numerous studies from a variety of ecocultural settings have supported the original hypothesis that relative levels of field dependence/independence are related to degrees of social conformity in social systems. Unfortunately, the majority of these studies were based on questionnaires; therefore, the investigators did not observe the activities, skills, or contexts in which their subjects were actually being socialized. In view of the North American evidence of Witkin and Goodenough, plus an increasing number of cross-cultural studies which link perceptual-cognitive operations to specific training or experience, it is difficult to determine if general socialization strategies per se—whether strict or lax—can account for patterns in psychological functioning *or* performance (see, for example, Cole 1975; Cole and Scribner 1975, 1977; Adjei 1977; Berland 1977; Harris 1977, cited in Laboratory of Comparative Human Cognition 1979). Socialization activities or specific child-rearing practices are embedded in the diverse contexts of social organization within particular ecocultural systems. By far, the most extensive attempt to examine the total context of enculturation experiences in the determination of perceptual functioning has been Berry's (1976) ecological model of cognitive socialization.

Berry's Ecological Model

Recently Berry (1966, 1967, 1971a, 1976) has extended Witkin's theory of psychological differentiation to other socioecological settings. Eschewing the environmental determinism of cultural ecology (Vayda and Rappaport 1968; Damas 1969), Berry has demonstrated that "ecological demands" and "cultural supports" are major factors in determining the kind of behavior an individual develops. Following the early leads of Barry and colleagues (1957, 1959), Berry has emphasized the contrast between the cultural-ecological milieu of gatherers and hunters and that of agriculturalists and pastoralists and has demonstrated a relationship between ecological press (ecological variables) and sociocultural emphasis for particular perceptual-cognitive activities. "Typically, *high food accumulation societies* pursue agriculture or animal husbandry, or have a naturally provided abundance of food close at hand. Typically, *low food accumulating societies* pursue hunting or gathering as their main subsistence activities. The former are typically *sedentary* with a relatively *high population density*, while the latter are typically migratory with a relatively *low population density*" (Berry 1975:209). These adaptive strategies to ecological press have corresponding sociocultural milieus with socialization practices characteristic of their place on the ecological continuum. Witkin and Berry have summarized the significance of the relationship among ecology, subsistence strategy, and development of differentiation:

> The ecological demands placed on persons pursuing a hunting and gathering subsistence economic life style require the ability to extract key information from the surrounding context for the location of game and the ability to integrate these bits of information into a continuously fluctuating awareness of the hunter's location in space for the eventual safe return home ... These requirements may be satisfied either by direct perceptual learning or by early sensory tuning ... in a particular ecology or be mediated by cultural factors which are themselves an adaptative response to the ecological setting ... The mechanism here therefore involves perceptual learning, or early tuning, in addition to the cultural factors of socialization and social pressure. (Witkin and Berry 1975:16)

Berry (1975) has illustrated his "ecological model" for conceptualizing the interrelationships between ecological, cultural, and psychological variations in the development of psychological differentiation, as shown in Figure 3. A growing number of reports indicating high levels of field-independent performance among gatherers, hunters, and fishermen lends support to this aspect of Berry's model (see Dawson 1967a,b; Vernon 1966; Feldman 1971, and MacArthur 1971,

Figure 3. Ecological model: social and psychological correlates. (From Berry 1975:211; reprinted by permission of Sage Publications.)

	Low food accumulation (Migratory, hunting, gathering, low population density)	High food accumulation (Sedentary, agricultural, high population density)
1. Ecological dimension		
2. Social-cultural (frequently observed)		
a) Socialization (Barry, Bacon, and Child 1959)	Lenient, supportive	Harsh, restrictive
b) Family structure (Nimkoff and Middleton 1960)	Nuclear	Extended
c) Social structure (Pelto 1968)	Egalitarian, atomistic	Hierarchical, stratified
d) Social relations (Honigmann 1968)	Reserved, fragmented	Mutual dependence, integrated
3. Psychological (predicted)		
a) Perceptual-cognitive differentiation (cognitive style)	Field independent, analytic	Field dependent, global
b) Socio-emotional differentiation (affective style)	Independent, reserved, controlled	Group-reliant, outgoing, expressive
c) Response to culture contact (acculturative stress)	Low stress (from A), high stress (from B)	High stress (from A), low stress (from B)

1973a,b, 1974). Certainly among groups of hunters and gatherers, structural flexibility, organizational fluidity, high levels of spatial mobility, as well as greater perceptual field independence (cognitive restructuring skills) are adaptive. Among hunters, social and technical activities reinforce for greater individual autonomy and perceptual restructuring skills, whereas more sedentary populations depend on social-interpersonal skills that stress conformity and interdependence, with less emphasis on the restructuring that is characteristic of field independence. Altogether, the cross-cultural research record supports the assumption that more spatially mobile subsistence strategies such as hunting and gathering promote field-independent performance on psychological tasks compared to the performance of sedentary agriculturalists. These studies also indicate marked sex differences, especially between females in the two ecocultural settings.

Sex Differences

One of the most pervasive findings in studies of psychological differentiation in the Western world has been consistent sex differences on measures of perceptual-cognitive style.[8] Males perform in a field-independent manner relative to females on perceptual-restructuring tasks such as the Embedded Figures Tests which require suppression of responses to immediately obvious stimulus attributes in favor of delayed response to less obvious elements. Reviews of studies on the development of sex differences have demonstrated that differences in perceptual functioning may occur as early as five years of age and are usually pervasive by adolescence. In accounting for the nature of these differences, Faterson and Witkin (1970) and others have suggested that the same factors which account for variable perceptual habits across cultural groups operate within a culture to produce sex differences in field dependence/independence. As well, numerous cross-cultural studies have reported sex differences in perceptual-cognitive performance associated with different socialization experiences for males and females. Originally, Barry, Bacon, and Child (1957) found marked cross-cultural evidence for greater nurturance and responsibility/conformity training for females and encouragement of achievement and self-reliance for males. When the socioeconomic base of the society was also considered, there was a clear emphasis on obedience and responsibility training for both sexes in high food accumulating societies. Self-reliance and achievement were emphasized for females and independence/achievement for males in low food accumulating societies.

Following the lead suggested by Barry and colleagues, Berry (1966, 1967) found no significant differences between males and females on measures of perceptual style among the Eastern Eskimo from Baffin Island. Using the same perceptual-cognitive tasks (Vernon Embedded Figures and Raven Progressive Matrices), MacArthur (1967) replicated Berry's findings among the Inuvik and Tuktoyaktuk Eskimos. Both authors' results were consistent with Witkin's field-dependence hypothesis and the conclusions of Barry and colleagues regarding comparability in socialization emphases on individual autonomy for Eskimo men and women. More recently Berry (1971a), in a replication of his earlier Eskimo study, found no marked sex differences among the Arunta. MacArthur (1973a,b) in a follow-up study among Canadian Eskimo children and adolescents, found few sex differences in traditional measures of field dependence. Consistent with these findings, Feldman (1971), MacKinnon (1972), and Berry and Annis (1974) reported the absence of sex differences among other North American migratory-hunting Eskimo and Cree communities. While no marked sex differences on measures of field dependence have been reported for migratory hunters, recent cross-cultural studies on sedentary rural and urban populations have demonstrated a sharp contrast between sedentary and nomadic groups.

Witkin (1967) and Vernon (1965a) reported clear-cut and pervasive sex differences in field dependence for women in numerous cross-cultural studies among sedentary populations in England, Holland, France, Italy, Israel, and Hong Kong. Berry (1966) and Dawson (1967a,b) found women markedly more field-dependent than men in their respective comparative studies of Temne/Scottish and Mende/ Temne samples. Dawson found Temne women to be more field-dependent than Mende women, which he attributed to the fact that Temne women have a more dependent, traditional, conforming role in their community (Berry 1966). Recent studies by Okonji (1969) on Nigerian and Ibusa adults and by Berry (1971a) on a sedentary Felefomin community in New Guinea have found consistent sex differences in perceptual styles. Females have consistently been found more field-dependent than males in a Nsenga African sample (MacArthur 1974) and a sample of Tsimshian Indians in northern British Columbia (Berry and Annis 1974).

In their village studies relating social conformity to psychological differentiation in Mexico, Holland, and Italy, Witkin et al. (1974a) found marked sex differences for children aged ten to thirteen; however, the differences were not significant between low and high conforming villages. Similarly, in studies of sex differences in cognitive style in non-Western, urban-industrial settings, marked field dependence for women has been demonstrated in the relatively tight urban communities in the Middle East (Amir 1975), Japan (Kato 1965), Korea (Park and Gallimore 1975), and India (Pande 1970a,b; Pande and Kothari 1968).

The interplay among ecology, social organization, and socialization processes has been developed to explain the contrast between sedentary and nomadic groups on levels of psychological differentiation. Sex differences in perceptual style, which characterize sedentary groups, are not found among nomadic hunters and gatherers. In accounting

for the pervasiveness of sexual equality on measures of field independence among gatherers and hunters, Berry (1971a) and others have
speculated that field independence among these nomadic groups is
highly adaptive. To demonstrate this, Berry (1976) and others have
emphasized the significance of the nomadism of Eskimo and Australian Aborigines within a "relatively homogeneous" physical and cultural environment. On the basis of their findings, the authors have
argued that hunting (primarily a male activity) and gathering (primarily a female activity) place a premium on spatial articulation in
"highly homogeneous" terrains—deserts, tundras, or extensive snow
fields. To emphasize this relationship, they have contrasted these eco-
logically specialized groups with sedentary groups, rather than with
other nomadic hunters and gatherers, in "highly variegated environments." From these comparisons they have speculated that "the fos-
tering of articulation . . . is likely to be stronger (among hunters) than
in a society where the same need to travel is met by an environment
which is inherently articulated" (Witkin 1967). Although this may
well be the case, no evidence from hunting and gathering groups in
"highly variegated and inherently articulated" environments exists
(see Witkin and Berry 1975; Stewart-Van Leeuwen 1978). Nonethe-
less, the cross-cultural record consistently indicates marked performance differences between sexes in sedentary-agricultural groups characterized by tight social systems emphasizing hierarchy and greater
pressure for females to conform relative to males. In gathering and
hunting groups, sex roles are more egalitarian, and individual autonomy is emphasized for both sexes.

Contexts without Content

The evidence reviewed above, especially the cross-cultural record,
supports the contention of Witkin, Berry and their collaborators that
ecological and cultural experiences influence levels of psychological
performance on measures of perceptual field dependence/independ-
ence. In accounting for cross-cultural variability, Witkin and his collaborators, especially Berry, have postulated that the socialization activities of cultural groups as a whole promote particular modes of psychological functioning. A review by Goodenough and Witkin encapsu-
lates the current status of research relating these factors to variability
in perceptual-cognitive development:

> There is an obvious and even dramatic correspondence be-
> tween the autonomy-fostering socialization practices typically

found in hunting societies and the child-rearing practices that foster the ontogenetic development of a relatively field-independent cognitive style within a given cultural group. In contrast, the socialization practices of the typical farming society, which encourage obedience and limit separation from parental authority, are similar to the child-rearing practices that are associated with the ontogenetic development of a relatively field-dependent cognitive style within cultures. Also contributing to the development of a field-independent cognitive style among hunters during their lifetime may be the opportunities provided for direct perceptual learning available to them as they engage in search for game. Social structure, socialization experience, and ecological encounters may thus work in tandem toward the same developmental end of producing adaptive modes of behavior in the individual. Certainly, the results of cross-cultural comparisons of migratory hunting and sedentary farming groups are consistent with the conclusion reached in earlier sections that environmental factors operative during ontogeny play a key role in the development of individual differences in cognitive style. (Goodenough and Witkin 1977: 46–47)

On the other hand, the same literature in support of Berry and Witkin's cognitive socialization scheme explicates the role of specific training experiences in the determination of perceptual inference habits. Although sex differences are undoubtedly related to different values placed on female participation in subsistence activities, the specific content and contexts of these activities has been ignored by most investigators interested in experience and perceptual functioning. It will be recalled that in sedentary societies there is a tendency toward greater sex role differentiation than in more spatially mobile populations. These sex differences are interpreted in terms of general socialization strategies or patterns of experience within the total ecocultural milieu. At the individual level (which is the nucleus of Witkin's theory), these interpretations translate into diverse patterns of experience across a wide range of interpersonal and ecocultural settings within each social system. From this perspective, the same cross-cultural evidence may be used to argue that field dependence and independence are alternative modes of individual functioning within particular performance contexts. For example, field-independent perceptual skills have been shown to be adaptive for hunters in that they enable them to focus attention or disembed the target from its context.

But in other activities, such as distributing meat among the members of a hunting band, field-dependent skills would seem to be equally adaptive. Thus, it appears equally plausible that levels of psychological differentiation as indicated by field-dependent/independent perceptual performance are not attributes of individual systems per se, but contextual manifestations of how individuals utilize experience and skills in responding to the demands of each performance context. Unfortunately, we know very little about how different kinds and amounts of experience with the interpersonal and material composition of diverse behavioral contexts contribute to patterns of psychological performance. This is true for systematically assessed as well as diverse naturalistic settings. To unlock the "paradox" of how these interrelated factors operate in psychological functioning, I introduce the construct of cognitive amplifiers in the next chapter.

2

Cognitive Amplifiers

Over the years evidence has accumulated which supports Rivers' contention that psychological performance is influenced by individual experience and skills in diverse ecocultural environments. Because Rivers' early observations prompted this study and figure largely in my argument regarding cognitive amplifiers, his conclusions bear repeating. Like most ethnographers who have operated in unfamiliar ecocultural contexts, Rivers noted that both his Melanesian and South Indian informants attended to elements in the visual field with apparently greater visual acuity than himself:

> Although the visual acuity (in the strict sense) of the Torres Straits Islanders was not found to be in any way extraordinary, their visual powers were, I think, equal to any of those which have excited the admiration and wonder of travellers elsewhere.
>
> Travellers have repeatedly called attention to the way in which savages are able to distinguish birds among the thick foliage of trees, and the quickness of the natives of Torres Straits in this respect was very striking. The power of distinguishing boats at a distance was also remarkable. We usually found, however, that as soon as a native had seen a boat and pointed out its position to us we were able to see it, but while we could perhaps barely see the boat, the natives would describe its rig and in some cases knew what boat it was. Their visual accomplishments in this respect were obviously of a kind in which

> special knowledge would be of enormous importance. (Rivers
> 1901:42)

These personal, ethnographic observations prompted Rivers the
cross-cultural psychologist to suggest that:

> Travellers have generally failed to distinguish between the two
> chief factors upon which the power of distinguishing objects by
> sight depends; one, visual acuity proper, depending on the re-
> solving power of the eye as an optical and psychological mecha-
> nism, the other, which may be called power of observation, de-
> pending on the habit of attending to and discriminating any
> minute indications which are given by the organ of sense. An-
> other fact which travellers have usually omitted to take into ac-
> count is that the observations which have been held to show
> extraordinary sense acuity have been made in surroundings
> with which the savage is extremely familiar. A feat,which to the
> outsider may appear to depend on a marvellous degree of acute-
> ness of vision, may depend merely on a correct inference
> founded on special knowledge. (Rivers 1901:12)

Later, in comparing Muller-Lyer illusion susceptibility among the
Toda and Papuan, Rivers elaborated on the greater role of experience
and context, rather than psychological factors, in determining perceptual inference habits:

> The psychological factors upon which the illusion depends are
> however of a simple nature and affect both savage and civilized
> man, and the reason why the illusion is rather less marked to
> the Toda and Papuan is probably that which I have already
> suggested, viz. a difference in the direction of attention, the
> savage attending more strictly to the two lines which he is de-
> sired to make equal, while the civilized man allows the figure
> as a whole to exert its full influence on his mind. (Rivers
> 1905:363)

In keeping with Rivers' original observation, a steadily increasing
body of evidence now indicates that each perceiver is sensitized to external ecocultural as well as internal stimuli through sociohistorical
experiences and skills which "focus the attention" and provide "special knowledge" in the diverse contexts of psychological functioning.
This theme is characterized in the mainstream of perceptual research

by E. J. Gibson's (1969) demonstration that "skilled or unskilled perceivers" add nothing to the stimuli. Rather, skilled perceivers have previous experience which enables them to gain greater information relevant to the perceptual task at hand. As we saw in the last chapter, subsequent cross-cultural studies have focused on organism–environment interactions or task-specific activities in explaining perceptual inference habits. Although many of these studies cite Rivers' original conclusions regarding environment, experience, and perceptual inference habits, they consistently ignore his rather astute observation that organism–environment interactions, especially perceptual inference activities, are *socially mediated* through such processes as "pointing at" the pertinent stimuli in each ecocultural context. Thus the cognitive amplifier construct in this study, while emphasizing that ecocultural experiences, context, and task-specific skills are important in determining patterns of perceptual-cognitive performance, also stresses that psychological functioning is mediated through interpersonal processes. The concept itself is not original to this study, though my emphasis on interpersonal processes expands considerably on previous efforts to explicate environmental, cultural, and social factors in cognitive development.

Following Fortes' (1938) suggestion that investigations of specific cultural activities, rather than macro-ecocultural system comparisons, would generate better understanding of the role of "culture" in psychological development, Bruner (1966) and his associates extended their studies of concept formation in cognitive development to non-Western cultures. One product of these early intercultural studies was Bruner's conclusion that each cultural system emphasizes different paradigms of experience or "amplifiers" in intellective functioning which correspond with variability in cognitive development. In Bruner's words, "Man is seen to grow by the process of internalizing the ways of acting, imagining, and symbolizing that exist in his culture, ways that *amplify* his powers" (1966:320–321). For most anthropologists, this observation was hardly noteworthy; cognitive psychologists had rediscovered cultural relativity. However, over the next decade Bruner and his collaborators generated a "cultural experience" theme which bound together a wide range of diverse studies concerned with ecocultural experience and skills in psychological functioning, including the disparate approaches in Piaget's and Witkin's theories of cognitive development (Piaget 1969, 1970; Cole et al. 1971; Cole and Scribner 1975, 1977; Berry 1976, 1980; Serpell 1976; Dasen, Berry, and Witkin 1979).

The notion of amplifiers posited by Bruner (1966) encompasses the same general sequelae covered by Berry's (1966) concept of *cultural aids*. Stressing subsistence activities within ecocultural niches, Berry has demonstrated how such cultural aids as language, arts, and crafts, as well as specific socialization strategies, influence Temne and Eskimo perceptual skills. For example, in contrast to the Temne:

> [Eskimo] possess an intricate system of words, termed "localizers," which aid in the location of objects in space. These localizers form an integral part of the word; the use of them, and hence the distinction, is obligatory. These distinctions are not normally required of users in English, and so it is possible that the Eskimo possess a geometrical-spatial term system as complex as that of Western technical man . . . Eskimo, when compared to the Temne, have available a fairly complete system of words which aid in dissection of, and communication about, the space around them. It is also apparent that the Eskimo will find it easier than the Temne to pass on one of these distinctions and concepts to their offspring. (Berry 1966:212–213)

Certainly, Eskimo language skills concerning the environment are an example of a cultural aid or amplifier related to their subsistence activities. The relationship between such cultural skills and the larger ecosystem has been further elaborated in Gladwin's (1970) ethnography of navigation activities and cognitive maps in Micronesia.

The role of ecocultural experience, particularly the influence of specific skills and/or contextual determinants of psychological performance on measures of perceptual-cognitive functioning, was first systematically reviewed by Cole et al. (1971) and Cole and Bruner (1971). These studies demonstrated that the situations which regulate control and utilization of the resources in a culture will also influence the nature of perceptual-cognitive skills among its members.

In accounting for the nature of the relationship between cultural skills and the development of cognitive abilities, Cole and Bruner (1971) generated the notion of *amplifying tools*, a concept they credit to Levi-Strauss's (1963) definition of subculture. "What is called a subculture is a fragment of a culture which from the point of view of the research at hand presents significant discontinuities in relation to the rest of that culture with respect to access to its major amplifying tools" (quoted in Cole and Bruner 1971:874). Emphasizing the technological features, they define an amplifying tool as: "a technological feature, be it soft or hard, that permits control by the individual of resources, prestige, and deference within the culture. An example of [an American] middle-class cultural amplifier that operates to increase the thought processes of those who employ it is the discipline loosely referred to as mathematics. To employ mathematical techniques requires the cultivation of certain skills of reasoning, even certain styles of deploying one's thought processes" (Cole and Bruner 1971:240).

Had they added "in a number of domains where such patterns (mathematical reasoning) of psychological performance are pertinent to the perceptual or cognitive task at hand," much of the material in the last chapter, as well as the subsequent discussion on cognitive amplifiers, would not be necessary. However, their notion of "amplifying tools" raises the question of generalizability of task- or context-specific experience. In their example, one wonders if mathematic reasoning skills, which may have been acquired and/or utilized in a limited range of interpersonal as well as ecocultural contexts, will be generalized across the diverse social settings in which individuals psychologically perform. Cole and his associates illustrate this problem nicely in their discussion of "how the learning experiences provided by different cultures relate to the logical structure and content of specific cognitive patterns." For example, in discussing their observation that many naturally occurring social contexts among the Kpelle corresponded with various testing situations, Cole and colleagues concluded:

> Examples of the learning of rules, as well as learning to use these rules in a contingent way, are suggested by much ethnographic data describing social situations. Yet we have no tools for distinguishing social and nonsocial problem-solving in an analytic fashion. In fact, almost all experimental situations are *nonsocial* in the sense that their successful solution requires manipulations of objects or words abstracted from context, rather than relations with people. (Cole et al. 1971:220).

As these researchers and others have pointed out, it is one thing to identify a set of rules or pattern of actions as cultural aids or amplifying tools in a social system, and quite another to ascertain how they are manifested in diverse ecocultural contexts (including experimental settings) where they are acquired as well as utilized. More importantly, as they succinctly summed up: "cultural differences in cognition reside more in the situations to which particular cognitive processes are applied than in the existence of a process in one culture and its absence in another" (Cole et al. 1971:233).

The general notion of amplifiers has focused attention on the eco-cultural contexts as well as the content of cognitive operations, and it has stimulated research on how interpersonal processes associated with experience and skills in one setting contribute to patterns of psychological performance in other contexts.

Contextual Processes and Perceptual Skills

The importance of concepts like amplifying tools or cultural aids within a social system has been demonstrated by Price-Williams (1961, 1962) and his collaborators (Price-Williams et al. 1969) in their early studies of specific ecocultural experiences and performance on Piagetian conservation tasks. Price-Williams (1961) found that Nigerian children performed in a concrete-operational manner at a younger age than Western comparison groups. He attributed this to the fact that familiar testing materials were used. Although he emphasized the problems attending cross-cultural use of standardized stimulus materials, Price-Williams did not follow up on his observations of differential experiences in the Nigerian cultural setting which may also have contributed to precocity on the Piagetian conservation tasks. Subsequently, Price-Williams and colleagues (1969) and Ramirez and Price-Williams (1974), in a study of conservation among a sample of children from pottery-making families in Mexico, showed that these skills were associated with enhanced acquisition of conservation.

Along these same lines, Bovet reported that food-handling activities among Algerian females promoted concrete-operational performance. Compared to Algerian males, "women were extraordinarily skillful in equalizing the weight of the two clay balls used in the [conservation] experiment . . . weighing in the hand was an effective measuring instrument for them" (Bovet 1973:329–330). She noted that females were reluctant to offer perceptual judgments regarding equality without being permitted to actually manipulate the test materials. When allowed, females would initially give conservation judgments; however, when the investigator directed their attention to the dimensional alterations, their expressed judgments became ambiguous. Bovet concluded that in such contexts, the females in her sample appeared to rely on proprioceptive and intuitive skills associated with their day-to-day experience of handling food.

Dasen (1975) reported similar patterns of conservation performance among spatially mobile hunters (Australian aborigines and Canadian Eskimo) and sedentary agriculturists (Ebrie of the Ivory

Coast). More importantly, Dasen (1977c) found that patterns of cognitive performance in each social system were in keeping with Berry's (1975, 1976) ecocultural model and cultural aids hypothesis. Further evidence in support of extending Berry's ecocultural model and the notion of amplifiers to include Piagetian studies, which links psychological performance on Piagetian tasks to socialization strategies, has been reported in separate studies conducted in Ghana by Adjei (1977) and Kirk (1977). Adjei found that pottery making and handling enhanced concrete-operational performance on conservation of substance, weight, and volume among adults and conservation of weight among Ghanaian children. Adjei's as well as Kirk's studies contain detailed summaries of day-to-day activities in each cultural setting, which indicate that socialization strategies, especially patterns of mother–child interaction, influence psychological performance. For example, in one testing situation, where mothers assisted their children in performing a matching task, Adjei found that maternal activities such as insighting, socially reinforcing, participating or supervising, and the like, "appear to be the best predictors of the child's Piagetian cognitive task performance" (Adjei 1977:251). Kirk, using a puzzle assembly task, reported a comparable pattern of socialization strategies which corresponded with variable performance in cognitive functioning.

Recent ethological as well as laboratory studies of nonhuman primates (Harlow and Mears 1979; Altmann 1980) and a growing number of cross-cultural investigations of interpersonal processes related to problem-solving activities indicate that social structural and organizational factors within domestic groups influence patterns of cognitive performance. Investigations of intergenerational relationships, especially parent–child and older–younger sibling interactions, have shown that the social composition of learning and performance contexts promote different patterns of experience with and attention to details of the perceptual or cognitive task at hand. For example, Samuels (1980) has shown that the presence of older siblings increases infant locomotor exploration, object manipulation, and visual inspection of performance contexts. Similarly, Mugny and Doise (1978) have demonstrated that groups of children with diverse cognitive strategies perform better on spatial representation tasks than a group of youngsters possessing more homogeneous strategies. Increasingly, investigations have shown that enculturation activities within family domains, especially maternal teaching strategies, influence levels of psychological experience and patterns of performance on perceptual and cognitive tasks (Korner and Thoman 1974; Croft 1977; Laosa

1978a,b; Kagan 1979; Stevenson and Lamb 1979; Perret-Clermont 1980). These pioneering studies raise important methodological issues, but they also focus our attention to interpersonal processes and the total distribution of experience and skills within ecocultural contexts of perceptual or cognitive functioning that may influence individual levels of psychological performance.

Cognitive Amplifiers Redefined

The ethnographic reality of concepts such as cultural aids or amplifying tools per se is not particularly remarkable; every ecocultural system has a curriculum of basic experiences and attending skills provided through a variety of lifelong socialization strategies. What vary, however, are the patterns of individual *access* to, and experience with, the elements and skills making up diverse social and ecocultural contexts of psychological functioning. In this study the concept of cognitive amplifiers stresses that interpersonal processes within as well as across contexts may focus the attention in psychological performance. For example, in most of the populations previously studied by cross-cultural investigators, the ethnographic record indicates that ecocultural experience and skills have been mediated through interpersonal processes within socially embedded contexts. Throughout an individual's lifetime the interpersonal composition of learning as well as performance contexts varies according to such factors as age, sex, experience, skills, and the like. Consequently, interpersonal factors within social and ecocultural settings may point out or focus the attention in each context of psychological performance.

3

Research Setting and Methods

To examine cognitive amplifiers and patterns of psychological performance in diverse, naturally occuring contexts, I conducted an ethnography of perceptual-cognitive enculturation activities in four contrasting ecocultural systems in Pakistan: the Qalandar, who are peripatetic entertainers and animal trainers; Kanjar, nomadic artisans, dancers, and prostitutes; the Lahoria, traditional merchant families in the old city of Lahore; and Jats, sedentary agriculturists in Punjab villages. The study was conducted from 1971 through 1973, with brief follow-up studies in 1979 and 1980.

Nomads and Sedentists: The General Hypotheses

The social organizational and ecocultural systems of both peripatetic artisans and entertainers contrast sharply with those of the two sedentary communities. The Qalandar and Kanjar combine lifelong socialization and training activities related to diverse yet highly specialized individual skills with spatial mobility in their nomadic subsistence strategies. Their peripatetic lifestyle demands structural flexibility and organizational fluidity across a wide range of linguistic, social, and ecocultural settings. This pattern emphasizes flexibility in individual subsistence-related skills, and both males and females participate in public as well as private economic activities. Unlike more sedentary populations, neither the Qalandar nor the Kanjar produce or store food resources, relying instead on a range of flexible entertainment or craft-related skills to acquire resources on a day-to-day basis.

Sedentary rural and urban dwellers, on the other hand, rely on relatively more secure economic resources such as agricultural crops or market inventories in permanent settlements. Of course, village farmers have direct control over food resources. Sedentary communities in Pakistan are predominantly Muslim, and this is associated with considerable sex role differentiation, with females participating less actively than males in public, extra-household or village activities. Because their lives are bound to relatively permanent resources (shops and fields), their systems of social organization stress cooperation and long-term solidarity within and between domestic, family, and other kinship-based groups in each community. As contrasting ecocultural systems, the peripatetic niche of nomads and the sedentary niches of village and urban dwellers within the same southwest Asian culture area seemed ideal for comprehensive investigation of cognitive amplifiers.

Because there is an extensive ethnographic record on village and urban communities in south Asia, I focused on the ecocultural milieu of peripatetic artisans (Kanjar) and entertainers (Qalandar). Drawing on the ethnographic record, cursory reports by nonprofessionals as well as personal observations of nomad–sedentist interactions in south Asia in the early 1960s, I ranked each of the four populations tentatively along the ecocultural and psychological continuum comprising Berry's (1975, 1976) ecological model of cognitive socialization and psychological differentiation. Using a modified version of Berry's dimension, I ranked the four groups as follows:

	Settlement Pattern	
nomadic		sedentary
low food	Qalandar, Kanjar, Lahoria, Jat	high food
accumulating		accumulating

	Socialization strategies	
lenient		harsh
supportive	Qalandar, Kanjar, Jat, Lahoria	restrictive
independent		obedient
self-reliant		

	Family structure	
nuclear		extended

	Social structure	
flexible	Qalandar, Kanjar, Jat, Lahoria	stratified
egalitarian		rigid

	Social organization	
fluid—fissive and fusive loose egalitarian sex role	Qalandar, Kanjar, Lahoria, Jat	mutually dependent high solidarity tight male-dominant

Within the original parameters of Berry's model and in consideration of cross-cultural studies of both Piaget's and Witkin's theories of
cognitive development, the existing evidence suggested several primary hypotheses regarding cognitive amplifiers in each population
and likely patterns of psychological performance on traditional measures of perceptual field dependence/independence and Piagetian
conservation tasks:

1. Peripatetic artisans and entertainers (nomads) will per-
    form in a field-independent manner relative to sedentary
    rural and urban dwellers (sedentists).
2. Qalandar, as peripatetic entertainers and animal trainers,
    will perform in a field-independent manner relative to no-
    madic Kanjar, less mobile artisans.
3. Jats (village agriculturists), by virtue of their greater expe-
    rience in farming as well as intravillage activities, will be
    field-independent relative to Lahoria (urban dwellers).
4. Among the Qalandar there should be no marked difference
    between males and females on measures of perceptual in-
    ference habits at any age.
5. Kanjar females will perform in a field-independent manner
    relative to Kanjar males, because females manufacture as
    well as travel daily to sell wares, beg, dance, and prostitute,
    while males stay in camp caring for infants.
6. In keeping with evidence on sex differences from studies
    conducted outside Pakistan, sedentary males will perform
    in a markedly field-independent manner relative to seden-
    tary females.

Before examining the data results and their bearing on each hypothesis (see Chapter 8), I will describe the research setting,
methods, and measures of perceptual inference habits. Because my
primary purpose is to examine cognitive amplifiers in the day-to-day
contexts of nomad experience, I present a detailed ethnographic description of their ecocultural milieu. While I visited several hundred
villages in Pakistan during my travels with the Qalandar and Kanjar

and spent nearly six months in two villages collecting perceptual measures, my observations of village and urban enculturation strategies are at best cursory. Certainly they lack the validity of accounts recorded by professional anthropologists specializing on sedentary socialization activities in South Asia, such as Minturn and Hitchcock (1966), Gore (1977), Ghuman (1978), Graves (1978), and Kakar (1979). Consequently, I have relied on the ethnographic record of child-rearing activities in South Asia as well as my own observations in interpreting the quantitative data pertaining to the hypotheses regarding the sedentary comparison groups.

The Geographic Setting

South Asia is an area of notable cultural diversity, particularly in the varieties of nomadic artisans and entertainers. Pakistan (West Pakistan prior to the December War in 1971) is politically divided into the four provinces of Sind, Baluchistan, the Punjab, and Northwest Frontier. Approximately one-third of the eastern frontier with India is a cease-fire line which includes the disputed territory of Jammu and Kashmir.

Pakistan may be divided into three geographic regions: the northern highlands where the Himalayan Mountains meet the Hindu Kush; the vast, sparsely populated Baluchistan Plateau; and the Indus River plains, part of the larger western Indo-Gangetic lowland. More than half of Pakistan is rugged, mountainous terrain with narrow valleys and foothills. The balance consists primarily of the vast alluvial plain of the Indus River and its tributaries. This includes the plains and low hills from the Aravalli Range west to the Sulaiman Mountains, and from the Salt Range and Siwaliks south to the Arabian Sea.

From origins in the Himalayas, the Indus River and its tributaries flow southwest for a thousand miles to the Arabian Sea. The province of the Punjab, corresponding roughly with the upper Indus plain, varies in elevation from about 500 to 1,000 feet in elevation. The lower Indus plain corresponds generally to the province of Sind. It is lower in altitude than the Punjab, gradually declining to sea level at the coast. Both areas are irrigated by diversion canals, which has, however, resulted in acute flood hazards.

Temperature, Precipitation, and Seasons

Roughly speaking, Pakistan has four seasons: the dry cool winter from December through February; the dry hot summer from March through May; the summer rainy period from June or July through

September, the time of the relatively heavy southwest monsoon; and the fall rainy period from October through November, the season of the northeast monsoon, which is generally light, carrying slight but highly variable amounts of precipitation. The amount and intensity of rainfall deposited in both monsoons in Pakistan are much less than in India. With the exception of the northern mountain zones, the annual precipitation averages less than ten inches, and for this reason agricultural cropping is concentrated in areas where water is most readily available, particularly the Indus plain and the provinces of the Punjab and Sind.

The exploitation of these floodplains for increased agricultural productivity has great cultural significance for the distribution of settlements on the Indus plains. Extensive canal irrigation, beginning in the Mughal Period (sixteenth–nineteenth centuries) is associated with all the major rivers and most of their tributaries. The two types of canal systems are innundation canals, begun by the Mughals, which depend on seasonal overflow, and perennial canals, begun by the British in 1868, which are fed by deflecting water from the rivers. Before the partition of the Indian subcontinent in 1947, more than 33 million acres in the Indus plains were under the control of 16 barrages and 30,000 miles of irrigation canals.

While there is considerable interregional variation, Pakistan lies in what may be termed a warm temperate zone. Summers are hot, and winters are cool to cold. Jacobad in northern Sind in the Indus valley has June temperatures consistently reaching 120° F; the monthly day-to-night mean is 98° F. The Punjab is characterized by high summer temperatures, often accompanied by constant dry winds (*loo*). Maximum summer temperatures are often over 100° F. In the Sind, temperatures are less extreme, being somewhat modified by the Arabian Sea.

Settlement Patterns and Population Distribution

These physical features, of course, influence settlement patterns. Village and urban communities are closely bound to agricultural production in the more moderate areas of North-West Frontier Province, Punjab, and Sind. The irrigation systems have extended agriculture and sedentary communities into many areas traditionally exploited by pastoral nomads. Small agricultural villages are distributed throughout the Punjab and Sind, where soil and water resources support the majority of Pakistan's population. In 1972 the two provinces contained approximately 80 percent of the total population of some 65 million.

In the Punjab, the population density is high; approximately 470 per square mile, while in the Sind, this figure is 254 per square mile.

In the tribal areas to the west and north of the Indus plain, the mountain passes have determined settlement locations along trails, roads, and more recently, railways. On the plains, cultural settlements have always been confined to clusters along the Indus and its tributaries. Transportation routes have followed this network, connecting market areas that serve the agricultural settlements. As one travels through the villages and urban centers in the Punjab and Sind, it is readily apparent that this has historically been a zone of cultural integration. Persian, Greek, Afghan, British, and other foreign intrusions have left their mark, giving this region a special identity within the Asian subcontinent. A vital element within the socioecological system of the villages and urban centers of Pakistan has been the numerous groups of nomads.

Nomadic Adaptations in Pakistan

Until the past decade, there has been considerable confusion regarding the nature and distribution of spatially mobile groups in Pakistan, although nomadism as an adaptive strategy is very old in the Asian subcontinent. Traditional accounts of nomadic groups tend to consider all of them as pastoral tribes, but not all pastoralists in Asia are spatially mobile (for example,Todas), nor are all nomads pastoralists. Certainly, endogamous groups of artisans, entertainers, caravaneers, peddlers, dacoits, and other nonpastoral peripatetic nomads have been part of the Asian socioecological system for several millennia (Basham 1954; Berland 1977, 1978, 1979a, 1980). While this study is not concerned with the historical or prehistorical reconstruction of nomadic strategies in South Asia, an important distinction must be made between pastoral and peripatetic nomads.

Peripatetic and Pastoral Strategies

Most readers are familiar with numerous types of nomadic adaptations, including the gatherers and hunters.[1] Better known are the groups of pastoralists, such as herders of reindeer, camel, sheep, and cattle, whose primary economic resource is livestock. More widely dispersed than pastoralists are groups of peripatetic artisans or entertainers, such as the familiar circus performers, carnies, tinkers, and gypsy fortune tellers in the Western world. In Pakistan, peripatetic groups of snake charmers, trainers of performing animals, bards, magicians, acrobats, jugglers, dancers, musicians, beggars, smiths, potters, and weavers have been enduring elements linking villages and cities. While pastoralists and peripatetics both rely on nomadism, their subsistence activities are markedly disparate.

Peripatetic nomads rely exclusively on human social resources, whereas pastoralists depend much less on sedentary communities. Pastoral nomads, as food producers, have greater direct control over subsistence resources; peripatetics, dependent on sedentary and in some cases pastoralist populations, are not food producers. The resources necessary for herding activities and livestock management tend to relegate pastoralists to distal eco-niches peripheral to agricultural zones and urban communities. Conversely, the specialized economic activities of nomadic artisans and entertainers are proximal to sedentary groups within both rural and urban settings. The nature of herd and group interactions with sedentists tends to limit the total range of individual or corporate economic activities among pastoralists, whereas peripatetics frequently are versed in a wide variety of economic skills. With human settlements as potential resources, peripatetic artisans and entertainers also have greater spatial flexibility than pastoralists, whose decisions and movement patterns must be tempered by herding requirements. Peripatetic groups, sparsely scattered through larger socioeconomic systems, offer a wide range of services and products which are frequently socially and economically inappropriate in more sedentary communities. In Pakistan, a single small town or village may not be able to support a full-time metalsmith or a group of entertainers, whereas a network of these sedentary communities can support such specialized activities. These networks of human production and personal needs, such as entertainment, I have termed the *peripatetic niche*. As in most complex social systems, in Pakistan the peripatetic niche supports numerous, distinct groups of nomads (Berland 1979a, 1980).

Survey of Peripatetic Nomads

To determine the range and distribution of peripatetic nomads in Pakistan, I conducted an ethnographic survey from March through August, 1971. Based on a review of the literature and helpful counsel from government agencies, I defined several problems which had to be overcome before conducting the survey such as language capabilities and entree into the camps of nomads. I decided to limit the ethnographic survey primarily to the Punjab and Indus plain. As this would involve working with multilingual nomads in three distinct linguistic

zones (North West Frontier Province, Punjab, and Sind), I hired a
full-time research assistant/interpreter familiar with Pūshtō, Punjabi,
and Sindi.

To assist in gaining entree and acceptance from nomads and sedentists alike, I rehearsed an explanation of my purpose with my
assistant and forwarded a general statement of purpose to all district
police and military headquarters. When approaching informants, we
told them I was there to see how their children compared to children
of nomadic artisans and entertainers where I came from, as a teacher I
was interested in how they taught their children the skills and knowledge they needed. This approach proved to be very successful, particularly once the word spread that the foreigner was essentially harmless
and was truly interested in children and the learning and teaching of
skills.

Beginning in Peshawar, NWFP, and terminating in Karachi, Sind,
we followed the major rivers, highways, railways, and irrigation canals
in search of nomadic camps. Inquiries were addressed to sedentists
and nomads concerning both nomadic artisans and entertainers. The
survey brought us into contact with a large number of pastoral as well
as nonpastoral settlements. The results of the preliminary survey,
later confirmed during two years of intensive ethnographic study
among the Qalandar and Kanjar, indicated fifteen endogamous groups
of peripatetics exclusive of pastoralists. Excluding tent-dwelling
groups of nomadic beggars, the survey revealed the following groups:

1. The Bazigar, primarily Muslim tumblers and acrobats
    (among Hindus they are called Nats), are usually found
    in cities and towns performing for special occasions such
    as the horse and cattle show in Lahore. Some are seden-
    tary but most move from city to city following fairs and
    public events.

2. The Charan, (derived form Sanskrit *chara*—wanderer),
    confined to the Punjab and Sind, work as migrant agri-
    cultural laborers, often serving as carriers. I believe the
    Charan to be synonomous with the Banjara/Vanjari of
    India. When not working on the wheat and rice harvests,
    they do odd jobs and beg.

3. The Changar, easily confused with the Kanjar, are no-
    madic artisans who specialize in weaving reed baskets
    used by urban and village laborers. They also manufac-
    ture winnowing baskets and brooms and weave fishnets.

4. The Churigar are bangle and jewelry peddlers, either sedentary or nomadic. Most operate out of major urban areas, with single tents traveling through traditionally established village networks.

5. The Gogrā are Hindu and Muslim scavengers who are confined to the major urban areas. They gather garbage and discarded materials such as iron, rags, glass, and paper, which they accumulate and sell to manufacturers. They are the unofficial street cleaners. During the wheat and rice harvest, some tents travel from village to village working as sifters of grain.

6. The Jogi or *saperas* are Hindu and Muslim snake charmers and medicine peddlers. Found throughout the Punjab and Sind, they tend to concentrate in urban areas when not following the village harvest. The men show snakes, the women manufacture and sell medicines. Some tents also maintain hunting dogs for the amusement of villagers.

7. The Kanjar are best known as artisans who manufacture terra cotta figurines and sell them as toys. They also sing and dance, and outstanding musicians and dancers often migrate to urban areas. They also sell perfume and gather scrap paper, cloth, and reeds to make paper flowers and animals, which they peddle door to door. A segment of Kanjar also own small wooden and metal merry-go-rounds and sell rides to the children.

8. The Kochi are primarily an Afghan tribe of pastoralists, some of whom smuggle and sell illicit goods such as cloth, firearms, lumber, and opium. They should be considered caravaneers rather than nomadic artisans and entertainers.

9. The Kowli, or Ghorbati, a Muslim group of tinkers and traders, peddle pots and pans among villagers and pastoral nomadic groups in Baluchistan and Persia.

10. The Lohar (blacksmiths) are one of the major nomadic artisan groups, often called Lori in the southern Sind. Found in North India and Pakistan, these nomadic tinkers and smiths may also trade and deal in cattle, especially in North India and the Southern Sind (see Misra 1975; Ruhela 1968).

11. The Marwari peddle toys and knickknacks (combs, soap, razor blades) in the Hyderabad area of Sind.
12. The Mirasi are famous in Pakistan as genealogists. They are the bards of North India and also work as storytellers and impersonators.
13. The Oudh are pastoral but a small segment works also as caravaneers and professional thieves (*dacoits*).
14. The Qalandar are a major group of entertainers who show dancing bears and monkeys, sing, dance, perform magic, and work as impersonators.
15. The Sansis are primarily nomadic, unskilled laborers and beggars. Like the Gogrā, they travel from village to village to help harvest rice and wheat, mainly as sifters. Many deal in medicines and charms for a variety of diseases. They, like the Mirasi, may also be genealogists.

Throughout Pakistan, particularly among sedentists, these peripatetic groups are frequently lumped together under the term *khānābādōsh*, a Persian term incorporated into Urdu, Punjabi, Pūshtō, and Sindi, which glosses into English literally as "house-on-shoulder." The term is also used by the sedentary population to refer to a snail, a tramp, and to those who have no permanent place to live (those who carry their homes around with them). When used by sedentists, the term always carries a negative or derisive connotation; it is seldom used as a term of reference among peripatetic groups.

While all spatially mobile groups (including pastoralists) are generally categorized into the single concept of khānābādōsh, I found that most peripatetics have a more elaborate classification scheme to distinguish different nomadic activities from those of sedentary groups. Depending on the context, the term khānābādōsh may be limited exclusively to *pāryātān* groups, a usage which is analogous to terms outside Asia such as gypsies or itinerants. Among peripatetics I found a clear conceptual distinction between *chaupani* (pastoralists); *qāfīlā* (caravaneers, professional thieves, and smugglers); and pāryātān (nomadic artisans, entertainers, and peddlers).

Sample Selection, Contact, and Rapport

The widely dispersed nature of these groups, along with their fluid social organization and spatial mobility, created problems in selecting a group for intensive study. While any of the pāryātān groups would have been satisfactory for the study, not all were willing to accept our presence; others were too small for ease in observation of the independent variables (cognitive amplifiers) and measures of the dependent variables (perceptual field independence/dependence).

During the survey, the groups most frequently encountered were the Jogi, Mirasi, Kanjar, Lohar, and Qalandar. I ruled out the Kanjar, Lohar, and Mirasi because their camps were very small (averaging three tents); and they were openly hostile and suspicious of my intentions. The Jogi and Qalandar had larger camps (mean of five tents), but the Jogi were extremely suspicious, which left the Qalandar.

The Punjabi month of Bhadun (about mid-August to mid-September) is a relatively slow period for villagers in the Punjab. Egler (1960) has termed it a period of waiting: there is little work other than irrigation, ploughing of fallow fields, weeding, pasturing, and care of livestock. During this time the Qalandar converge on large cities to earn cash. Using Lahore as a home base, my research assistant and I made daily visits to Qalandar camps in and around Lahore. In early September we approached a camp to the south of Lahore which was composed of fifteen Qalandar tents. By coincidence, we had encountered five of these tents earlier during the survey near Rawalpindi. We visited the camp daily for two weeks, concentrating our questions and interests on animal training practices. I then asked for permission to purchase a tent and live next to them in order to save transportation costs. Permission was granted, and full-time fieldwork among the Qalandar commenced in October, 1971.

To the best of my knowledge and that of the Qalandar with whom I lived and traveled, no other non-Qalandar, either Asian or European, had ever lived in their sociocultural milieu. Entree into the Qalandar world was slow and painstaking, and when finally granted, it was contingent on four promises: (1) never to divulge the nature of their language (Qalandari, more often called Farsi, is unwritten; Farsi here means "the language which others cannot understand"; see Grierson 1922 for an interesting discussion of Gypsy languages comparable to Qalandari); (2) never to reveal the exact source of their bears and monkeys or to divulge their cost; (3) always to disguise the amount of cash and kind earned by an individual or tent; and (4) never to report to the police or other authorities about things they should not know.

A unique set of circumstances early in the research helped me gain rapport with the Qalandar. Shortly after we moved in with the camp and while preparing to move north after the rice harvest, the Pakistan–India war broke out. Caught near the Indian border, forty tents of Qalandar were forced to remain in an exposed area during this period. We were subsequently bombed and strafed by both sides and suffered a few losses. This situation created a strong sense of shared experience between the Qalandar and myself. I was subsequently adopted by them and thus became privy to such information that an outsider is normally forbidden to know. Throughout the research period I kept a flat in Lahore, where a single tent of Qalandar would often visit overnight. This provided an excellent opportunity for candid discussions of subjects that could not readily be discussed in the camp setting.

Research Method and Materials

Along with a female full-time research assistant I lived in a tent and traveled with the Qalandar for fourteen months. During this period we used two tents, a Western or Pakistan army-type tent with a canopy in front to provide shade and a standardized testing context, and a Qalandar tent, which was used for traveling because it was easier to assemble and also less conspicuous. We walked with the group, carrying equipment on three donkeys. Traditional ethnographic information was collected on kinship, economic, political, and other material with a view toward a general ethnography. Early in the investigation, research was focused on subsistence activities and the division of labor by sex. The Qalandar understood the purpose of the specific and general questions relating to skills and training, as these topics are vital to their livelihood. While establishing rapport with individuals, we concentrated our inquiries on the training and maintenance of the dancing bears and monkeys, balancing goats, and fighting dogs. To better understand the animal training process, I traveled to Peshawar with several Qalandar and purchased a ten-month-old Kashmiri black bear. Learning to train this bear was very helpful in understanding skill-training and also provided much amusement for the Qalandar.

Socialization and Child-Rearing Practices

Observations and questions relating to child-rearing practices were organized and collected along the lines suggested by Whiting et al. (1966). It was impractical to record detailed descriptions of interaction patterns simultaneously with observation of behavior, because as professional entertainers, the Qalandar were acutely aware of being observed and would regulate their behavior accordingly. Instead, by participating in these activities I was able to observe behavior sequences, which had to be recorded later.

The Language Barrier

The Qalandar speak the languages of the areas in which they travel. Most Qalandar speak Punjabi, Hindi, Sindi, Urdu, and Rajasthani fluently, in addition to their own language. Baluch and Pāshtō are also spoken, although less fluently. Most of the research was conducted in Punjabi at first, and later in combined Punjabi, Urdu, and Farsi. My assistant and I did not know all of the languages spoken by the Qalandar, and when they wished, the Qalandar would switch to a language unfamiliar to us.

Fieldwork through Space

The fluidity of social organization and spatial mobility posed many obstacles to observation. However, by frankly discussing these issues with the Qalandar early in the research period, we were able to overcome many difficulties. Four of the most troublesome problem areas were: being identified as partial to one side in a dispute; deciding which group of tents to travel with when a group split up; sharing and receiving food and gifts; and explaining our presence among the Qalandar to the sedentary population. Each of these potential problems was resolved in the course of fieldwork.

From the beginning it was determined that we were present to learn and not to teach. We agreed never to share information gathered from one informant with another. This ulimately resulted in a reciprocal agreement: as guests, the investigators would not interfere, and as hosts, the Qalandar would not abuse our guest status by trying to involve us in their disputes. This was successful to the point that we witnessed major social infractions (including murder and theft) and were not expected to participate in the final resolutions. When camps divided, we decided to move with the larger segment generally; however, if an infant was born or new animals were being acquired for training, we would stay with that segment. From time to time we would pack up on our own and join another group, generally in response to information about someone having a baby, getting married, or dying. On several occasions this involved renting a truck, loading our animals and equipment, and traveling several hundred miles to join another group.

Sharing food is important among tents camped together, and disputes about selfishness, unequal shares, and so forth were a major source of internal tension and ultimately fission. From the beginning it was decided that we would share food at a different tent each day. Thus we ate whatever a particular tent was serving in exchange for an equivalent amount of our uncooked food. We did make tea twice a day which was shared with all present in a camp.

Initially, we encountered considerable hostility from sedentists because we were studying khānābādōsh children rather than their own. The Qalandar finally decided we should tell the sedentists that we were studying the bears and monkeys, not the children. Given the "pariah" status of nomadic artisans and entertainers, it was not surprising that this explanation was extremely satisfactory, even applauded, among the sedentists.

By following the major segments of the initial group contacted at Lahore, we ultimately were able to make contact with 800 tents of Qalandar, primarily in the Punjab and northern Sind. Movement was confined primarily to major roads, canals, and railway lines. Our regular contact was with 105 tents throughout the research period. During the fourteen months of field research, we traveled over 5,200 kilometers, approximately 1,800 kilometers on foot. Our travel routes are indicated by the black arrows on the map (Figure 4).

Perceptual Inference Habits

The specific activities and skills related to particular socioecological contexts were analyzed from three perspectives: how the individual is socialized into these skills; how access to and experience with these skills is related to the division of labor by sex and age; and how these skills are expressed and maintained on a day-to-day basis. Observations on the three variables—subsistence activities, child-rearing practices, and sexual division of labor—were organized along the lines recommended by Whiting, Child, and Lambert (1966), Barry, Bacon, and Child (1957), Minturn and Hitchcock (1966), and Gladwin (1970).

As indicated in the review of literature, a number of studies have demonstrated that variations in learning environments produce variations in perceptual-cognitive skills. As environmental demands effect certain adjustments in social organization, they enhance specific psychological adaptations. Individual patterns of experience within these realms are related to socialization activities and interpersonal processes within a given ecocultural context. Cross-cultural variation in psychological performance in measures of psychological differentiation as well as Piagetian conservation tasks, at both the individual and group level, has been shown to correspond with cognitive amplifiers in diverse socioecological systems. In order to systematically assess perceptual inference habits related to both Piaget's and Witkin's theories regarding the role of experience (cognitive amplifiers) in psychological functioning, we selected a battery of perceptual-cognitive tests to be administered to samples from each population (Qalandar, Kanjar, Lahoria, and Jat).

As previously discussed, one of the common denominators of Piaget's and Witkin's theories is the notion of perceptual-cognitive articu-

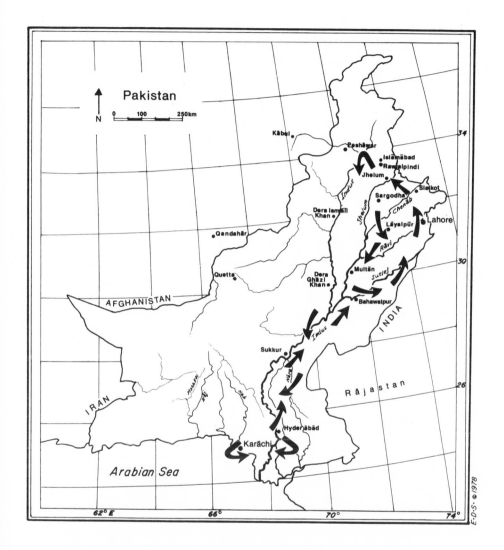

Figure 4. Map of Pakistan, showing Qalandar and Kanjar travel routes.

lation. Young children (preoperational in Piaget's terms) tend to be less articulated relative to older children and adults. Articulation involves the analysis and structuring of the environment so that parts of the perceptual field are experienced as delineated and discrete (field-independent); less articulation is characterized by perception of the field as a whole (global or field-dependent).

In a discussion of Piaget's developmental scheme, Witkin et al.

(1962) pointed out that the same trend is found in the development of psychological differentiation: children tend to be less articulated early in their perceptual development and become more articulated as they grow older. Both Piaget and Witkin have argued that articulation in perceptual-cognitive functioning involves perceptual disembedding. In turn, competence in perceptual disembedding is associated with disembedding in nonperceptual tasks. In discussing the research on the Embedded Figures Test (EFT), Witkin et al. (1971) found that performance on the test was related to performance in a broad array of other perceptual tasks requiring disembedding, especially the Muller-Lyer illusion and other related measures. This is supported by the research of Piaget (1967, 1969), Piaget and von Albertini(1950), Piaget, Vinh-Bang, and Matalon (1958), and Witkin et al. (1971).

In a replication of Piaget's work on perceptual illusions and of Witkin's research on field independence, Gardner (1957, 1961), Mercado, Ribes, and Barrera (1967), and Robinson (1972) have demonstrated that response to the Muller-Lyer illusion is essentially a perceptual and scanning task related to the level of field articulation. Poor performance on the EFT or on the Children's Embedded Figures Test (CEFT) and the Muller-Lyer illusion can be related to inefficiency in attending to relevant cues and in disregarding irrelevant cues.[2] Piaget(1950, 1969) and others have shown that this "attending efficiency" is also related to the kinds of perceptual processing involved in the conservation tasks; preoperational children often rely on perceptual cues in explaining nonsimilarity in conservation.

In the present study, an effort was made to delineate those factors which have been demonstrated to influence variation in psychological differentiation. Toward this end, ethnographic observation and systematic assessment were focused on those activities and skills related to basic subsistence strategies. While these measures assess different aspects of the perceptual-cognitive domain, they are treated in this study as interrelated measures of the dependent variable, perceptual inference habits. Thus a wide range of tests was available. Due to the operational limitations of the field setting, measures of perceptual differentiation were selected for their interrelatedness, while still tapping a broad spectrum of the behavior in the perceptual-cognitive domain.

Samples

We acquired measures of perceptual inference habits from the two peripatetic populations, Kanjar and Qalandar, while living and traveling with them. While living among the Qalandar during the first field trip, we frequently shared camp areas with groups of Kanjar.

Over time we developed rapport with these people, and on four different occasions lived with them for periods ranging from several days to three weeks. During these sessions perceptual measures were collected, along with observations of enculturation activities. Additional ethnographic information was gathered from Kanjar as well as Qalandar on subsequent field visits in 1979 and 1980. (A long-term comparative study of manufacturing activities among Kanjar, village potters, and carpenters is scheduled for 1982–1985.)

During the first year we visited more than 150 villages in the Punjab and Sind, which enabled me to select two villages as comparison populations. In the second year my sample was two adjacent villages, one with primary school, one without, composed primarily of Jat farmers. The general locations of the two villages, in the Gujrat district of the Punjab, are shown on the map. The urban sample of Lahoria was contacted through my research assistant's agnatic relatives and other friends with kinship ties to families in the walled city of Lahore.

Tests

One of the most difficult and initially frustrating tasks was developing a battery of tests that would be sensitive to the dependent variable but acceptable and practical in the disparate ecocultural milieus. Before systematic assessment of perceptual inference habits was begun in earnest, we administered a battery of traditional measures of perceptual style and conservation to a sample of semi-sedentary Qalandar and villagers in the Karachi area. The initial battery included:

1. Embedded Figures Test (EFT) and Children's Embedded Figures Test (CEFT)
2. Perceptual Illusion Battery (Segall, Campbell, and Herskovits 1966)
3. Kohs (Wechsler Adult Intelligence Test) Block Designs
4. Conservation Indices

The EFT and Block Design tests proved to be unacceptable measures. On timed tests the villagers, and especially Qalandar, couldn't agree on what "work as quickly as you can" meant. Unschooled villagers varied on these cards from a few seconds to more than six hours. The Qalandar saw no reason why they shouldn't work on reproducing a design for several days or longer if necessary. In fact, one of the Qalandar informants took a set of blocks and was still working on the designs seven years later. Time was a factor on the EFT as well, but also the detail on each stimulus card became blurred by dirt and indistinguishable after being handled several times. Because they were not used to following the "rules" of testing situations, the use of the "pointing stylus" with the EFT was anathema to the Qalandar, as was my direction to leave the cards on the table and only look at them. Several, in an effort to heed my concern about not touching the cards, used knives to point; and once the figure was disembedded, they liked to cut it out and show me exactly what it looked like "out of context." (Knives were occasionally used to trim off half of a block to make it "fit" in reproducing the pattern of the Block Design test as well.) While I did not have an unlimited supply of these two tests, I had no intention of telling a Qalandar what he could or could not carve on!

Both nomads and sedentists related well to the stimulus materials in the Perceptual Illusion Battery (Muller-Lyer and Sander parallelogram) and the CEFT. Following Price-Williams (1961, 1972), we used local, familiar materials in the conservation tasks. Examples of each test series are included in Appendix 2.

Materials

To ensure comparability of test results, the equipment was standardized, as were the positions of the researchers and the subject. A modified television table with a flat, light gray nonglare top was used as a testing surface. Four rattan stools (*muras*) of varying height were used to assure standard perceptual distance between eye level and the stimulus material on the table.

For the peripatetic and village samples, all tests were administered under a protruding flap at the front of the tent. By closing the front of the tent the subject was less distracted by activities surrounding the testing situation. For the urban sample, the tent was not used. Instead, the table, seats, and canopy were set up on the roof of a house in the old city of Lahore. (House roofs are often recreational areas for families as well as sleeping areas during the hot season.) In each setting, all tests were given outdoors during daylight hours with Shell No-Pest Strips hung on the tent canopy poles to keep flies out of the visual field and away from the stimulus materials. However, this was not always successful, and the flies were a great source of distraction within the peripatetic samples.

Test Presentation

To insure standardization, tests were administered in the same order for all subjects: Illusion Battery, CEFT, and conservation tasks. The total testing time varied with age and subjects, with a range of 60 to 180 minutes. Throughout the testing situation a flexible approach was taken: if informants appeared to misunderstand the instructions or the situation, directions were repeated as often as necessary. A break was taken between tests if the subjects appeared tired or irritated. All subjects were tested individually, and the orientation of the two researchers relative to the subject was held constant.

Subject Variables

All subjects participated on a strictly voluntary basis. Each individual was asked if he or she would like to play some games that children and adults in other places and cultures play. The notion of competitive and skillful performance on games (*khel*) is an ancient concept in South Asia. A variety of cognitive games in the chess category, as well as games of perceptual-motor skills, from trick knot-tying to shell games and the like, are part of both the nomad's and sedentist's cultural heritage. Individuals were not paid for participating, although candy and cigarettes were given to each subject at the end of the testing session. Because subjects were selected on a strictly voluntary basis, it was impossible to systematically match or control subjects on the key variables of age, education, and sex. However, every effort was made to solicit volunteers representing the range of these variables. All subjects were fluent in Punjabi, so all test directions and test-related interviews were conducted in that language. The directions were translated into Punjabi without difficulty, and we were satisfied that the subjects understood the nature of the tasks they were asked to perform. For several of the urban informants, however, who were more comfortable using Urdu, directions were translated and interviews conducted in Urdu.

Characteristics of the Samples

The basic age, sex, and educational characteristics of the four sample groups are summarized in Table 1. Formal education is reported in years completed. The Pakistani school system is divided into four levels: primary (grades 1–5); middle (grades 6–8); high and intermediate (grades 9–12). In the village situation, only primary school children were available for testing. All levels were available in Lahore.

For the sedentary samples, school records, parents, and others could provide accurate ages, but among the nomads age determination proved to be a problem. Nomads measure time by seasonal change, which controls agricultural production and nomadic movement. A common annual benchmark is Ramadan, a major Muslim religious period. Births are not officially recorded nor are birthdays recognized; thus, when an informant says a child is five years old, he

Table 1. Statistical characteristics of the four sample groups on three important demographic variables.

Variable	Sample groups			
	Qalandar	Kanjar	Village	Urban
Number	95	37	68	66
Age (in years)				
mean	21.80	13.78	14.53	16.70
s.d.	17.28	7.81	9.94	10.19
minimum	4	5	5	5
maximum	80	40	55	43
Education (in years)				
mean	0.0	0.0	1.21	3.92
s.d.	0.0	0.0	1.47	4.23
minimum	0.0	0.0	0.0	0.0
maximum	0.0	0.0	5.0	12.0
Sex				
no. males	37	16	36	31
no. females	58	21	32	35

means that five wheat or rice harvests have passed, which approximates one year in the Western sense. However, for older informants (twenty to eighty years) estimations of age were very vague. Generally, they had to guess their age. The informant's parents or elder siblings were consulted, and inquiries were made concerning historical and social events at the time the child was born. Many cited a war, a district fair, a flood, or an election, as reference points. Such information was collected for each informant whose age was ambiguous and then cross-referenced with known historical accounts, such as newspapers and census records. The ages reported are thus as accurate as possible. Readers familiar with attempts to systematically assess psychological performance under naturalistic conditions are aware of the problems involved. Because I established excellent rapport with my informants, I am confident that the test results are reliable.

II

The People in Context

4

The Peripatetic Qalandar:
Time, Space, and Structure

Like Rudyard Kipling's Kim, hundreds of generations of South Asians have been entertained by groups of peripatetic Qalandar. Among the lettered and the illiterate, wherever there has been a settlement of people, children have pleaded with parents and *ayas* for permission and a few *annas* to see the Qalandar monkey and bear show. In addition to performing with trained animals, the Qalandar are also skilled magicians, jugglers, acrobats, dancers, musicians, impersonators, and beggars.

Historical Perspectives

While there is some evidence that the Qalandar have been in the South Asian subcontinent since the late Vedic period, written accounts or ethnographies of them are virtually nonexistent. Most of the information in the social-historical accounts of regions administered by British colonial officers is confined to the late nineteenth and early twentieth centuries. The earliest British accounts identify the South Asian Qalandar with the Kalandar of Sir Richard Burton's *Arabian Nights* (1934), which characterizes them as horse thieves, Muslim fakirs, or leaders of performing bears and monkeys. Crooke's description is typical:

> The Qalandar is a lazy, swindling rascal, some who go about with snakes; others with tame bears and monkeys. He wears round his neck several strands of white stone or beads and

glass. He also carries a bead rosary (*tabish*), and usually on his right wrist two or a single brass bangle . . . He announces his approach by twanging the *damary*, or little drum, shaped like an hour glass . . . Those who have monkeys, the male being called Maula Bakhsh and the female Zahuran, make them dance to amuse children . . . Those who have bears make them dance, and allow for consideration little boys to ride on their backs, which is believed to be a charm against small pox . . . They also sell some of their hair, which is a favorite amulet against the evil-eye . . . Some go about as ordinary beggars. (Crooke 1896:186)

In justifying his classification of Qalandar as a criminal tribe, Crooke states:

This tribe, or rather the numerous groups composing it, proceed through districts disguised and call themselves Langre Qalandar or Rohillas of Rampur. In Rampur and the neighborhood they use the former, and towards Lucknow the latter. They travel about in the cold and hot weather, but in the rains they settle down and occupy themselves in begging. Their wives and children accompany them, but they do not encumber their movements with any luxury, such as cattle, furniture, etc., having only one or two ponies for the transport of their personal effects, in addition to which, hidden among their quilts and blankets, are reins, ropes, and headstalls for the stolen ponies . . . They pass the night under trees or in the fields, or, if near a populous place, in a convenient grove. During the day, disguised as beggars they mark down the horses and ponies which they purpose to steal. When they obtain a fair number of animals, they pass off as horse-merchants, and make their escape as rapidly as possible. (Crooke1896:187)

Although Crooke's account was written more than eighty years ago, it reflects the present-day perception of the Qalandar held by the sedentary population, including many officials, in the Punjab and Sind. This is partially the result of ignorance and superstition and partly of Qalandar efforts to maintain a mystique about themselves.

Many popular accounts link the origins of the Qalandar to the fourteenth-century Muslim saint Bo Ali Qalandar, who died in the Sind in 1324. While some devotees of Bo Ali Qalandar are labeled "Qalandar," they are not Qalandar in the sense of the tribe (*quam*) or of the occupation and skills of nomadic entertainers. When asked by outsiders about their origins, Qalandar frequently claim to be followers of Bo Ali Qalandar or devotees of Qalandar Lal Shah Baz, a saint who arrived in the Sind during the Arab conquest of Muhammad bin Qasim in the eighth century. While Qalandar are frequently followers of a number of *pirs* (holy men or spiritual guides) and saints, these origin stories are fictitious accounts used to satisfy or manipulate gullible outsiders.

Qalandar have numerous stories explaining their nomadic origins. Two of the most common ones, collected from older informants, are given below.

> During the period of Sikander [Alexander], before Jesus or Mohammed (peace be upon him) our forefathers were zamīndārs [landowners] living a very happy life with land and many cattle.
>
> One day a woman among our ancestors was preparing the evening meal at her house. There was a knock at the door. When she opened the door, there stood a beggar asking for something to eat. "Go and beg from other places first," she said, "my food is not prepared yet. But come back later." Some time later the beggar came back, but just at that moment the woman burned her hand and so she shouted at him, "Go away, you are like a dog sitting there begging."
>
> Before he left, the beggar gave her a *bedua* [bad wish] and said, "Your entire family will always wander around like a dog begging for food."
>
> When her husband returned, she told him what happened and related the bedua. He laughed and said it was just a foolish beggar. A few months later, a big disaster came and destroyed all the buildings, crops, and animals, and the family was starving. The entire *biradari* [brotherhood] met and discussed the beggar's bedua. They decided to search for the beggar and apologize for the woman's sharp words.
>
> After searching for many years they found the beggar and cried at his feet to please turn away the bedua which brought the disaster. The fakir told them that a bedua cannot be called back from God and that they would always have great disasters in their lives. "However," said the beggar, "to help you earn a daily living take this bear and this monkey, train them, and they will earn your bread. You will not earn much, but you will

not die of hunger. If you want more than bread, all of you, children, women, all people, will have to do many things and share together, otherwise you will always have only bread to eat."

Since that time our life is dependent on our animals. We always have to move for two reasons. We cannot perform animal shows in one area every day, and if we have land, a disaster will come and destroy us. See there [we were camped near Lahore], where the factory is. We used to camp there where the ground was high and good. They forced us to move here when the factory was built. Everywhere we go, new things force us to move our camps. The beggar was right, a disaster always comes when we stay a long time in one place.

A second common origin story goes thus:

Before the period of the English Raj, our forefathers were involved in robbery and killing as a hobby. One day after the English came, an official was killed by one of our people. The police came to arrest them, but the biradari had guns and daggers and they killed all the police. The next day the English brought their army and cannons and blew up the village.

Most of our ancestors were killed, but a few were able to run away. After running for many days they got tired and hungry. Where they stopped there was a khānābādōsh camp. They were frightened of the khānābādōsh but so hungry they decided to send the three most beautiful people—one man and two women—to ask for food.

The khānābādōsh leader gave them food and a mat to sleep on. When they woke they learned that the khānābādōsh were Warrach Qalandar who perform monkey and bear shows.

This leader offered to let them live with them and learn how to earn food from showing dancing bears and monkeys. They leader told them that as long as they wander with bears and monkeys the police would not notice them because people see only the animals.

They learned to do all these things and intermarried with the Warrach. Since that time we have been Qalandar who earn our bread from bears and monkeys.

These myths contain important clues toward understanding Qalandar economic and social structure. Like the Rom, tinkers, and

Figure 5. A Qalandar drum.

other nonpastoral nomads of Asia and Europe, the Qalandar maintain themselves as an economic parasitic group within a sedentary society. As a peripatetic population vis-à-vis sedentists, the Qalandar are considered a pariah group. This has produced a strong sense of group identity and contributes to the viability of their subsistence strategy as entertainers within the socioecological milieu of sedentists. This strategy depends on a complex utilization of human social resources, specifically, the sedentists.

Identity

Most sedentists hear a Qalandar before they see one. Each Qalandar male announces his presence by playing a small, hand-held drum (*dug-dug-gee*), which is an hourglass-shaped cylinder with leather drum heads at each end (Figure 5). This drum has a high and distinctive clack which can be heard for a quarter mile or more. Besides signaling the presence of a Qalandar, the drum serves other important functions. Each man's drum has a distinctive tone which identifies him to other Qalandar working in the same area, which is particularly important when they are working in different parts of a neighborhood separated by streets and houses. The drum is also used as a percussion rhythm instrument which, along with songs and stories, accompanies the performing animal and children. In addition to the dug-dug-gee, many men, especially the bear owners, carry bagpipes, and the distinctive sound of each bagpipe also signals a particular man's presence. The sound of bells, often used as decorations for trained goats, dogs, and monkeys, combines with the cacophony of drum and bagpipe to stimulate the curiosity and interest of young and old alike.

In the villages a Qalandar man is usually accompanied by a child between three and seven years of age leading a bear or monkey, along with a goat and a dog. In dress, the Qalandar are rather nondescript compared to other nomadic groups. Each man wears a turban, a long shirt, and a dhoti. Footwear, highly variable, ranges from simple leather slippers to army combat boots, either obtained in lieu of cash for a performance or retrieved from refuse. With the exception of being accompanied by trained animals, the appearance of the Qalandar is similar to that of most poor or service zats in the Punjab and Sind. This invisible social status is a highly adaptive aspect of Qalandar economic activities such as begging.

In marked contrast with the mud and brick residences of the village and urban sedentists, the Qalandar social unit is the tent (*puki* or *tumba*), of a form that is fairly common among nomadic artisans and entertainers throughout Asia and Europe (see Figure 6). Termed a Gypsy Bender Tent, it is similar to the tent used by Pardhis in the Vindhya Mountains of India and that of the Rom in the New Forest and Surrey areas of Great Britain.

The style and shape of each Qalandar puki is a family's identifying signature. Close inspection shows that each tent is slightly different from all other tents, and its characteristics can be read from consider-

Figure 6. A Qalandar tent with the side cloth rolled back.

able distance. This is particularly important in helping members of disputing tents to avoid one another.

The puki is an efficient form of shelter against the elements. The withies, made from eight curved pieces of bamboo, are tied together at the top with strips of cloth or leather. The main cloth spread over this skeleton is in one piece but composed of five individual layers of cloth, with each layer consisting of hand-stitched pieces of material; the result is a unique patchwork design for each tent. Small cloth ropes sewn into the main cloth secure it to the poles. As sections of the main cloth wear out or rot, they are replaced; all five layers are thus replaced approximately every five years. The inside layer of each tent cloth is often made from brightly colored materials cut into a variety of geometric forms. The assembling and dismantling of tents is a cooperative effort by all its members and by other camp members who have finished their own tents. Both sexes sew and repair the tents, although women tend to do this more than men.

The typical Qalandar tent, weighing from 11 to 18 kilos, can be assembled or dismantled in about thirty minutes. When traveling long distances with one-night stops, many families frequently have a smaller, simplified tent of the same general design. Individual Qalandar serving as lawyers and judges also use the simplified tent when they travel alone to settle disputes.

During warm periods the front and back of the tent are left open. Frequently during very hot periods, an entire side is folded up to give maximal ventilation, or a family may dispense with the tent for a night and camp in the open. During cold and rainy periods, the tent flaps are closed to form four fairly well-insulated walls. During the monsoon, groups often remain sedentary or, as water accumulates, move to higher ground. These moves are more difficult because when soaked, the tent quadruples in weight.

The space within the tent is commonly organized in a standardized pattern. Cooking materials are placed at the left (occasionally right) front of the tent. A *charpoy* (cot of woven jute string with a wood/bamboo frame), is placed at the back of the tent; valuable or perishable possessions are also placed here. In the center and front portions of the tent, cotton rugs (*dari*) or jute mats are laid flat on the ground. This and the entrance area are the main social sections for the family. A visitor is usually confined to the entrance and front sections; a family member is always between a visitor and the charpoy, where valuable possessions are kept. The daily social area becomes the nightly sleeping area. Blankets and quilts are spread on top of the dari, where the entire family sleeps together. Prepubescent children often sleep beside their parents. Mature children sleep with their heads against the wall opposite their parent or sibling of the opposite sex. There is a common joke that fathers have sexual intercourse with their daughters and mothers with sons by "mistake" on very dark nights. A shallow pit for the fire is scooped out at the center near the tent entrance. Great care is taken in managing the fire since it is the most common and dangerous threat to the tent. While the arrangements within the tent are generally stereotyped, they vary slightly depending on the size of the family and its possessions. The placement of tents and items within tents are practical considerations which have no ritual significance.

Space

Qalandar use the terms puki or taber to indicate both household and tent and also to count the number of tents present in a group. The distribution and movement patterns of tents are determined by a number of internal and external factors. External factors relate primarily to economic and social requirements. Because the Qalandar are entertainers, the demand for their skills is determined by the availability and duration of resources among sedentists, which depends on the seasonal harvests. Intensive mobility coincides with the wheat harvest (*rabi* or *hari* crops) from early April to mid-June and the rice harvest (*kharif* or *sauni* crops) from early September through early November (see Figure 7), when tents travel daily along irrigation canals, railway lines, roads, and lanes connecting different villages. Daily movement declines immediately after the harvests, and the Qalandar camp for two or three days in a particular village. These longer camp periods coincide with the major marriage periods among villagers, when there is a great demand for the Qalandar entertainment skills.

The travel route and social structure of the tents that move together, particularly during harvest periods involving high mobility, are predetermined during continual negotiations among tents. The camp structure is based on a balanced distribution of bears, monkeys, and donkeys among the tents. The ideal unit for maximal exploitation of human resources in the average village, is two or three tents with monkeys and one tent with a performing bear. During cycles of intensive mobility great effort is made to promote good relationships among the tents traveling together, because disputes producing segmentation result in deleterious economic consequences.

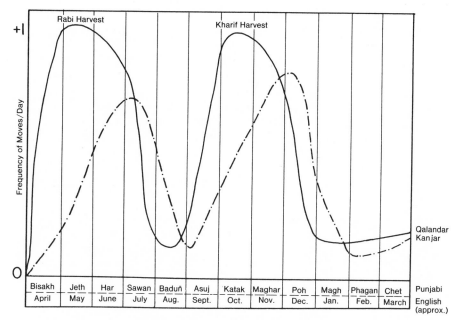

Figure 7. Relative mobility patterns of Qalandar and Kanjar.

The routes taken by groups seeking wheat and rice are usually pre-determined but may vary from year to year. The reason is that, although most tents have never been a part of the traditional village system of crop distribution in the Punjab and Sind, many have developed regular patron–client relationships with minor landlords. The farms owned by the zamīndārs form a route along which tents must travel during the harvest seasons. Following the harvests and marriage periods in the villages, Qalandar converge on urban areas, where they sell the surplus rice and wheat they have collected and begin entertaining for cash.

The success of this adaptive strategy is suggested by its antiquity, To the sedentary population, the Qalandar derived their identity from their animals, tents, and entertainment skills, and their social structure is a complex composite of these factors. It is not feasible for them to remain in one area, because the income from their bears and monkeys is not sufficient to support a family's needs. Consequently, a family uses other subsistence skills and relies on the economic cooperation of all tent members. Their specialized subsistence skills and their intensive spatial mobility expose Qalandar to a variety of sociocultural and ecological niches, ranging from open vistas in desert areas to highly carpentered sedentary ecologies. In addition, they encounter sociocultural diversity among the sedentary populations within each setting. Their survival as peripatetic entertainers depends on behavioral flexibility in adapting to diverse socioecological systems. In order to understand the importance of flexibility in their social and economic organization, and how this contributes to individual behavior, it is necessary to examine the role of animals.

Animals

Each tent depends on its animals, particularly the donkey as a pack animal. Among the Qalandar studied, each tent had an average of two or three donkeys, with a range of one to five. On a day-to-day basis the donkey transports household possessions; while young children and old people guide the donkey along the route of travel, other individuals are free to beg and entertain. The donkey is particularly valuable during the harvest seasons, when the average tent earns seven to ten *maunds* (one maund = forty pounds) of both rice and wheat, which the donkey must carry. Some Qalandar purchase additional donkeys for the harvest period and then resell them. When the tents travel from village to village in the rural areas, grass and fodder for donkeys are readily available along roadsides, canal banks, and railway lines. Most villagers allow Qalandar to graze their donkeys in the harvested fields where they camp. In cities and other areas where this is not possible, family members, particularly women and mature girls, must travel considerable distances to cut public grass. Frequently females arrange with landlords to cut their grass in return for sexual favors. Horses are sometimes used in place of donkeys, but they are less efficient as pack animals and are primarily prestige possessions.

With few exceptions, all tents maintain one or two goats, ideally, one male and one female. Goats serve two important functions; the lactating females are a source of milk for infants and young children, and goats are trained to do balancing acts as part of the entertainment repertoire. Goat kids are retained as replacement stock or sold for cash. On rare occasions, such as circumcision ceremonies, or weddings, an individual will kill a goat and distribute the cooked meat to the camp. Goats are not usually eaten unless they are sick, dying, or too old to work.

Donkeys and goats are not branded, ear-marked, or decorated with any special identification. Their owners work closely with them and can readily identify each of their animals, as well as those belonging to the biradari members. None of these animals are given a name other than a reference to its sex, such as *bakri* (female goat) or *bakra* (male goat). Tent members often develop strong emotions about their animals, and their welfare and comfort receive high priority. It is common for owners to weep when an animal is sold, sick, or dying.

Two sizes of dogs are kept by the Qalandar. Small dogs are trained to dance on their hind legs, walk on their front legs, and mock-fight with the monkeys. These dogs are taken out of camp as part of the entertainment act. Many Qalandar also keep large dogs to protect the camp. They are trained to stay close by the tents and to serve as early warning systems. They first bark at and eventually attack any stranger who is not signaled as "O.K." (*theek-hai*) by a camp member. Dogs, like other animals, are not named; however, since the British period, many of the performing dogs are called Jack.

Some Qalandar keep other animals, including the Asian badger, weasel, porcupine, and miscellaneous nonpoisonous snakes, as pets for their own amusement or more often for display in the urban areas, where children are less acquainted with common wildlife. Older men may keep parrots and chukars in cages. Years ago chukars were used as decoys for fowling, a custom still prevalent in the NWFP.

The three most important animals in Qalandar entertainment routines are the Asian brown bear, the Kashmiri black bear, and the rhesus macaque. They predominate in Qalandar origin myths and give the Qalandar their distinctive identity among other peripatetic entertainers in South Asia.

When an individual has acquired a new animal, all tent members contribute to its maintenance and training. Recognizing its economic significance, they grant the bear a prime social position within the tent. The bears, monkeys, and dogs are not grazed or allowed to freely roam in search of food. Instead they often eat the same diet as the people. Tender leaves, berries, and insects are occasionally used to supplement the diet of bears and monkeys; however, these foods are seasonal and scarce. Most of the time they are fed dal, chapatis, and assorted fruits and vegetables which are begged or purchased from markets. A common expression among Qalandar is "We cannot eat if our animals don't eat first." Indeed, all animals are given priority in the distribution of food. On numerous occasions when food supplies were scarce, I observed Qalandar going without food while a bear or monkey was fed.

Donkeys and horses do not compete for food with the Qalandar, although they are grazed or fed on purchased fodder before the human members of a tent eat. The distribution of these animals and their related skills among tents is an integral factor in the organization and structure of Qalandar society.

Social Structure

The extremely fluid nature of Qalandar social organization and their movement patterns made it very difficult for me to conceptualize a model of their social structure, so I had to rely on Qalandar conceptualizations. They explain that to be a Qalandar is to earn a livelihood by showing performing bears and monkeys. While they also use a number of other economic strategies, such as begging, magic acts, and acrobatics, their unique identity is derived from the fact that only Qalandar have performing animals. Not all Qalandar work with performing bears or monkeys, but every individual has the necessary training and experience to earn a livelihood with these animals if he chooses. Once I had purchased a bear and learned how to handle him in a few standardized show routines, my informants announced, "Now you are a Qalandar."

My informants explained that all Qalandar are considered one qaum (tribe or nation), divided into a number of zats. Qalandar conceptualize their qaum as a tent made up of strips of cloth sewn together, each strip of cloth representing a different zat. The common thread binding them is their specialized skills as entertainers with monkeys and bears. A survey of the 105 Qalandar tents and their genealogical records showed that seventeen different zats were represented. The zat names are fairly common today among historical and contemporary sedentary rural and urban castes in Pakistan (Wikeley 1932) and lend some credibility to Qalandar stories about their sedentary origins. Each Qalandar traces zat membership through his or her father back to some common ancestor who, they claim, was a landlord or famous nomad. Very often their genealogical reckoning goes back to a group of brothers and sisters who were forced into a nomadic lifestyle because of fission in the ancestral sibling group. Qalandar informants readily admitted they did not know who their apical ancestor was and joked that no one really knows.

Unlike the larger sedentary population in the Punjab and Sind, for the Qalandar the notion of zat has very little meaning in determining social organization. The relative insignificance of zat as a structural principle in determining camp composition is related to a number of factors, including organizational fluidity associated with spatial mobility and Qalandar notions regarding parenthood and sibling groups. It is my impression that they use the notion of zat as a descent principle primarily to establish a common heritage with the sedentary population in an effort to escape their pariah status. Like other nomads, the Qalandar rely on flexibility in social organization, emphasizing the weakness or absence of strong political authority or hereditary office, pliability in group membership, and individual as opposed to lineage or group skills in basic subsistence activities. Instead of stressing descent group solidarity, they emphasize their notion of biradari as an organizing principle within the qaum.

Qalandar use biradari in three distinct yet related ways, depending on the context. Occasionally, when external political threats, such as war, threaten large numbers of Qalandar, biradari is used synonymously with qaum. More commonly it refers either to all Qalandar who have fairly frequent contact with each other or to individuals who are camped or traveling together. Implicit in this use is the notion of *biradarānā* (brotherliness), a spirit of group cooperation and support. In some respects biradari is structurally analogous to the anthropological notion of maximal and minimal lineage. In the sense of camp structure (*dēhrā*, a cluster of tents) biradari is constantly changing because of fission and fusion among the tents, the basic social component of the society.

The tent as a social unit is built around the family of a man, his wife, and their unmarried children. In over eight hundred tents visited, there were only eighty-five instances of an extended family group occupying a tent; these represented orphaned children and widowed or infirm elders who were unable to maintain their own tent. The members of a tent are the commensal group. The only corporate property is the tent itself, which is a gift to the bride and groom from their close kinsmen. When two families desire to arrange a marriage between their children, they often camp and travel together. Once the marriage arrangements have been finalized, one form of courtship is for the intended bride and groom to construct their tent with the aid of their relatives. In severe and violent marriage disputes leading to fast divorce or separation, the couple often abandons the tent. In that case, uninvolved relatives often keep the tent but may burn or break it into parts which are distributed among both sides of the family.

All other property and animals are individually owned. The daily utilization of an individual's resources is decided jointly by the members of his tent; however, each member has the right to withhold or specify how his or her possessions are to be used. In addition to the tent, the necessary equipment such as blankets, clothing, harness, and pots is kept to a minimum because of their nomadic lifestyle. The household necessities can be carried by family members and two donkeys.

Ideally, each tent is an independent economic unit, and it is not uncommon to see single tents traveling and working as discrete segments separate from other Qalandar. More often, however, two or more tents will make alliances and travel as a group or camp. The number of tents in a camp depends on many factors, such as season, rural or urban setting, proportion of bears and monkeys, and the relationships among the tents.

In periods of high mobility, as during the wheat and rice harvests, the average camp has three tents (range: one to seven). During periods of less mobility and in urban centers, the average is five tents (range: one to forty or more). Camps of more than forty tents are extremely unusual except when the Qalandar have been confined by outside political force, as during a war. Internal fission usually operates against large camps because they are socially volatile and economically inefficient. During the India-Pakistan War in 1971, more than sixty tents were compelled to camp together for two weeks near the border in the Punjab. Although they were in an exposed area near a battle zone, more Qalandar were killed and injured in disputes among themselves that in bombing, strafing, or shelling. Casualties would have been much greater, but the Qalandar finally convinced the military authorities that "we will kill each other if we have to stay together . . . We do not have a way to control our behavior under these circumstances." That casualties from internal confrontations were not even higher may be attributed to the fact that the Qalandar were busy keeping their animals from killing one another in the air raid trenches.

Kinship is always a component of the alliance among tents; because of biradari and zat endogamy (and exogamy), every Qalandar is related to nearly every other Qalandar in a number of different and involuted ways. Kin affiliation beyond the tent depends on how an individual wishes to trace affiliation at any given time, based on what will best serve his or her interests (and the interests of those he or she wishes to affiliate with). While always manifesting elements of kinship, camps are organized by decisions relating to economic resources and skills. Regardless of the camp size, duration, and season, however, any Qalandar camp is based on choice and represents an alliance among the tents comprising it.

Structural Flexibility and Organizational Fluidity

Where zat membership is determined by birth and is immutable, bira-dari and camp affiliation involves choice. Each Qalandar considers this resource potential vis-à-vis his sedentary clients and his pattern of mobility, as well as the Qalandar with whom he wishes to affiliate or avoid. The crucial point stressed here is that tent alliances and locations are almost always a matter of individual choice, and these choices have a very strong influence on decisions concerning movement and affiliation. As nomads, Qalandar can always move and affiliate with or avoid particular people. This flexibility in social organization is structurally manifested in the deemphasis on lineage (zat) solidarity while ambiguously defining yet emphasizing the notion of biradari.

Relationships among tents are extremely unstable because of fission and fusion among them. Each tent is potentially an economically independent unit whose internal organization and alliance with other tents is based on individual judgment. The process by which Qalandar tents ally themselves is the key to their social organization. Tents within a camp continually reaffirm their alliance by a number of alliance strategies, especially economic and sociopolitical support, food sharing, engagements, and marriages.

As professional entertainers, Qalandar are always conscious of the distribution and nature of the skills and resources in a camp. A camp of only monkey or bear owners, or a concentration of skilled acrobats, is economically inefficient and creates excessive competition for a limited resource—the attention of their sedentary audience. Consequently, friendships, common interests, and kinship are often sacrificed for more practical considerations, especially during the high-mobility, high-income harvest periods. Often a tent alliance during the harvest season is not structurally duplicated in the urban setting. While these practical resource considerations are important, tent alliances are also determined by kinship principles. Most Qalandar camps have tents representing adjacent generations based on affiliation between parents and the tents of their married children. This organizing principle is based on beliefs about human behavior and the role of children vis-à-vis parents.

The Qalandar believe that God (Khudappa) created children to serve their parents. From birth onward, children are expected to serve their parents, particularly older children with greater earning capacity. During the early years of growth and learning, parents are very loving and supportive of their children. The parent–young child (ages three to ten) relationship is often referred to as a *guru–chela* (teacher–student) bond. As children approach puberty and their skills produce substantial income for the tent, the parents' nurturant behavior is replaced by dominance and constant reminders of the children's obligation to parents for feeding and training them. In addition to demanding help and comfort, parents also manipulate the older children for purposes of self-interest and self-aggrandizement. Children are thus perceived both as economic burdens and as social and economic assets. While mastering the skills necessary for a particular economic strategy, the child is considered a liability. When he is capable of working and contributing to the daily maintenance of the tent, the child is highly valued. The notion of lifelong responsibility to the parent is a core cultural value among Qalandar.

However, there is a contradiction between this value and the behavioral reality associated with fluidity in social organization. Once a child has acquired rudimentary subsistence skills, he is capable of economic independence from his natal tent, and consequently parental authority is weakened. The child and his parents must reconsider the child's economic skills in terms of the existing distribution of resources in a camp and the tent's potential alliances. This emphasis on individuality and flexibility is manifested in several Qalandar laments regarding alliances (especially camp membership) with mature children. Older informants often expressed the fragile nature of this relationship by analogy to a batch of bird eggs: "I give birth to a batch of baby sparrows. Most get sick and die, the others eat my food until they are strong, then the bastards fly away."

Qalandar are keenly aware of the need for social flexibility, especially in camp structure. The most commonly used expressions regarding fission in a tent or camp are: "Every person most follow his own stomach" and "Everybody is a friend to his own means." Consequently, while children are expected and desire to maintain relationships with their natal tent, the exigencies of their nomadic lifestyle make these alliances extremely difficult to maintain. While parents desire to maintain close affiliation with their children, they realize that tent survival is enhanced by successful alliances with other tents, and the most desired means of establishing such alliances is through engagement (*mang*) and marriage (*wai-al* or *shadi*).

Marriage, Fusion, and Fission

Engagement and marriage planning occupies a large part of Qalandar life. Regardless of the age of the prospective partners, all engagements and marriages are arranged by the parents or, if the parents are not available, by the parents' siblings or the prospective partners' older siblings. Occasionally there are love (*mastānā*) marriages; however, these are extremely rare and short-lived. When a couple enters into an unarranged or unapproved marriage, the biradari may declare them *hukka-pani-bund* (literally, "waterpipe is closed"), and they are ostracized from all Qalandar affiliation. Most commonly the deviant couple is denied economic cooperation and camp affiliation. The severity of this social reprimand is usually effective in deterring and reversing deviant behavior.

The considerations in engagement and marriage planning are the economic advantage of the parents and their siblings more than the compatibility of the prospective husband and wife. This strong economic element is reflected in the large numbers of engagements and divorces. Most alliances between tents are sealed or symbolically insured by the two tents announcing an engagement between children. If the alliance is successful and the engaged children are old enough (postpubescent), the marriage takes place. However, most children are engaged many times before they are old enough to marry. Although informants usually lose count, they estimate that the average child is engaged more than thirty-five times between conception and the first marriage following puberty. One tent engaged a particular child with two different tents on the same day. In the morning, Tent A engaged their eight-year-old daughter to a boy in Tent B. During the ceremony (simple sharing of food and tea with great expressions of love and affection between tent members), the wife of Tent A abused another child in Tent B. A fight broke out, and the engagement was broken off. That afternoon Tent A made a new alliance with Tent C and affirmed this new relationship with an engagement the same evening.

Once a marriage has been agreed upon, the tents involved usually travel and work together. During this period the *bovar* or brideprice is negotiated and an initial payment is paid to the bride's tent. While Qalandar express a preference for boys, girls and women are recognized as greater economic assets in the daily maintenance and subsistence of a tent. The bovar is considered recompense for the economic loss incurred by the girl's tent. After marriage the couple's parents try to cooperate in their newly formed alliance, but this tent cluster is seldom able to stay together for long. Because children are supposed to serve their parents first, constant quarreling and bickering among the three tents about the married children's real or anticipated unequal distribution of time between their parents results in camp fission. To ameliorate this conflict-producing situation, the Qalandar ideal is for married children to spend six months camped with the wife's parents and six months with the husband's parents. This strategy is never satisfactorily worked out, and occasionally one or each set of parents demands a divorce and the return of its child. This pressure on married children takes many forms which create tension and conflict within the new tent as well as between their natal tents. Argument, failure to share, and resource considerations are typical reasons for conflict within any of these tents or between individuals from separate tents. Tension and the potential for fission always exist.

The response to this kind of conflict is fairly stereotyped and goes through the following stages. First, other biradari members in the camp try to smooth conflicts into compromises. If they are unsuccessful, the disputing tents will move apart or form new or brief alliances with other tents. Depending on the outcome of the dispute, a divorce may or may not be sought. If the dispute is resolved, the couple remains married; if it is not resolved, parents begin the search for new alliances, that is, new spouses for their children.

In addition to parental pressure, a common source of conflict between a husband and wife is the failure of one to contribute his or her share to the tent. Actually, threats of divorce and separation are much more common than actual divorces. In most cases, the bovar must be refunded, which has a tempering effect on disputes. The money for brideprice is seldom available within the husband's tent. Instead, when a marriage is planned, the husband's uncles and aunts, brothers and sisters, and other biradari members are asked for loans or financial support for the bovar payment to the wife's family. Because other biradari members have a vested economic interest in the success of a marriage, every effort is made to settle disputes before they grow into major social divisions or infractions, such as divorce, injury, or murder.

Disputes and other social infractions that cannot be worked out informally by the camp members themselves are sent before the biradari *panchayat*, a formal jural session composed of camp members and/or other Qalandar who are respected for their fairness. The ruling on a dispute from a biradari panchayat is binding for the litigants. Punishment for most social infractions consists of public apologies, payment for damages, and fines. Payments are standardized by the severity of the infraction and are annually prorated on a sliding scale determined as a proportion of the cash or cash equivalent earned by the offended party during the previous two harvests. For example, if a man beats his wife and she complains to her family, the biradari panchayat, after hearing all the arguments, may fine her husband a proportion of her family's earnings from the previous rice and wheat harvests. The proportion (usually in the range of 5–10 percent) is based on the severity of the beating. Thus, if the wife's family collected three hundred pounds of wheat and two hundred pounds of rice, the fine would be based on the cash equivalent of this amount at current market prices. If a man kills his wife, the fine is usually seven times the total amount earned in the previous harvests. This amount and the manner of payment is flexible, depending on the circumstances motivating the killing.

Qalandar marriages are extremely fragile and behaviorally volatile, although to a lesser degree than are engagements. In the survey of 105 tents, the average number of marriages was three to four for each adult Qalandar, with a range between one and eleven. Husband, wife, or parents can institute a divorce. In a first marriage, the parents often demand a divorce, especially if no totally dependent children are involved. The usual motivation is the parents' discovery of a better alliance. The loss or return of the bovar is compensated for in the new marriage agreement. In a marriage involving dependent children (infancy to three years of age), the husband's family is less inclined to demand divorce, because the bovar is not returned. The wife's family, although it retains the bovar, is disinclined to assume responsibility for a daughter with a dependent child. In second and subsequent marriages, wives tend to instigate divorce more often than husbands or parents. Third and subsequent marriages are more stable for several reasons: the children in the couple's parents' tents have assumed greater economic worth, and by this time the husband and wife have children of their own, which they use to create alliances with other groups. Also, it is not uncommon for a third or even a fourth marriage to be between individuals who were married to each other before. One informant had been married to the same patrilateral parallel cousin three different times.

In an analysis of the genealogical records of these tents over four and five generations, the predominant marriage pattern is between children of siblings or patrilateral and matrilateral first cousins. When asked about "rules" that might regulate marriage patterns, informants specifically pointed out that they do not have marriage rules. Qalandar explain marriage choices thus: "There are people you cannot marry because it is shameful [*sharm*, used in this context to mean "too disgusting to think about"] and other people whom you may or may not wish to make a marriage with—it all depends." Among Qalandar, incest (sexual relations and/or marriage) is limited to adjacent and same generations of sibling groups linked by a natal tent: one's parents, one's siblings, one's parents' siblings, and the children of one's siblings.

Sexual fidelity is expected between husband and wife. Sexual liaisons outside of marriage are discouraged, but the prohibition is not strictly enforced. The main practice is to take great care in not being caught in a sexually compromising situation. When found out, the guilty parties are brought before the biradari panchayat, publicly scolded, and sometimes fined. Sexual liaisons and marriage outside the Qalandar qaum with other khānābādōsh or *gadja* (sedentists) are strictly forbidden unless related to survival of a group or tent. A woman who enters into such a relationship is sought out by the biradari, most often her brothers, and if she does not break off the relationship and return to her tent within a few days, she is severely beaten and/or killed. Because Qalandar are considered socially inferior to all other Muslim and Hindu *zats*, opportunities for sexual liaisons outside the qaum for men are practically nonexistent; however, Qalandar males will occasionally enter into sexual liaisons with other khānābādōsh.

These rules and actual marriage patterns reflect the fission and fusion processes characteristic of Qalandar social organization, and they offer some insight into an aspect of those processes that is easily missed in cursory examinations, namely, the importance of the sibling group. Of all interpersonal relationships, the most valued, loved, and respected are those between brothers and sisters within a tent. With the possible exception of some married couples, siblings are together more than any other age or sex group. Membership in the sibling group is determined through both the mother and the mother's husband with emphasis placed not on descent but on association with the mother from birth. Children are considered siblings (*dūdh-ka-bacha*). While most children nurse only from their mothers, a child who nurses from another woman is considered a member of the sibling group of her tent. Siblings usually share the same tent before marriage; however, it is not uncommon for children of one tent to have siblings in other tents.

Before marriage the sibling relationship is very close and affectionate and is reinforced by mutual support vis-à-vis the parents, especially as children reach marriageable age and must leave the tent. Parents love their children, but they view them as means to an end, as social and economic resources to be manipulated for economic survival. Infants and young children, like naive bears, monkeys, and other animals, must be molded (socialized) as quickly as possible to become contributing members of the tent. This process emphasizes sibling solidarity and is expressed in a common Qalandar analogy about how family life reinforces sibling feelings for one another.

> Our families are like a monkey show. Two monkeys [the children] are tied together and expected to perform and feed the *bandarwālā* [the monkey trainer]. The bandarwālā is constantly pulling on their ropes and poking the monkeys to make them perform better. No matter how hard the monkeys work, the bandarwālā never has enough and is always demanding more. It is the monkey's *patlag* [obligation] to do these things, but he also has a duty to run away. The monkey is never able to satisfy the bandarwālā—the more the monkey does or the more he runs away, the more he is pulled, prodded, or hit with a stick. This is why monkeys hold each other when they are not working.

Qalandar marriages and other alliances between tents are responses to external demands as well as adaptive responses to internal sources of fission and fusion. What appears structurally to be continuity between generations is, in fact, an attempt by each generation to ensure flexible socioeconomic organization by maintaining solidarity and continuity within the sibling group. Structural features fuse with organizational behaviors to produce the fission and fusion characteristic of Qalandar social organization. No move, marriage, or other social response is necessarily decisive and immutable. Along with specialized subsistence skills, this flexibility reinforces for individualism as a personal as well as a social trait.

5

On Being a Qalandar: Subsistence Skills and Strategies

In Pakistan the Qalandar performing bears, monkeys, goats, and dogs distinguish them from other nomadic and sedentary entertainers. No longer found in the more densely populated areas, these animals have a novel appeal among sedentists and when trained are valuable sources of income for the monkey trainer (*bandarwālā*) and bear trainer (*bhālūwālā*).

Monkeys and Bears

Each tent has either a bear or one or more monkeys. The two are seldom owned together and never tied together because it is easy for a bear to injure or kill a monkey. The Asian brown bear is a rare species; among the Qalandar it is outnumbered four to one by the Kashmiri black bear. The rhesus macaque, although no longer found in the Punjab, remains fairly common in the mountainous areas to the north. Both bears and monkeys are acquired very young from a group of semisedentary Qalandar in the NWFP, who specialize in acquiring wild animals. Mountain tribes (Kohistanis) trap bears and monkeys and sell them to the Qalandar as well as to professional dealers for cash. The animals are caged and transported to semipermanent camps in the Peshawar valley, where they are given their first training.

Before being sold to other Qalandar, the bears are conditioned to be led and to stand on command. At five to ten months of age the bears have their canine teeth removed, and a silver ring is inserted into the nose. These experiences are very painful and traumatic for bear and

Qalandar alike, and it is believed that the men who perform these mutilations must never own adult performing bears. It is said that the bear never forgets those who have hurt him and will kill them upon reaching maturity. Monkeys are not mutilated in any way. When captured, they are kept caged or tied. Their initial training by specialized Qalandar consists of being broken to a collar lead and conditioning to sit, lie down, and roll over at a verbal command. After this training, word is sent through other Qalandar that the monkeys are available for purchase. Entertainers who need replacement or additional animals then travel into the Peshawar valley to negotiate the purchase of a bear or monkey.

The purchase of a new monkey or, even more, of a bear involves many extremely complex social and financial arrangements. Monkeys are less expensive, with one brown bear worth about twenty fully trained, healthy monkeys. The more common black bear is worth about twelve to fifteen fully trained monkeys. A four- or five-year-old trained monkey will pay for itself in an average of eight months. Because they are no longer found in the Punjab and Sind, bears have greater appeal to the sedentary village and urban dweller, and a bear owner consequently earns more than a monkey owner; however, the training and maintainance of bears poses special problems.

Training begins immediately when a very young or juvenile animal is acquired, following a traditional respondent-conditioning paradigm. Unsolicited or volitional behavior from a monkey or bear is consistently negatively reinforced by severe beatings, especially on their sensitive noses. Appropriate respondent behaviors, most often elicited by poking the animal with a stick and pulling with a rope, are verbally reinforced and occasionally rewarded with small portions of foods. The animals are given regular practice sessions when not in day-to-day use. This training continues throughout the animals' tenure among the Qalandar and involves the entire membership of the tent and often children and adults from other tents. While the acts the animals perform are fairly standardized, each animal trainer is known to possess some special skill or rapport with an animal which others observe in hopes of improving their own performance routines.

When asked what being a Qalandar means, a Qalandar always specifies familiarity with entertainment routines and skills in using trained bears and monkeys. They are quick to add, however, that income realized from animal routines is seldom sufficient to support a tent throughout the year and that additional income strategies are vital for their survival. Thus, in addition to performing acts, Qalandar are also skilled as magicians, dancers, musicians, comedians, acrobats, jugglers, impersonators, and beggars. Each Qalandar is familiar enough with the skills involved in these activities to earn income or to teach them to naive or less experienced individuals. Many specialize in a particular activity, for example, juggling, and become highly skilled experts who are sought after as teachers or by tents desiring to affiliate with them because of their extra appeal to audiences. The skills associated with their entertainment activities determine the *geist* or the Qalandar cultural milieu, and a description of them here is essential for understanding how these social and technological skills amplify perceptual and analytic processes associated with the ontogeny of psychological differentiation.

The Bandarwālā

At some time in their lives, all Qalandar participate as bandarwālā, either before audiences or within the camp (see Figure 8). The bandarwālā is the most frequently encountered Qalandar in the Punjab

Figure 8. A bandarwālā and his monkey.

and Sind. Less expensive, easier to maintain and handle than bears, the rhesus macaque is trained to perform a number of standardized routines as part of the bandarwālā's act, which are usually parodies of human situations and include the monkey behaving like a frightened soldier (limping, shooting, surrendering); village guard (strutting, beating with a stick); husband being forced by his wife to visit his mother-in-law (being dragged, nodding head, rolling over), and the like. The monkeys are often dressed in costumes made from children's clothes. Other props, limited to items which can be conveniently carried, include miniature stools, eyeglasses, assorted hats, and toy guns, all of which will fit into the Qalandar *jamel*, a special leather shoulder bag. The jamel also holds a begging bowl, food bowls for animals, and sufficient space for payments received in kind, such as portions of rice, flour, or cast-off clothing. In addition to performing monkeys, the bandarwālā also may have a goat trained to perform balancing acts, a dancing dog, comedy performance (*bacha jhamura*) with an accompanying child, and sleight-of-hand or magic routine.

The combinations of animals handled by the bandarwālā is difficult to control—especially during performances in congested areas—and successful management depends on knowledge and experience with the animals in the group. Less experienced bandarwālā confine their routines to single monkey performances. Unless especially gifted as a dancer, acrobat, or juggler, every Qalandar child, especially males, begins as a bandarwālā. By age ten, he has been constantly exposed to other bandarwālās and has received organized training and practice sessions using his father's animals or those of other close biradari members, including performances before family and other camp members. He also is given the responsibility of sharing entertainment activities with an experienced bandarwālā.

At puberty he receives his first monkey and is expected to work independently. For his first few solo performances before the public, his father, mother, or another experienced individual follows him about to observe his behavior, remaining at a distance or blending with the audience. After each performance, the novice and his observer critique his activities, analyzing his timing, aggressiveness, animal handling, choice and execution of routines, and sensitivity to such audience characteristics as age, sex, caste, and class. For example, an animal routine poking fun at mother-in-law/daughter-in-law relationships at a household with a new, in-marrying daughter-in-law might offend the family, whereas in a family with established in-law relationships, such parodies would be entertaining and heartily rewarded. To aid them in being sensitive to a household, neighborhood, or village milieu, the

Qalandar rely on information gathered from shops, barbers, peddlers, and servants, as well as information collected during previous visits. Qalandar are very sensitive to individual and group differences in behavior, based on previous experience and extensive analysis of conditions in varied settings. Material possessions, accent, physical condition, complexion, and such, all provide the trained observer with valuable clues about an audience. For this reason, Qalandar are reluctant to perform in public areas where they have little knowledge of or control over the audience, preferring to work inside a household compound or yard.

As the young bandarwālā acquires experience and confidence, he is able to earn more income, which he uses to acquire additional animals. Those willing to take the risk and who can marshal sufficient resources will try to become bhālūwālā, trainers and performers with bears.

The Bhālūwālā

The Asian brown bear and the Kashmiri black bear—rare, large, and potentially dangerous—are extremely appealing to urban and rural dwellers throughout South Asia. Consequently, the bhālūwālā's routine is the most costly and dangerous yet most lucrative entertainment among Qalandar (see Figure 9). The bears have particular difficulty in adjusting to the heat and the hard-surfaced roads, so they are very irritable and prone to unprovoked attacks on other animals or humans

Figure 9. A bhālūwālā and his trained Kashmiri black bear.

within striking distance. These bears weigh between 250 and 350 pounds, and their claws are clipped at the tips but not removed; children and adults who work with them have extensive scars from injuries inflicted by the swipe of a paw. A blow by an angry or playful bear can kill a man or child; death may be almost instantaneous from a broken neck or more protracted from internal bleeding or secondary infection from severe wounds. I estimated that 10 percent of those who work with bears die from their injuries. Only very alert and quick individuals avoid serious or fatal injuries. The bhālūwālā has to be constantly on guard against his bear's attack or flight, and when a tent is traveling, care is taken to keep bears and other animals separated.

Being a bhālūwālā requires great strength, cunning, and knowledge about an individual animal and consequently, bears are worked and trained almost exclusively by mature, experienced, and healthy men. Although it is usually discouraged, women often train experienced bears when their husbands are away, tired, or sick, but only if mature children or other camp members are present. Though bears may be extremely dangerous, supervised infants and young children from the bhālūwālā tent are encouraged to be around them to increase mutual familiarity. Children are forbidden to ever punish or strike an animal and are encouraged to feed and pet bears, because one of the popular activities in the bhālūwālā's routine involves the bear and child.

The bhālūwālā, unlike the bandarwālā, does not include other animals in his entertainment routines. Most often he uses a bagpipe for musical accompaniment and carries a jamel to hold props and earnings. Many include a young child (age three to five) in their acts involving the bear as well as for comedy routines A bear is primarily trained to dance, march like a village or household guard or a soldier with a stick or wooden rifle balanced on his shoulder, move as if riding a bicycle, and perform other simple acts. At the conclusion of the routine and with economic encouragement from the audience, the bhālūwālā will perform two additional and more dangerous acts. In the first, a mock wrestling match, the bear, standing on his hind legs, is grasped around the waist and chest and wrestled in a circle and ultimately (if the bear allows it) to the ground. In the second performance the bear sits and the child places his head or neck in its mouth. The bear gently grasps the child's neck in its mouth and rises to stand on all fours.

The child is especially vulnerable during this activity, and both he and the bhālūwālā are extremely sensitive to the most minute behavioral changes in the bear. On one occasion, Raja, a four-year-old boy, was working with his father and a large Asian brown bear. At the moment Raja placed his neck in the bear's mouth, a woman in the audience threw her shawl over her shoulder, apparently startling the bear. Seeing this, Raja lunged forward, but not before the bear had wrenched his head to one side and swatted Raja in the leg. Raja's neck was wrenched and lacerated, and his tibia appeared broken. Despite obvious pain, he circulated among the audience to collect the earnings. Then he was carried back to camp and examined closely by his father and his mother's brother, also a bhālūwālā. His neck lacerations were minor, and they joked about how the "flowing blood had drawn extra money from the audience"; however, his fibula was broken. His parents set the leg, supporting it with hard pieces of goat skin bound tightly with strips of cloth. The following morning, the father repeated the routine with his bear before the entire camp. At the close, Raja limped up to the sitting bear and placed his neck in its mouth. At the successful conclusion he was loudly praised by those present, who concurred that both Raja and the bear had salvaged their self-respect (*issat*) and could work effectively together. Because he was genuinely crippled, Raja accompanied his mother to the market, where his condition would make him appealing as a beggar. His five-year-old sister accompanied her father as part of his bhālūwālā routine.

Among many traditional sedentists, it is believed that the bear's claws and hair have special powers which protect against illness and the evil eye (*badi nazar*), and bhālūwālā save claw clippings, which they sell for protection against smallpox and cholera. A small lock of bear's hair is believed to be potent in protecting young children from the evil eye, and a ride on a bear's back protects as well as aids in curing a multitude of diseases. Occasionally a sedentary family will bring a sick child to a Qalandar camp in the hope that a bear will help in restoring health. Qalandar often refuse to take money for this service. Instead, they later find out whether the child lived or died. If the child lived, they visit that house and surrounding area regularly.

Another source of income is from renting bears (and other trained animals) to motion picture companies. Almost half the feature films made in Pakistan about village life include brief scenes including Qalandar and their bears and monkeys; however, this provides only sporadic and low-paid work. Thus, income from the last two sources is extremely variable, and Qalandar survival comes primarily from entertainment routines.

Trained bears are particularly susceptible to disease and intestinal disorders associated with worms. A man who loses a young bear is seldom able to recover or accumulate sufficient funds to purchase a new one. The longer a man works with a bear, the more opportunities there are for severe or fatal injuries to his family or himself. This fear of crippling injury or death ultimately determines a man's tenure as a bhālūwālā. With increasing age, his stamina decreases and his fear increases to a point where he can no longer effectively control himself during performances or training sessions. A few men have turned to eating opium to bolster courage; however, depending on his age and health, a man may sell or trade his bear to a son or relative and resume other economic activities to support himself. Most often he will become a judge or lawyer or return to being a bandarwālā.

Bacha Jhamura, Singing, Dancing

The *bacha jhamura* (joking child), a comedy routine performed by Qalandar only, is a series of brief, humorous dialogues, most commonly between an adult bhālūwālā or bandarwālā and a child (usually three to six years old of either sex). With the adult sitting and the child standing facing him, the following represents a typical *bacha jhamura* routine between a father and son:

Father	Bacha Jhamuray!
Child	Waa Waa!
Father	Is a sheep bigger or a lamb?
Child	Lamb!
Father	Is father bigger or son?
Child	Son!
Father	Is teacher bigger or student?
Child	Student!
Father	I am your father.
Child	I am *your* grandfather!
Father	Is mother bigger or daughter?
Child	Daughter!
Father	How many wives you have?

Child	Two!
Father	Where do they sleep?
Child	On *charpoy!*
Father	Where do you sleep?
Child	In the fireplace!
Father	Why did you perform this?
Child	For my stomach!
Father	Now Jhamuray, say salaam to everyone.

Occasionally a widow and her child or an elder and a younger sibling will perform *bacha jhamura*. Because all children learn the routines by rote, a man without young children often borrows a child from a neighboring tent. By age four, all children have learned at least a half dozen of these brief routines. Most are based on parodies of established social roles, especially authority in sex-role relationships. Along with hand clapping and other physical manipulations that teach rhythm to the infant and young child, systematic training in these standardized verbal responses begins with the child's first language development.

Along with *bacha jhamura*, Qalandar children learn to sing and dance (*nātā*). Their songs and dances fall into three discrete styles: traditional Qalandar; traditional village and regional; and popular and contemporary music, often related to motion picture themes and preferred by the more modern sedentists, especially urban dwellers. Public performances are limited to the traditional village and contemporary styles; their own music and dancing are performed only within Qalandar camps. Public musical performances are occasionally part of animal routines, but more often are limited to special engagements at weddings and other celebrations among the sedentary population. Singing and dancing performances are not regular sources of income, and only prepubescent children and older males dance before the public; Qalandar consider it shameful for women to dance outside the camp milieu. Young, attractive (light and clear-complexioned), and graceful boys between six and eleven years are selected and trained, most often by their mothers and other female dancers. Their dance routines are very stylized, demanding coordination and control, and it is not uncommon for six-year-old children of both sexes to possess the grace and sensorimotor control of mature, professional dancers.

Magicians, Jugglers, and Acrobats

In addition to bacha jhamura and *nātā*, Qalandar children also learn basic magic skills (*judugar*) or sleight-of-hand manipulations, which are part of performing animal routines and are performed specifically at sedentists' weddings, birthday parties, and similar occasions. When not otherwise occupied, adults and older children frequently use acts of legerdemain to amuse infants and toddlers, and by puberty, children are expected to be sufficiently skilled in sleight-of-hand skills to perform before the public. The tricks in the Qalandar's repertoire are fairly simple and standardized, with little reliance on extensive physical apparatus. These routines include ball, coin, and cigarette manipulations; cup and ball routines (shell games); handkerchief or silk tricks; turban cuts and rope tricks; and basket tricks and other illusions.

Sleight-of-hand skills depend on pure manual dexterity, emphasizing speed, coordination, and control of perceptual-motor processes. They involve presenting sequences of manipulative activities requiring intense concentration and simultaneously generating deceptive or misdirection cues such as false movements, patter, and comedy. Qalandar stress the importance of deception (*fareb*) in magical activities; they exploit established or create new perceptual-cognitive associations by specifically focusing or misleading the audience's attention during physical manipulations or routines, for example, by looking up in the sky or pointing away from the manipulation. Although these deceptive activities are standardized, Qalandar are sensitive to such audience characteristics as social class, occupation, age, education, and other factors which might influence memory, attention span, and associations. Qalandar attribute the success of these routines to their clients' inability to inhibit (*roknā*) the influence of deceptive manipulations or previous associations (*mila raknā*).

The sensorimotor and perceptual-cognitive skills related to sleight-of-hand and dance activities are behavioral characteristics also utilized by Qalandar in their entertainment strategies as jugglers and acrobats. Although they are not as skilled as full-time professional acrobats and jugglers in traditional urban centers, Qalandar include feats of balance and simple juggling routines (*bajiger-nutt*) in their repertoire and perform publicly on special occasions, especially in rural areas. In contrast to their sedentary counterparts, Qalandar emphasize individual skills rather than team activities, such as bending over backward, feet flat on the ground, and grasping the ankles or picking up a cloth lying on the ground. One of the more popular balancing acts with numerous variations requires two boards (3 feet by 4 inches by 1 inch) arranged in the shape of a cross, with ten full glasses or cups of water placed an equal distance apart on them. From a sitting position, the juggler balances all this on his head, rises to a standing position without support of his hands, then dances in a circle without spilling any water. While all Qalandar receive training in bajiger-nutt skills and many practice it for their own amusement, only very talented children perform before the public.

The entertainment strategies discussed above, especially the bandarwālā, bhālūwālā, nātā, judugar, and bajiger-nutt, emphasize individual skills demanding sensorimotor coordination, concentration, and practice. Two additional subsistence activities, impersonation routines (bērūpiā) and begging, are based exclusively on sensitivity to and manipulation of human social resources outside the Qalandar cultural milieu.

Bērūpiā

Bērūpiā (Sanskrit: *bahu*, "many"; *rupa*, "forms"), denoting an actor, mimic, or more correctly, an impersonator, is an ancient entertainment skill found only on the Asian subcontinent. Because of its antiquity and the unusual nature of the perceptual cognitive activities and skills involved, I discuss it here in some detail. The role of bērūpiā in contemporary Asian society is best captured by Prakash Tandon in the autobiography of his childhood in the Punjab:

> A Behroopia's specialty was to disguise himself and act a role in such a realistic manner that people did not suspect it to be play-acting. He might arrive at a party as an old toothless hag, and no one would know until the end, when he suddenly threw away his garb and declared that he was a Behroopi. People used to be so taken in that they would gasp with wonder and reward him suitably. (Prakash Tandon 1961:81)

While there are many cursory historical accounts of this skill, the best description for the Punjab is that of Ibbetson:

> One of the favorite devices of the Baharupias is to ask for money, and when it is refused, to ask that it may be given on

condition of the Baharupia succeeding in deceiving the person who refuses it. . . . Some days later the Baharupia will again visit the house in the disguise of a peddler, milkman, etc., sell his goods without being detected, throw off his disguise, and claim the stipulated reward. (Ibbetson 1911:133–134)

Working as a bērūpiā is a matter of individual Qalandar choice and aptitude. When a young man decides to pursue this skill he is often apprenticed to an established or retired Qalandar bērūpiā; occasionally he will go and live with a Mirasi bērūpiā guru (teacher) during his training period. The range of his impersonations depends in large measure on his complexion, height, and facial structure. Many a young man begins as a female impersonator but switches to more masculine roles as his beard and voice mature. Characters most commonly impersonated are policemen, government inspectors of measuring devices such as gold/silver scales in commodity markets, women, insane persons, holy men, landlords, army officers, doctors, zāmindārs, and old women. A bērūpiā must always carry a comb, lipstick, mirror, face powder, and mascara, as well as the clothing, such as dresses, suits, and shoes, and props such as a gun, briefcase, and eyeglasses, that are characteristic of the role he intends to play. General knowledge is acquired from ascending generations who have had experience in dealing with a wide range of individuals in those roles. In selecting individuals to impersonate, a bērūpiā often unobtrusively observes people from a distance. Qalandar bērūpiās constantly work on improving their impersonation skills; regional accents are practiced, clothing and props are continually refined to ensure cultural credibility. Impersonations are rehearsed before camp members and other bērūpiās who openly critique the performance. A detailed knowledge of social roles and values in the more diverse sedentary society is also a crucial requirement.

While each routine is idiosyncratic, the basic interpersonal strategy is stereotyped. A Qalandar dressed as a poor beggar first approaches an individual to beg money or food; if refused, the bērūpiā informs the individual that he will return and deceive the ungenerous one into giving him money or food. He then returns after a few days or even several weeks as a bērūpiā to deceive or get a promise of money from the individual. When the money (or kind) is handed over, the bērūpiā casts off his disguise and demands payment because he has successfully deceived the person. Most individuals taken in by a bērūpiā pay in proportion to the degree they have been deceived; the more successful the deception, the greater the reward.

In South Asia the bērūpiā is distinguished from the professional con artist (*badmash* or *char-sau-bis*). Since the British period a bērūpiā in the Punjab is supposed to carry a police identity card specifying that he is not a char-sau-bis. Qalandar bērūpiās commonly carry testimonial books with letters of praise from those they have successfully fooled. A successful bērūpiā earns about as much as a bhālūwālā and derives great personal pleasure from his successful impersonations, which are based on specialized knowledge about behavioral characteristics associated with social roles, as well as specific information in individual strategies as a professional beggar.

Begging (*faqir*), another major economic strategy, is a highly developed skill used throughout the year, but most intensely when the Qalandar are camped near the urban areas to obtain cash, food, clothing, and other daily necessities. The cycle of begging is closely related to the lunar months of the Muslim calendar, especially the periods with special religious holidays. Several of these holidays are especially favored by Qalandar because the well-to-do are most generous in their distribution of food, cash, or clothing. These holidays include: Id Milad (the Prophet's birthday); Id (marking the end of Ramadan); Id-ul-Bakr (month of Haj); Maharram (month of mourning for Imam Hussain), followed by Safar (month of great hardships in the history of Islam); and Rajjab (commonly called the month of *zakat* or alms). Rajjab marks the period when Muslims assess their wealth and property and distribute 2½ percent of its value to the poor, sick, widows, and other needy. Zakat is the fifth pillar of Islam, and people believe that by giving alms their property becomes purified and blessed. The Qalandar make a point of being in wealthier neighborhoods during these festival periods.

Qalandar also try to capitalize on regular religious occasions when people give alms as part of their normal *fitrana* obligations. This includes giving charity on the eleventh day of each new moon and giving alms before joining the Friday Eid prayers. Most Qalandar in Pakistan claim to be Shiah Muslims and devotees of Imam Hussain, the son of Ali and grandson of the Prophet, but in reality they tend to be religious pragmatists—Sunnis, Shiahs, Ahmadiya, or Christian, whichever affiliation best serves their purpose. Many informants were bitter about the partition of India, because they missed the Hindu festivals and seasonal pilgrimages that they covered before strict border controls prohibited free movement between India and predominantly Muslim Pakistan.

Normal everyday begging is usually confined to market areas. Women with infants and those young children not accompanying the bears and monkeys or tending donkeys visit markets and bus or railway stops to beg. They beg cash from shoppers and travelers, and food from merchants, the source of most of the fruits and vegetables in their diet. While all Qalandar beg, it is the women and young children who provide the tent with most of its daily requirements. Old people no longer able to keep up with the extensive mobility maintain themselves exclusively by begging. This strategy is possible in Muslim Pakistan and Hindu India, where there is special compassion for the aged, hungry, crippled, and destitute women and children. Qalandar discuss the skills of successful begging at length and teach them as separate economic strategies. Children learn how to dress and make up their faces to enhance a hungry or sick look and practice walking with a limp or on a crude crutch. Mothers beg with infants, and older siblings beg with baby brothers and sisters.

Girls between eight and puberty occasionally combine sexual joking with their begging strategies. They watch for small groups of high-school-aged urban boys, especially schoolboys walking home through relatively isolated areas. One or two girls will walk beside them and make sexual gestures and jokes, which most often relate to the boys' desire to view or touch a girl's vagina. Most boys are so embarrassed that they will pay the girls to be quiet and go away. More aggressive youngsters are coaxed into a field or behind a wall with promises from the girls to expose or allow finger penetration of their vaginas for a prepaid sum. Having collected the money, the girl instructs the boy to sit on the ground. The girl may then lower her *shiliwar* (baggy trousers), exposing her vagina for a few seconds, or more likely, money in hand, run away. A more aggressive girl may encourage the boy to expose his penis before letting him momentarily insert a finger into her vagina before she runs away. Girls enjoy recounting these immensely humorous episodes to their families and other camp members. The income derived from sexual joking is less rewarding than the intense pleasure the girls derive from manipulating and humiliating the boys. Like the bērūpiās, they enjoy being the center of attention and source of mirth among camp fellows. Individual feats are praised regardless of sex, age, or relative status, and Qalandar emphasize the importance of each individual's contribution to the survival of his tent.

Division of Labor

Flexibility in behavioral skills is manifested at the individual as well as corporate level in their division of labor. A formal analysis of the manner in which individuals are assigned to subsistence activities is summarized in Table 2. Both sexes participate in most activities approxi-

Table 2. Qalandar division of labor by sex and age.[1]

Activity	Age		
	0–7	7–14	14–20+
Food preparation			
Preparation	D	D	D
Cooking	D	D	D
Killing, butchering	C	C	C
Tent maintenance			
Repair (sewing)	C	E	E
Water fetching	C	C	C
Fuel fetching	C	C	C
Cleaning	C	C	C
Clothing repair	—	C	C
Laundering clothes	C	C	C
Material culture			
Bag making	D	D	D
Rope cordage	E	E	E
Playing musical instruments	C	C	C
Political activities			
Lawyer (*waikel*)	—	D	D
Judge (*munsub*)	—	—	D
Primary economic skills			
Bhālūwālā	C	A	A
Bandarwālā	C	A	A
Musician-singer	C	D	A
Dancer	C	D	A
Magician	C	D	A
Bacha jhamura	C	—	C
Juggler-acrobat	C	D	D
Bērūpīa	—	A	A
Beggar	E	E	E
Sexual joking	B	B	B
Care of animals			
Dogs	C	C	C
Goats	C	C	C
Bears	C	C	D
Monkeys	C	C	D
Horses	C	C	C
Donkeys	C	C	E
Chickens	C	C	C

Table 2, *continued*

Activity	Age		
	0–7	7–14	14–20+
Pets (snakes, birds, badgers, porcupines, weasels)	C	C	C
Milking	C	C	C
Grass collection	C	E	C
Supervised grazing	C	E	C

1. A = exclusively males; B = exclusively females; C = approximately equal participation by both sexes; D = predominantly males; E = predominantly females.

mately equally, and young children are actively involved in all spheres
of economic activity as well as decision making. Skills which are limited to one sex are bērūpiā, for males only, and sexual joking, females
only. In tents with bhālūwālās and bandarwālās, men are generally
the exclusive animal performers before the public, although women
commonly assist in the daily training of bears and especially of monkeys. In fact, when a man is not working with his monkeys, his wife
often takes the opportunity to formally instruct their children in basic
bandarwālā skills.

Men do most of the food preparation and day-to-day cooking for the
tent. When Qalandar travel exclusively during the harvest periods,
wives prepare breakfast (tea and any food left over from the previous
evening meal), while husbands feed and prepare the animals for the
day's travel. Women usually go begging early in the morning and late
in the afternoon. When camped near urban centers, the women go out
to beg more often than the men go out to entertain with their animals,
and as the women's economic contribution is then greater, the men
actively participate in food preparation and infant care.

If a tent or camp member has not returned to camp within a few
hours after dark, other camp members begin to be concerned. If a
child or man does not return, camp members go to search, but if a
married woman does not return, there is great hesitancy about
discussing her absence and general reluctance to go in search of her.
Women must often extend sexual favors to zāmindārs or village over-
seers in return for grass for the animals or food for the family, and
these sexual encounters, unlike sexual joking among unmarried girls,
are *never* discussed between a man and wife, brother and sister, or father and daughter. Husbands worry about their wives and privately
express disgust about these unions, but no matter how worried or
angry a husband is, he never includes these liaisons in family argu-

ments. Occasionally, when he expresses his jealousy or anxiety to his father or another senior biradari member, he is sympathetically reprimanded and reminded that his stomach is full, his animals and children have enough to eat, and "each individual must follow his own stomach."

While women go out almost daily to beg and cut grass, men vary the amount of time they spend as entertainers with their animals. About half of the men go out every day, while the other half go out two or three times a week. Most often husbands go out to entertain because their wives threaten to beat or leave them. A wife's common refrain until her husband has gone is: "You lazy bastard! Go bring food for us. Are you going to feed your animals your own flesh and blood!" When a man has not worked for several days or has returned with less food and cash than expected, his wife tries to shame him into contributing more. She first attracts other tent members' attention by screaming abuse at him: "You shit-faced son of a pig, seed of dirt, sister fucker . . . You don't earn anything! Have you no shame? The animals are hungry, the children are hungry—the tent needs repairs . . ." If the man has worked hard and is not holding out he will retort: "Stop barking! Your vagina (mouth) is on fire. A penis as large as a tree cannot satisfy you!" His wife most frequently replies: "You go and fuck your mother—she has a bigger vagina. You smell like a rectum and your penis is covered with lice!" This pattern of abuse often degenerates into laughter as each uses increasingly foul abuse. On some occasions the abuse leads to physical attack, with the wife most often striking her husband with a stone or stick. These fights are usually broken up by other camp members. Most often the relationship is back to normal within an hour. Sometimes, however, the man or woman will pack up and leave until tempers have calmed down.

In the economic activities described above, earnings are divided among the individuals who have worked together. Shares are usually equal for adults and children over six. Smaller shares are given to very young children, and infants receive nothing. A child or adult working alone considers all income in cash and kind to be exclusively his or her own, to be consumed or distributed among tent members as he or she chooses. The much expressed, but seldom practiced, cultural ideal regarding food and income is that all resources should be given to the mother or wife for distribution. This ideal is approximated in an individualistic manner. During the day, those who have earned cash and food often consume or hide a portion in their clothing before returning to camp, then give the balance to the mother or wife to save, prepare, and distribute. Each member of a tent accuses every other member of being selfish and holding back. From time to time this abuse shames an individual into relinquishing his personal cache, but this is exceptional. Because abuse and accusations about hoarding may lead to physical attacks by fellow tent members, most individuals try to consume most of their daily earnings before returning to camp. Uncooked foods are considered the common property of the tent. The distribution of food within and among tents symbolizes individual efforts to maintain tent and camp solidarity. Daily variability in the food available for distribution contributes to either fission or fusion in camp.

Qalandar believe that the relationship between husband and wife is based on economic cooperation and mutual support. Husbands and wives are expected to cooperate in maintaining their tent and giving support to their parents, siblings, and children. Public authority and decision making are ideally supposed to be vested in the men, but informants readily admit that private and real authority is held by women. The dominant social position of females is best summarized in the following expressions frequently used by Qalandar men: "This is the time of women's rule . . . The women will take us to our graves . . . money is like a *pir* (holy man), wives are like a trick (*bahana*); you follow them both."

Men constantly complain that their wives expect too much work from them, and individuals spend a great deal of time arguing about the responsibility for obtaining and distributing resources. These arguments both within and between tents are often harsh and are expressed in a pattern of abuse which is characteristic of interpersonal relationships in a Qalandar camp to the extent that they consider abuse a valuable social skill. One informant explained that "our children first learn to abuse, then learn to talk."

There are no apparent distinctions of age and sex in the pattern of abuse. Every Qalandar abuses every other Qalandar, explicitly and without hesitation. Abuse terminology relates to sex, sexual organs, urine, feces, and so on. For each polite term or construct describing a sexual act, there are scores of slang terms for the same concept, each of which can be ranked by the severity of the intended abuse. A few of the most common abuses used between tent members on a daily basis are listed in English below:

Dyad	Abuse
Young son to father, to get or distract attention	My penis is in your mother's vagina!
Young daughter to father, when being scolded	Stop barking . . . go put your head in your mother's vagina!

Dyad	Abuse
Sister to brother, expressing anger or affection	You have a face like a monkey!
Sister to sister, expressing anger	Your face is like a big vagina with lice in it!
Elder sister to younger, unmarried sister, expressing anger	Stop barking or I will tear your vagina open and enter into it!
Mother to daughter, expressing displeasure	You are made of feces!
Husband to wife, expressing anger about requests or demands	Your face is like a big vagina!
Husband to nagging wife	Stop barking and go fuck a dog!
Wife to husband, expressing anger	Go and fuck your sister (or mother)!
Father to daughter, to stop annoying him	Put your finger in your vagina!

Abuse is used in practically every setting and serves to release tension both within and between tents. As some artisans take pride in their technological skills, Qalandar take pride in their ability to generate creative abuse. Perhaps more important, their readiness to abuse without consideration of status or rank reflects their belief in basic equality among all individuals.

These subsistence activities and patterns of social organization are the stuff of Qalandar survival. As peripatetic entertainers, Qalandar rely on successful execution of routines involving skills which require constant practice, reevaluation, and planning. Each set of skills involves unique, specialized behavior emphasizing flexibility and a broad spectrum of sensorimotor and perceptual-cognitive activities.

6

On Becoming a Qalandar: Socialization and Child-Rearing Practices

Qalandar believe that all children are gifts from God, and parents consider them as potential economic resources. Child-rearing practices emphasize individual development and basic sociotechnological skills. Each Qalandar is perceived as a unique individual to be trained and encouraged throughout life in those basic skills which best fit his or her age, ability, and temperament. Parents consider it their obligation (*patlag*) to nurture and teach these skills. It is the child's obligation to learn and use them to support themselves and contribute to their natal tent.

Qalandar believe that the individual's temperament and basic skills change with age and experience. Consequently, throughout their lives they evaluate one another to obtain the best fit between an individual's ability and those skills best suited to earn a living. Their emphasis on the unique status and flexibility of each individual is demonstrated in the often-quoted saying: "Panjun unglian baraber nahee handyan"—No five fingers are alike.

This emphasis on individual variation in ability and temperament may be related to the lack of terms in their language for the different stages or periods in life. When asked what the most important times in a Qalandar's life are, all agree on birth, marriage, and death, the major events that set the parameters within which an individual is socialized into the cultural milieu. The behavior patterns between these major life events correspond with five stages in individual development: infant, birth to three years; young child, four to seven years; *chela* (student), eight to puberty; adult, marriage (fourteen to forty); and old age, forty to death. The notion of chronological age has very little meaning among Qalandar. As a child matures, his status relates to his kinship position as well as his socioeconomic potential and abilities. As discussed earlier, one of the most striking features of Qalandar social organization is the inclusion of infants and young children in all spheres of sociocultural activity. While stressing individuality, Qalandar, from birth through death, are integral members of a wide range of socially organized task and family groups.

Pregnancy and Childbirth

Women often are not sure they are pregnant until the end of the first trimester, although they suspect pregnancy once they have missed their first period. When a woman is confident she is pregnant, she immediately informs her husband and other camp members. This is to protect the pregnant women from *parchhanwā*, the evil shadow of a woman who has recently had a miscarriage or stillbirth. If the parchhanwā falls on a pregnant woman, it will, according to belief, cause miscarriage or stillbirth. Pregnant and parchhanwā women avoid each other so that the latter will not be in the former's shadow. Besides avoidance of parchhanwā, the two most important restrictions during pregnancy relate to dietary restrictions and abstinence from sexual intercourse. Pregnant women are supposed to avoid "hot" (*safra*) foods, that is, most meats, nuts, and certain other high-protein foods, because they are believed to cause miscarriage. They are supposed to refrain from sexual intercourse to avoid miscarriage, but there is great variability in the actual practice of these taboos.

During the last month of pregnancy a woman tends to stay closer to camp and often restricts her daily activities to shorter periods of begging, grass cutting, and wood gathering. If an older, experienced midwife is not available, word is sent to another camp for a midwife. Most often a pregnant woman camps with or near her mother, who serves as the midwife. During labor and birth the woman is confined in a comfortable position within her tent, accompanied by her mother and/or the midwife. Her husband and children (if any) squat in front of the sealed tent, and the women inside report on the progress of the birth through the tent flaps. When the infant is born, the husband announces its sex and general condition to the camp. He is then expected to give the cash value of a baby monkey or goat to the camp members to buy food for a celebration. Inside the tent the midwife buries the afterbirth, bloody clothing, and rags under the floor of the tent to keep dogs from eating them, bathes the mother, and wipes the baby clean before placing it next to its mother. Small, light bells are tied to the infant's wrists and ankles. The mother or other attendant frequently strokes the infant about the face and gently massages the feet, hands, and legs. These physical manipulations elicit responses from the newborn which are perceived as recognition signals of the parents' affection and concern.

A mother's breast milk is believed to be safra for seven days following birth, so the baby is fed a mixture of water and brown sugar by dipping a twisted cloth into an open cup of the *gurpani* (sweet water or *sherbet*). Because the cup is exposed to flies, newborn babies frequently develop intestinal infections, and many die of marasmus and dehydration within two to three weeks. Between 60 and 65 percent of all babies die within the first month to six weeks of life. Because of the high infant mortality rate, babies are often not given a name until they are a year or more old, but may be given a nickname (*larkāi-kā-nām*), usually a term for a common animal or insect, such as *chiri*, sparrow; *chicher*, leach; *kerri*, ant. These larkāi-kā-nām often stay with a child until he is married. Not uncommonly, adults address each other by their nickname in a joking relationship.

Infants are fed frequently, and a breast or bottle of milk is always given on demand. Because of poor diet related to food restrictions during and immediately after childbirth, a mother frequently has insufficient breast milk. Consequently the breast is often supplemented with goat's milk or buffalo milk purchased from *Gujjars* (nomadic goat or buffalo herders) or tea shops. At approximately two or three months, the infant is given tea (rich in sugar and milk) and introduced to solid food, most often dal and rice mixed with milk. During the first year or two the mother, and often older, nonlactating women in the camp, let the infant use their breasts as pacifiers. Plastic, honey-filled pacifiers are purchased from the market as breast substitutes, especially after the first teeth appear. Independent of teething activities, infants are allowed to manipulate and chew on a wide variety of objects, including pieces of cloth, sticks, and practically anything that is not easily swallowed. Since a newborn baby is believed to be particularly susceptible to a number of spirits and ghosts (*jinns, bhuts, cherals*) and the evil eye (*buri nazar*), many charms and amulets (*tabiz*) are placed on him for protection. Also beads, bells, pacifiers, and the like are tied around his neck so the infant has something to manipulate and pay attention to.

Depending on the difficulty of the delivery, the mother is usually up and round the next day. While a woman is considered unclean (like a pig) for forty days, her polluted state pertains only to prohibition of sexual intercourse during this period. On several occasions when a camp moved, women with newborn babies were seen to get up and walk for many miles. If she is extremely weak, a woman may ride on a donkey or, if that is not possible, her tent remains behind. The infant is carried on the hip in a sling or arm cradle by the mother or other camp members. Occasionally the infant is placed on top of a donkey and secured to the household possessions; the caretaker walks along-side.

Infancy

Because of the high rate of infant mortality and beliefs regarding the baby's vulnerability to buri nazar, the infant is confined fairly closely to the tent for the first few weeks, and all members of the tent and close relatives from other tents care for him constantly. When the mother goes out to the toilet or to visit another tent, he is cared for by his own or other tent members, who take turns watching the baby, fanning flies from his face, singing, and performing other nurturing activities, which include fondling, kissing, tickling, and leg massage. When left alone during naps or a brief emergency within the camp, he is placed in the *jhūlā*, a patchwork cloth hammock suspended by ropes from the tent ridgepole. During the first seven to nine months he is frequently placed in the jhūlā to sleep during the day, but at night he sleeps next to his mother on the ground. Infants, though often asleep, are constantly sung to and talked to by parents and sib-lings. Very commonly, if a baby is crying, all family members take turns through the night holding the baby cradled in his or her lap and singing lullabies. The Qalandar expect babies up to nine months or a year to cry, and they never scold or speak to them harshly. After the baby begins to crawl (about five months) and walk (nine to ten months), adult abuse and scolding are common, but never in extreme anger. By the time the infant is three or four weeks old, he has become an integral member of the camp. Instead of spending most of his wak-ing hours with his mother or older siblings, he is now passed from one tent member to another. When sleeping, he is returned to the jhūlā in the family tent or held by an old man or woman. Until he can support himself in a sitting position (about four months), he is placed in the jhūlā when left alone, where he is very safe for a number of reasons. Within the tent, the jhūlā is suspended about two feet above the ground, which provides shade and allows air to circulate around the baby while keeping him out of easy reach of snakes and insects. While alone in the tent and in the jhūlā, the baby is never out of earshot of other camp members, but if they should be remiss, the tent dogs bark and warn the camp of unfamiliar animal or human intruders.

The Infant's Perceptual World

From the moment of birth, the Qalandar infant enters into an environment of extremely complex and variegated stimuli. To understand the nature and intensity of stimuli impinging on a week-old infant lying in a jhūlā, I spent eight hours lying in a comparable position in a Qalandar tent. The visual field is represented in Figure 10.

To the reclining adult, the patchwork roof of the Qalandar tent represents scores of geometric forms in variegated colors which change with the movement of the sun and clouds. The elasticity and curvature of the tentcloth change the shapes with bursts of wind. The field of stimuli surrounding an infant is much too complex to describe in detail here. Instead, I ask the reader to imagine the variety and intensity of sights, sounds, and smells that emanate from and around a Qalandar tent, including traffic (automobiles, trains, buses, *tongas,* cycles); animals (goats, dogs, monkeys, sheep, camels, horses, donkeys); humans and their paraphernalia (bells, clothing, music, radios, laughter); and so on. Out of this mélange the infant learns to recognize the familiar stimuli, such as parents' voices, the sound of camp dogs, the particular bray of each tent's donkeys, or the unique chatter or each monkey.

A Qalandar also provides additional stimuli for the infant. By the time the child is a month old, and frequently at birth, a parent ties strings of light bells on his ankles and wrists. As he grows older, his parents and siblings spend hours dangling brightly colored objects before him, encouraging him to "look" and "grasp." Parents and other camp members frequently use sleight-of-hand routines to amuse infants and toddlers. Frequently held in people's laps in a sitting position, the child is exposed to nearby activities such as magical acts, as well as events related to camp maintenance and entertainment routines. When transported, infants are always vertically positioned, allowing exposure to a broader, more distant, and variegated sensory-perceptual world. This systematic stimulation begins in the first month and continues through puberty.

Free Soiling

Infants are not diapered and are generally left bare from the waist down. Most wear second-hand or begged clothing. Infants and toddlers are often dressed in a shirt or short dress, so that clothing below

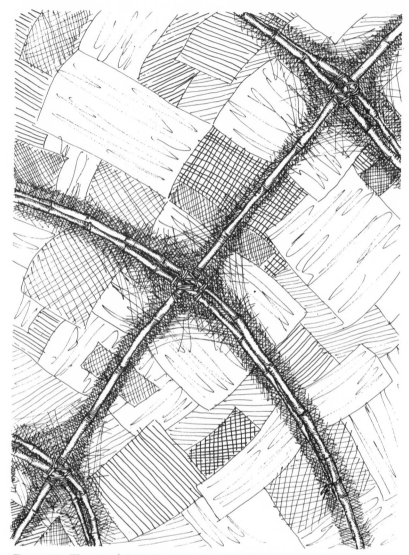

Figure 10. The visual field of a Qalandar infant lying in a cradle.

the waist will not interfere in free soiling. When babies urinate they are simply turned away from the individual or group, most often toward the front or back of the tent. Defecation is handled less casually—infants and young children are grabbed up and spirited outside to the front or rear of the tent. Parents and siblings try to anticipate a bowel movement, and many infants spend long minutes suspended above the ground in a squatting position being encouraged to move their bowels. During the night, and when carrying an infant for long distances, family members place rags between themselves and the baby.

No systematic effort is made to toilet train an infant until he can walk, which is between nine and ten months. By this time he has learned the verbal command to "sit still," and the family has begun to more accurately estimate the timing of bowel movements. Once he can squat and walk without support, he is led outside the tent and told to defecate. If he does not, this procedure is repeated at regular intervals until he does. When he defecates as instructed, he is warmly praised by all present. If he fails to defecate outside the tent and messes himself and/or others within, adults or older siblings wipe up the feces with cut grass and throw it outside the tent or into the fire pit. By the time he is thirty months of age, the child will go outside the camp to defecate. Until puberty, children are allowed to urinate within the camp; after puberty males and females go separately away from the camp for elimination.

Infant Handling

There is no shame attached to genitals or elimination for Qalandar children. Genital manipulation is common in infants, and both sexes frequently explore each other. Adults are greatly amused when young children try to copy the moves in sexual intercourse that they have observed among adults and animals. Qalandar will often use these episodes as catalysts for abuse or sexual joking among themselves. Women frequently draw an analogy between a young boy's ineptitude in intercourse and her husband's; for example, "No matter how still I lie, he can do nothing!" Sexual joking is common and uninhibited in front of children. Its importance in Qalandar life is reflected in the saying that "everyone follows his own stomach, and when the stomach is full, they follow their genitals." Masturbation is discouraged for males, because it is believed each individual has a given, unrenewable amount of semen.

Qalandar seldom bathe infants more than once or twice in the first year, although they frequently wipe clean the hands, mouth, and genital area. This deemphasis on cleanliness relates to two important elements of their customs and beliefs; namely, that infants and young children are more appealing as beggars if they are dirty and that dirty, unattractive infants are less likely to attract the attention of someone possessing the evil eye. Older children and adults, who also bathe infrequently, wash the genital area daily as part of the normal toilet associated with defecation. At other times they wipe their hands and face clean with a damp cloth. While many adults wash with well water, the location of the camps means that bathing is confined to rivers, tanks, and canals. Older people are modest in bathing and always remain fully clothed.

Clothes are washed regularly with soap and water. Individuals take responsibility for washing their own clothes, with parents and older siblings washing an infant's clothes. From an early age Qalandar learn to express their individuality in their clothes and their manner of washing them. Each individual develops a unique rhythm in pounding clothes as he washes them which, like the rhythm of his drum, represents his "signature."

Though their role is less than that of the women, older men and male siblings (between eight and twelve) spend a great deal of time taking care of infants. During the day, when husbands and wives are busy, older men who no longer entertain with animals and are not otherwise occupied frequently care for camp infants. Most often, however, an infant accompanies his mother as she goes to beg and cut grass. When an infant can support his head (about one and a half to two months) he becomes a part of the primary economic routine of begging. Until he can walk (about eleven months) and imitate morphemes as a bacha jhamura at about thirty-six to forty months, his primary activity outside the camp is to go begging with his mother or occasionally an older sister. Before he can walk, his mother carries him straddling her hip, her arm around his back for support. During the process of begging, he is held out or pinched so he will cry and whimper. Thus, from birth, the infant is not only included in the cultural milieu of the camp but also is exposed to the sedentary milieu as a participant in begging. Until he can crawl at about six months he is primarily a passive recipient of this stimulation; however, systematic manipulation of his behavior begins in the first months of life.

The Qalandar actively encourage infants to participate in and explore the world, with few restrictions on active participation. To encourage an infant's socialization, parents and especially older siblings systematically train infants to become independent, contributing members of the tent and camp.

Systematic Training

While most infants and children are expected to learn from imitation and example, certain early behaviors receive systematic training, with the most obvious strategies directed toward accelerated development

Figure 11. A Qalandar woman teaching a young child to dance.

of gross and fine motor behaviors. To encourage crawling, a two- or three-month old infant is placed in a prone position, and a sibling holds food or a pacifier just in front and above him to encourage him to raise his head and chest to get it. When he is five or six months old and on all fours, his teacher holds food or some other desired object just out of reach in front and above him to stimulate him to crawl and grasp for his reward. Later, when he begins to bear some weight on his legs, his mother or a sibling grasps him under the arms and, while singing, rocks him from foot to foot to teach him rhythm and balance (see Figure 11). On his back on the ground or in the jhūlā, and later when he begins to sit without support, he is constantly trained and entertained with brightly colored objects such as bells and food to encourage his grasping and fine motor development. When he begins to crawl he is allowed to explore the tent and camp, with the only restrictions being to avoid donkeys, bears, and monkeys which might cause injury. Frequently, after the child has learned to stand and crawl, a parent or sibling holds out food to encourage the child to walk. During this period parents, siblings, and other camp members are very supportive of the infant. As he begins to toddle, they spend many hours patiently supporting and encouraging him to walk independently. In all learning situations, they encourage him to develop new behaviors and systematically reinforce them, with either nonverbal reinforcement (candy, food, hugs, and pats) or, almost always, with verbal reinforcement ("*Shabash!*—"bravo," "well done!"). As he gets older, they gradually replace physical rewards with verbal reinforcement and other indications of approval and support. By age three, children are given a share of the earnings from entertainment routines performed with adults. The child is free to use these earnings as he chooses. Food is most often shared with the tent, while cash is hoarded or used to purchase candy, fruit, and cigarettes, which most youngsters begin smoking by age five.

While young children may be verbally scolded for inappropriate behavior, the emphasis is on encouragement and reward of desired behavior. Verbal abuse is most frequent when parents lose their temper; however, in two years of observations, I saw young children struck or beaten on only five occasions. These beatings, in the form of a spanking across the back of the legs, were all associated with the child's mistreatment of animals or younger siblings. Other camp members readily praise appropriate behavior but are reluctant to punish children from other tents, because this often leads to disputes between adults.

The Young Child

From about three to eight years of age, children are incorporated according to their abilities into two regular economic activities, begging and bacha jhamura. By four years, they have learned the basic bacha jhamura routines, and those who are best and considered the most appealing to sedentary audiences work with their fathers or other camp relatives who are bandarwālās or bhālūwālās. Children who are less attractive because of dark complexion, pockmarks, and other defects work as beggars, alone or with their mother or older sibling. When children are not engaged in begging and bacha jhamura they are expected to assist in cutting grass, gathering wood, and other work necessary to maintain the tent. During leisure time they occasionally play games, such as marbles, "tent," and tag. Most often, however, they sit beside their parents or other camp members as they arrange marriages, groom each other by removing head lice and giving leg massages, and discuss decisions and problems about life and survival in general. Also during this period adults instruct and encourage children in balancing acts, dancing, and basic sleight-of-hand procedures. Each child is observed and evaluated by his parents and other camp members, who decide which skills he should concentrate on to develop expertise. In selecting his entertainment skills, each child is expected to follow the counsel of his parents and other biradari members. Young children who have exceptional skills and abilities then begin specialized training as acrobats, singers or dancers, bērūpiās and so on.

Qalandar have learned through generations of experience that very young children, women, and old people are much more successful as beggars than older children and men. Therefore, children between eight and thirteen years of age are considered *chela* (students) who are to concentrate on developing expertise in entertainment skills, especially if they are boys, and on taking care of younger siblings and the tent while parents are away during the day. Included in entertainment skills for all males are those for bandarwālā, magic acts, and the control of balancing goats. About this time most boys receive a naive monkey and/or goat from their parents to begin training and incorporating into an act. This requires several years of intensive practice, and the older boys are frequently confined to camp during this period. First as infants and later as chela, children most often have contact with the second ascending generation, because it is usually the grandparents who are available during the day to instruct and help the novice bandarwālā, bērūpiā, nat, or bazigar. When an older child's mother is around, it is she who most often forces the child to practice the necessary skills.

While older girls are also encouraged to participate in these activities, they usually continue to beg, either with the mother or in pairs, or they work at sexual joking. Posing as mother and child, they frequently take infant siblings and beg with them. Like older boys, girls are expected to care for the tent and younger siblings. A girl's tent will not consider arranging a marriage for her until a boy can support himself as an entertainer. Once girls have reached puberty (about twelve to fourteen years of age) and the boys can support themselves as bandarwālās or bērūpiās, their marriages are arranged, and the cycle of alliances and training is generated anew.

Summary

Qalandar infants and children are recognized as potential economic resources upon which tent and social survival depend. Toward this end, child-rearing practices for both sexes emphasize early development of the skills associated with subsistence activities and the qualities of self-reliance, independence, initiative, and aggressiveness. Children are trained for and assigned tasks which contribute directly to their own welfare and to the survival of the tent. From a very early age the child recognizes that the tasks he is assigned represent an important contribution to his own and his family's survival. Consequently, the social world of the child and the adult are the same. This contributes to perhaps the most striking characteristic of Qalandar children—their self-assurance. This stems in large part from child-rearing practices which emphasize that each child, regardless of sex and special abilities, should be exposed to and trained in the basic skills of the nomadic entertainer. These specialized skills, along with the animals and the nomadic lifestyle give a Qalandar child his identity in the larger sedentary world and within his own cultural milieu. The importance of this milieu to the individual is summarily stated in the following Qalandar tale:

> We are khānābādōsh. We go place to place and fight a lot but still we live together and intermarry. If somebody gave us enough food and land and asked to stay in one place we wouldn't be happy there. You [the investigator] can understand this because of your experience living and traveling with us. Staying in one place is not our pattern or system.

> There was a jungle in which many bulbuls [birds] used to live. There they were free and happy, singing and fighting together. One day a king passed through that jungle and trapped a bulbul and took her to his palace. He made her a golden cage and had his servants prepare delicious food for her. Whenever it was meal time, the bulbul would just sigh and say: "Oh! This cannot compare with Bulkh and Bukhara's food." Whenever the bulbul said this, the king would order even more and better food for her to make her happy.

> One day when the king came, the bulbul spoke to him: "Oh King! Bulkh and Bukhara's food is so much better it cannot be compared." The king thought about this thing, and the next day he asked the bulbul to take him to see this place and the food. The bulbul thought about this thing and on the next day agreed.

> After a very long walk, the bulbul and the king reached the same jungle. There were thousands of bulbuls happily singing. The king listened for a long time. Then the king let the bulbul go. She flew up and sat in a branch of a tree above the king. In a beautiful voice she said to the king: "I was not happy in your golden cage or with the delicious food you offered. See! I am happy in this jungle where I have many friends and relatives.

This is the way of our life; it is the way we are raised, and it is the way I like to live.''

No matter how nice the food and house, we are happy to live together, to travel together, to fight each other, and to marry together. Such is our nature.

Indeed, their varied subsistence activities and the diverse contexts in which they are acquired and performed emphasize sensorimotor, perceptual-cognitive, and interpersonal experiences and skills which contrast sharply with those of more sedentary populations. Qalandar also differ from other peripatetic groups sharing the same eco-niche, especially artisans and craftsmen; whereas artisans rely on the manufacture and sale of material resources for their survival, the primary resources of Qalandar are individual social skills.

7

Peripatetic and Sedentist Comparison Groups

For comparative purposes, as well as better understanding of the relationship between task-specific skills associated with subsistence strategies and patterns of psychological performance, I gathered comparable measures from a sample of Kanjar, spatially mobile artisans who exploit the same socioecological niche as the Qalandar. For contrast, samples of sedentary agriculturalists, Jats, and traditional urban dwellers, Lahorias, were studied as well.

The Kanjar

Like the Qalandar, these nomadic artisans have long been an integral part of the South Asian cultural setting. Today, as in centuries past, Kanjar women wander the streets and narrow lanes in villages and cities calling out, "Gugu ghoray lay loa" ("Take the toys"). In response, young children beg their parents for money or items to exchange for the clay and reed toys (gugu ghoray) being offered for sale. Adults also respond to the Kanjar refrain to obtain the baskets, brooms, ropes, fishnets, papier mâché horses, and paper flowers which the Kanjar make. Older men quietly chuckle and wives look askance at their husbands, for Kanjar women are also professional prostitutes.

The Kanjar in the Punjab and Sind follow essentially the same pattern of mobility as the Qalandar. During the major harvest periods they travel from village to village selling their wares. Between harvests they concentrate on the periphery of the urban centers. Frequently,

Figure 12. A Kanjar tent.

Qalandar and Kanjar share the same lot or field for their camps. During these periods I was able to visit Kanjar tents and observe their technological skills as well as observe the cultural milieu of their camps. The Kanjar tent is made from reeds (see Figure 12); their camps (tent clusters) are smaller than those of the Qalandar; each camp is composed of only one or two tents (observed maximum, three).

Because they are artisans, the basic social and technological skills of the Kanjar contrast sharply with those of the Qalandar, but the most striking feature of their cultural milieu is the division of labor by sex. On a day-to-day basis, the men stay with the tent and care for infants and young children. Kanjar females, on the other hand, are away from the tent during most of the day, peddling toys and other products among the sedentary population. Compared to the men, the women appeared to be much more aggressive, mobile, and independent both within and outside the camp. In contrast to the Qalandar, sex roles were marked, with females apparently having greater access to the major social and technological skills than men, certainly greater spatial mobility, and more experience with the social and technical skills involved in the manufacture and marketing of their basic subsistence resources.

Spatial mobility is essential for Kanjar survival,and their mobility pattern is determined primarily by the markets for their products and services. Kanjar informants related their movement patterns to the need to establish new markets once an area had been covered. Because tents are autonomous and camps small, fission within the camp cluster plays a minor role in mobility and flexibility of the social organization. The basic structures underlying Kanjar social organization are the zat and the biradari. Kanjar refer to their social system as a qaum composed of many zats. The zats tend to be associated with primary subsistence strategies or occupations (*kusub*) such as gugu ghoray makers and makers of papier mâché horses and paper flowers. Among the Kanjar there is a marked tendency for zat and biradari endogamy.

The basic social, economic, and commensal unit is the tent, consisting of a woman, her husband, and their unmarried children. The tent or camp is the optimal socioeconomic unit. Thus, Kanjar economic strategies necessitate maximal dispersion of tents throughout the larger sedentary population, which emphasizes the tent and the distribution of skills among family members. The emphasis on tent independence is reflected in Kanjar marriage patterns and values concerning the relative economic potential of males and females.

Among other peripatetic artisans and entertainers, it is jokingly said that Kanjar are endogamous for two reasons: they sell their beautiful girls, and the ugly ones are too expensive. Kanjar bovar or brideprice is very high, often amounting to the equivalent of two or three year's cash earnings for the groom's tent. A marriage always creates a new tent or family, which becomes an economically independent social unit. Because females are so highly valued as daughters and wives, the most common marriage arrangement is between children of siblings, especially of brothers and sisters. One female informant explained their marriage system in this manner: "The only way I can avoid paying a fortune for my son's bride is to make his marriage with my brother's daughter and to give my daughter to my brother's son. We call this *wady dee shadi* or exchange marriage." Unless a tent has sufficient cash for bovar, the wady dee shadi prevails among Kanjar and appears to account in part for the small size of camps. All tents camped together were negotiating or involved in wady dee shadi marriages.

Subsistence Activities and Division of Labor

There are three major sources of cash and kind income among the Kanjar: sale of gugu ghoray and other products, begging, and prostitution. As indicated in Table 3, these activities are primarily controlled by females. Males are primarily responsible for daily tent and camp maintenance, animal care, and nurturance of dependent infants and young children. Kanjar men, especially husbands, earn a little cash from the sale of papier mâché horses, begging, and some cock fight-

Table 3. Kanjar division of labor by sex and age.[1]

Activity	Age		
	0–7	7–14	14+
Primary economic skills			
Gathering clay	D	D	D
Gathering firewood	D	D	D
Gathering paper, scraps	C	C	C
Gathering reeds (*sirki*)	D	D	D
Molding clay figurines	E	E	E
Decorating clay figurines	C	C	C
Firing clay figurines	C	C	C
Making paper flowers	C	C	C
Making papier mâché	C	C	C
Selling *gugu ghoray*	B	B	B
Selling paper flowers	E	E	E
Selling papier mâché	C	C	C
Beggar	C	C	C
Prostitute/dancer	C	B	B
Musician	A	A	A
Care of animals			
Dogs	D	D	D
Donkeys	D	D	D
Horses	D	D	D
Chickens	D	D	D
Grass collection	D	D	D
Supervised grazing	D	D	D
Food preparation			
Preparation	D	D	D
Cooking	D	D	D
Tent maintenance			
Repair	D	D	D
Water fetching	D	D	D
Fuel fetching	A	A	A
Cleaning	D	D	D
Clothing repair	D	D	D
Laundering clothes	D	D	D

Table 3, *continued*

Activity	Age		
	0–7	7–14	14+
Material culture			
Bag making	D	D	D
Rope cordage	D	D	D
Musical instrument mak-			
ing	D	D	D
Political activity			
Lawyer (*waikel*)	—	—	E
Judge (*munsub*)	—	—	E

1. A = exclusively males; B = exclusively females; C = approximately equal participation by both sexes; D = predominantly males; E = predominantly females.

ing; however, the control of economic resources and income rests with females.

The primary function of Kanjar males is to support the females. As infants, the males are socialized in activities related to caring for the tent and animals, and collecting materials such as clay, reeds, and scrap paper for manufactured products such as gugu ghoray. They frequently are carried by older females or siblings for begging activities in urban markets.

When old enough to walk without support, young boys will frequently accompany their mother or older sisters as they travel about selling their wares. While adult males do not participate in these activities, Kanjar believe that all of their members must be familiar with these strategies. By age four, males are encouraged to beg in the markets when not engaged in other activities.

In addition to these activities, many young boys are trained to become musicians so that they can provide musical accompaniment for the dance routines of their mother, sisters, and future wife. More skilled individuals are encouraged to leave the peripatetic lifestyle and seek work as professional musicians in houses of prostitution to gain sufficient cash for the brideprice, which must be paid before marriage. A man is constantly reminded that his *roti* comes from the hard work and sacrifice of the females in his life. Within the daily camp milieu there is a general atmosphere of equality between sexes; however, compared to females, Kanjar males appeared to be very passive and cooperative. The dominant role of females is openly manifested during disputes, marriage planning, and disagreements regarding economic considerations, such as cash distribution or decisions about tent alliances and movement patterns.

As might be expected, female infants are much more desired than males among the Kanjar. When a girl is born, there is much celebration and happiness; when a male is born, there is no celebration at all. Until she can walk on her own, the female child spends most of her time with her father and older male siblings. As she begins to walk, they begin to train her in singing, dancing, and the making of gugu ghoray. When she is old enough to walk long distances, she is expected to accompany her mother or older female siblings during the day. During these trips she is taught and observes the strategies involved in selling, begging, and prostitution. By the time she reaches puberty the Kanjar girl is expected to be able to support herself and her family with these skills once she is married.

When not engaged in peddling, the women manufacture products for sale. These work periods also provide opportunities for them to instruct young children in the manufacture of their products. Males mix the clay and water, and females manufacture, as well as instruct children in the molding skills necessary to produce miniature pots, pipes, horses, camels, and other objects. When fired, these become toys for sedentary children. Both sexes use reeds and wattled cane to weave stylized baskets and mats; plaited straw is woven into rattles or fans for infants, while string or *munj* grass is woven into fishnets and ropes. In addition to these activities, mothers teach young girls to dance and sing.

Kanjar girls are constantly evaluated by their mothers and mothers' sisters as potential professional dancers and prostitutes. Young, fair-skinned, smooth-complexioned, and talented girls are marked early in their lives for sale into professional groups of prostitutes and dancers in the major urban areas. These economic arrangements are usually made by the parents through contacts with their own siblings who are already established in these areas, for example, in the diamond or gem market in Lahore. Once sold into professional communities, these women seldom maintain contact or correspondence with their natal group.

Like other specialized artisans and entertainers, the Kanjar express their values in those activities most central to their socioecological adaptation. Kanjar child-rearing practices emphasize the development of the skills necessary for subsistence. Since the tent is the primary economic unit, emphasis is on cooperation and individual support in tasks affecting the well-being of its members. Very early in their development children are incorporated to adult activities. Young children are also encouraged to develop the basic skills related to procurement of raw materials such as grass, reeds, and clay, and manufacture of products for sale. Within the tent there is a spirit of equality and cooperation, although sex roles are sharply marked. While both sexes have experience with manufacturing skills, males are socialized to be supportive and cooperative in their behavior and are involved in tasks that ensure the daily maintenance of the family tent. Females, on the other hand, are socialized to be aggressive, self-reliant, and independent, traits that are essential for those who peddle products, beg, and prostitute.

Like the nomadic Qalandar, the Kanjar represent a thinly dispersed population whose basic social unit is the tent. Patterns of social organization both within and between tents must be elastic and adaptable to afford the wide contacts and available markets necessary for their survival. On a day-to-day basis, Kanjar females travel greater distances and have more interpersonal contact with the diverse sedentary population than do males. The behavior skills demanded in their daily subsistence activities appear to reinforce their greater independence, self-reliance, and aggressiveness relative to males. On the basis of these cursory observations it was expected that Kanjar females would be field independent relative to males and that the Kanjar as a cultural group would be field independent relative to illiterate sedentists.

Rural Sedentists

In an effort to obtain measurements of perceptual-cognitive performance from a less fluid social system with more rigid sex roles, measurements of field independence were taken from a small sample of sedentary village farmers or Jats.

Land Tenure and Village Organization

The villages of the Punjab and Sind, which range in size from several hundred to a thousand or more inhabitants, have been a part of Asian civilization since the fourth millennium. In discussions of ancient India, Basham and others describe a village pattern which differs little from that of Pakistani villages today:

> The village was a cluster of huts, small and large, often grouped round a well or pond, near which was a small open space with a few trees . . . The villagers formed a self-conscious community, and often had an energetic communal life . . . This vigorous corporate life continued into the Middle Ages . . . village coun-

cils took an active interest in the communal welfare, dug and renewed reservoirs, made canals, improved roads, and cared for the village shrines . . . Most peasant holdings were small, and were usually worked by the owner and his family, but there were a few large farmsteads, the owners of which cultivated their estates with hired labor. (Basham 1959:190–191)

The crops grown in ancient India were much the same as those grown in this region today. Barley and wheat are grown in the north, rice in the irrigated plains, and millet in the drier areas. Sugarcane is widely grown, as is sesame for oil. Peas, beans, and lentils are commonly grown everywhere. Although soils have been depleted of their nutrients, the crops, seasonal cycle, and the basic activities of the village agriculturalists have changed very little in the Indus plain.

Villages in this region may be classified into four types based on patterns of land ownership: those owned as large estates by individual landlords (*zamīndārs*); those owned by a single lineage of small landholders; those owned by several lineages; and those owned by two or more zamīdārs plus a mixture of smaller landholding lineages. The major form of land tenancy is the *batai* ("to share", usually 50/50) system, in which the zamīndār lease land to farmers (mostly Jats). The contractual relationships between zamīndārs, cultivators (Jats), and service castes (*kammis*) is similar to the jajmani system found throughout North India. Examples of customary services and payments in a Pakistani village are summarized in Figure 13.

Most villages in the Punjab consist of mud or clay houses. Each family possesses several houses, which are usually surrounded by high, clay walls. Frequently, these walls are contiguous, so that the entire village appears to be walled. The landholdings of the residents surround the village like the spokes of a wheel, which they work as tenants for large zamīndārs. The social organization within and between villages is by hierarchical relationships between extended families, representing traditional zat or jati systems.[1] The basic distinction among social groups in the village is between landholders and traditional craftsmen or kammis. The more prominent and prosperous zamīndārs are titled *chadharis* to distinguish them from lesser owners, tenants, and sharecroppers. The kammis represent a hierarchy of service castes ranked within the village according to their occupation—barbers, carpenters, weavers, blacksmiths. In most regions of the Punjab, the majority of the landholding farmers and tenant farmers are Jats, who are considered to be an indigenous caste of cultivators, although the distinction between Jat farmers and Jat nonfarmers

Figure 13. Customary services and payments in a Pakistani village. (After Ahmad 1974; from *Peoples of South Asia* by Clarence Maloney. Copyright © 1974 by Holt, Rinehart and Winston, Inc. Reprinted by permission of the publisher.)

Kammis	Services to tenant-farmer	Payment
Household		
Lohār (blacksmith)	Maintains agricultural implements	1 paropī of all grains; 4 topās of wheat in addition;3 sīrs cotton per plow; Rs. 2 for sugarcane per plow (recently instituted); money payment for making new implements
Tirkhān (carpenter)	As above	As above
Nāī (barber)	Shaves, massages, acts as messenger at births, marriages, or deaths; circumcises	As above; paid cash and grain on ceremonial occasions; amount varies according to his status
Kumbār (potter)	Formerly made bowls for Persian irrigation wheel; few specific functions now	
Kumbār (teamster)	Carries loads of wheat, sugarcane, fodder	1 topā per pakkā maund for carrying load; 1 topā for having come to carry load
Mehnatī musallī (winnower)	Winnows	1 topā per pakkā maund
Mocī (cobbler)	Repairs shoes	While wheat is still in field collects 4 gadīs; 8 topās from each tenant house
Mirāsī (genealogist)	Serves as genealogist and bard	4 topās of wheat

Kammis	Services to tenant-farmer	Payment
Wazān kāsh	Employed by each pattī head to distribute wheat and cotton to landlord, tenants, servicing people; one person in each pattī	½ paropī per pakkā maund
Musallī (sweeper)	Employed by the two landlords to keep the derā clean, wait on guests, keep hukkā ready, and so forth	1 topā from each tenant of landlord's pattī
Village		
Pīr	Full-time religious devotee or saint	1 marlā of any crop; 1 topā of wheat; 1 sīr of cotton
Faqīr	Takes care of village saint's tomb; acts as host in annual fair	3 topās of wheat; anything left on tomb, such as cash, food, oil
Maulvī	Leads prayers, performs marriages (previously both maulvī got from all tenants; now each mosque identified with a landlord's pattī)	1 marlā of any crop; 1 topā of wheat; 1 sīr of cotton; cash at marriage or death
Dholī (drummer)	Announces special occasions; wakes people for sehrī during Ramadan; acts as chief drummer at marriages	4 gadīs of wheat; cash at marriages

Note: Weights and measures in Punjābī villages differ from the Pakistan government standards. The basic unit of weight in Pakistan is the sīr, but in villages it is the topā, a metallic bowl containing 2¼ sīrs. 1 sīr = 2.057 pounds; 1 topā = 2¼ sīrs; 1 pakkā maund = 40 topās; 1 kaccā maund = 40 sīrs; 1 paropī = ¼ topā; 1 gadī = 1 topā (gadī is a cloth bundle; when referred to in distribution it means that the grain is mixed with hay).

is vague. The traditional association of the Jat with cultivation is summarized in the Punjabi village proverb, "The Jat's baby has a plow handle for its plaything."

While villages may differ somewhat in appearance, average size of landholdings, and economic and social structure, the pattern of daily living varies little throughout the region. Overall social organization is hierarchical; however, ideological and symbolical aspects of the Muslim caste (zat) system differ from that of the Hindu system. Caste hierarchy in the Punjab and Sind, based on secular status and occupation, is probably the most important indicator of social status. Generally, these Muslim castes have not retained the Hindu purity and pollution restrictions in social relationships. Nevertheless, concepts about defiling occupations persist: groups such as cobblers, sweepers, and other untouchables are subjects of discrimination. The notion of an unclean occupation exists but not that of an unclean caste. In a study of Jalpana, Ahmad reported that he could find no consistent behavior patterns between different zats in the village: "Everyone prays together and smokes together. But when landowners and cultivators sit around smoking the hukkā, the former put their lips to the spout, while the latter smoke by holding the spout in their hand and drawing the smoke through the hollow of the fist. People also eat together ... irrespective of biradari or zat." (Ahmad 1974:156) Whether the concept of zat is precisely analogous to that of the Hindu *jati* is an interesting question which, however, must be deferred for later study. Significant for the present study is that the ideology of hierarchically ordered, primarily endogamous, hereditary groups is strong in Pakistan.

Domestic Group Organization

The individual within the village social milieu obtains both identity and importance as a member of a household (*khandan*), based on blood ties between males; household and zat affiliation are determined patrilineally. The household ideally consists of a man, his wife or wives, his single and married sons, their wives and children, and his unmarried daughters, as well as other relatives, such as a widowed or divorced sister or daughter. Marriages serve as links between households both within and between villages, creating alliances which are expected to endure throughout a lifetime.

The parents arrange children's marriages, with considerable effort made to find suitable and compatible mates. Women are one of the links through which households maintain alliances; however, in contrast to other parts of South Asia, in the Punjab a woman seldom relinquishes her rights as a member of her father's or sibling group. Consequently, wives frequently return to their natal households for visits or if mistreated by their affinal kinsmen. To help ensure good relationships between households related by marriage, families commonly participate in gift exchanges on all important ritual occasions. The alliance aspect is predominant in the marriage arrangements and in the ceremony itself, a ritual that emphasizes that the marriage is between families and not simply between individuals.

The honor and integrity of the household rests primarily in its daughters; thus, great care is taken to control their behavior—especially prior to marriage, when female virginity is essential. Women usually marry in their teens or early twenties; the average groom is six to seven years older than his bride. After marriage, the wife remains in her husband's household under the scrutiny of her husband's mother and/or her husband's father's mother. Often isolated from regular contact with her own family, a woman makes the most difficult adjustments of her life during the first two or three years of marriage. A new wife is the least valued individual in the husband's household. Very often the relationship between the bride and her husband's mother is characterized by tension and animosity. To avoid this potentially destructive situation, parents frequently arrange their daughter's marriage to the household of close relatives or biradari members, where reciprocal, amicable relations already exist with the husband's mother. In most marriages the wife does not begin to have any status, security, or authority in her husband's household until she bears a son.

Sex Roles and Division of Labor

In the Punjab villages of my experience, men are more highly valued than women. It is commonly assumed that males and females are totally different kinds of creatures; women are generally believed to be weaker and less developed than men. In mind, body, and spirit, women are believed to be less disciplined, more sensual, and more dependent on others (usually males) for protection from their own impulses and the advances of strange men. To protect one's daughter or sister from shame or immodest behavior is to protect the honor and integrity of the family. The difference in status of the male and the female pervades all social relationships, as shown by the welcome extended to a newborn son. When a son is born, there is usually much celebration, including drumming, singing, and public announcements, but when a daughter is born, the occasion is more quietly observed, if celebrated at all.

Figure 14. The Jat farmer's seasonal round of activities. (From Degler 1960: 204; reprinted by permission of Columbia University Press.)

Punjabi months*	Farmer's seasons	Seasonal activities
Bisakh	End thirteenth month (to April 21)	Scarcity of good food
Jeth	Summer harvest and planting (April 22–June 7)	Very intensive work. Cutting of maize, millet for fodder, wheat (main crop of year); payment of house *kammis* and others. Planting of cotton, fodder, millet, maize. Dry weather; frequent irrigation
Har	Leisure, marriages (June 8–July 8)	Little work, plentiful food. Season of country fairs, marriages. Cutting of tobacco just before rains begin
Sawan	Monsoon rains (July 9–Aug.14)	Period of anxiety: hope and fear because of rains. With first rains, planting of paddy begins. Irrigation if rains delayed
Bhaduñ	Waiting (Aug. 15–Sept. 14)	Very little work besides care of cattle, ploughing of fallow fields, weeding paddy
Asuj / Katak	Autumn harvest and planting (Sept. 15–Nov. 30)	Period of very intensive work. As soon as fields dry after rains, commence ploughing. Harvesting of millet, maize, rice. Planting of autumn crops of wheat, barley, gram, lentils, fodder, chilies
Maghar / Poh / Magh	Winter, marriages (Dec. 1–Feb. 28)	Period of little work on land, except care of cattle, cutting fodder, weeding crops. With rain, fodder abundant; otherwise scarce. After rains, ploughing of fields for spring planting. Picking of cotton, chilies; cutting of sugarcane begins and continues into next period. Main period of craft activities in village
Phagan	Spring planting (March 1–31)	Moderately hard work. Planting of tobacco, sugarcane, maize and millet for fodder, vegetables
Chet	Thirteenth month	Little work except care of cattle and harvesting of lentils, gram, barley

* Months follow Gregorian calendar.

The value placed on males is reflected in infant mortality rates. Minturn and Hitchcock (1966) reported that infant mortality for males was 25 percent, for females 41 percent and this pattern is reflected in the historical census records (see Galt 1913; Blunt 1931; Bean 1974). My own cursory observations and discussions with nomads tend to support the notion that these figures indicate greater concern for males rather than deliberate neglect or infanticide of females. However, while traveling with Qalandar we found fiv·ₑ corpses of apparently abandoned neonates, all female. These different values for males and females are common in the ethnographic literature on South Asia and are easily seen in domestic arrangements and child-rearing practices. Minturn (1963) and Minturn and Hitchcock (1966) report that in many North Indian villages men and women live in separate quarters. While prepubescent children are often allowed more freedom of movement, in many households social distance between the sexes is maintained by separate living spaces. In the Punjab village the strict physical seclusion of women, purdah, is relaxed, though close public contact or cooperation between members of the opposite sex is discouraged. Among poor villages sex roles may be slightly relaxed, but division of labor along sex lines remains fairly rigid, especially in household and infant maintenance activities.

The activities of Jat farmers are closely tied to their land and to seasonal variations in crop harvests (see Figure 14). The two busiest periods are the summer and winter planting and harvests. Egler has one of the best descriptions of the Jat farmer's activities, and I quote from her description of an annual cycle for Moala village in some detail:

> The much awaited monsoon brings hope on the one hand and despair on the other. The farmer is full of hope, for the rains mean enough water to start the planting of the paddy, but if the rains last too long this means flood, and flood is destructive. It may demolish his house, destroy his fields, leave the standing sugar cane and fodder covered with mud, and carry away the straw stored for the cattle.
>
> Nevertheless, with the first shower he is busy planting the paddy. After that, until the early fall, he has little to do except for the routine work of caring for his cattle, cutting and preparing fodder for them, weeding the paddy fields, and, if there is a long interval between the rains, irrigating the fields. Thus, between his hopes and fears, the time goes on, and if the monsoon rains do not cause devastation he has his autumn crop of paddy and also millet and maize.

The autumn harvest, *kharif*, also known as *sauni*, starts in the middle of September and continues through November. This is a very busy season, for the farmer has both to harvest the crops in the different fields as they ripen and to prepare for sowing the fallow fields that have been lying under water during the rainy season and are now drying out. If the soil has retained the dampness of the rains, it is easier for him to plough, but if it has not rained, the soil is dry and he has to irrigate these fields, which is extra work and takes much time. It takes at least sixteen hours to irrigate each field. With a plough drawn by a pair of oxen, it takes him one day to plough each field at least four or five times. In these fields he sows the main crops of the year—wheat, barley, and gram. At the same time he also plants the winter vegetables—carrots, turnips, radishes, cauliflower, and lentils. Also in the late fall the paddy is ripe and he must harvest it. So this is a period of intense activity; when the farmer may need all of the twenty-four hours of a day for work. If he can get it, he asks for help.

The season of intensive work is followed by a period of relative rest, the three winter months, when, if it rains, as it usually does, the crop sown in the fall will grow abundantly, producing plenty of fodder for the cattle. However, if it does not rain, the farmer must irrigate the wheat and the other crops, the vegetables, and also the fields which are to be ploughed and prepared for the early spring sowing. If it were not for the lack of fodder, this would be an easy period for him. If he has stored enough wheat, barley, and gram, he grinds them coarsely and mixes them with hay to feed his animals. They are then well fed. But usually he does not have enough; then he cuts off the tops of sugar cane and collects grass, if there are lowlands nearby, but he still has a hard time keeping his animals fed.

In the early spring, he plants sugar cane, tobacco, fodder, chili peppers, melons, and summer vegetables in the fields, and he has to manage by borrowing—but no one has enough to lend anyone else. Though it is a brief period, it is a difficult one and seems very long.

Then in the summer, the wheat, barley, and gram are again ready to be harvested. This is the summer harvest, *rabi*, commonly known as *hari*, the busiest period of the year for everyone. The crop must be cut, threshed, and winnowed, and all the people who have been working for the farmer during the year must be paid in grain. The grain for the year must be stored away, as also the straw for the animals. During this busy period of harvest, he has also to irrigate the fields of tobacco, chilies, sugar cane, fodder, and summer vegetables, which he planted in the early spring, for now the days are hot and dry. He also plants a nursery for the paddy, cotton, and the fodder which he always needs for his cattle.

After he has stored the wheat and has collected the tobacco, the farmer has plently and for one month there is not much to do, except for the routine work of weeding, turning the soil, irrigating, and taking care of the cattle.

This is the month of country fairs which the farmer attends, where he listens to music anad singing, watches wrestling, horse races, and native games, eats sweets and fruits, and enjoys life thoroughly. Then the work cycle begins anew. (Egler 1960:50–53)

From my peripatetic perspective, Egler's account is typical, and the cycle for Moala is close to that found throughout the Punjab and northern Sind, although there is considerable annual and seasonal variation.

The Jat samples were all minor landowners and farmers who survive on agricultural produce, primarily wheat, sugarcane, maize, corn, rice, cotton, and various pulses. The daily activities of males relate to their fields and draft animals.When they are not engaged in agricultural pursuits, the men stay together and discuss problems of caste or village concern. While females occasionally assist in picking cotton or collecting pulse leaves, their primary responsibility is handling and processing harvested resources. Women also spin cotton, make and repair clothing, and manufacture dung cakes for fuel in addition to caring for the children. Most of these activities are social, involving all the women from the household as well as from other families in the village. Older children frequently accompany the same-sex parents, while young children and infants are the primary responsibility of their mothers and other females in the family.

Enculturation for Sedentism

The most striking characteristic of child-rearing practices and children's behavior patterns, compared to those of peripatetic groups, is the emphasis on deference, obedience, and dependence. Minturn (1963) reported that Rajput parents in Khalapur emphasized obedience, politeness, and peaceableness for children. Deference and obedience are stressed in training the child, especially the female, to be suitably observant of the hierarchy of family relations. Children should, above all else, be obedient and respectful to elders. This notion dominates South Asian cultural values and is maintained in the manner by which adults discipline and reward children. Village children seldom, if ever, are praised to their faces, because that would emphasize a sense of self-importance which is antithetical to maintenance of authority and loyalty within the hierarchy of family relationships.

Dependence is encouraged in village children; they seldom receive any specialized trianing or practical experience with tasks emphasizing responsibility. Children's chores are irregular and brief, and young children are seldom assigned tasks for the purpose of developing a sense of responsibility. Children are expected to learn by imitation, and there is very little formal instruction for either sex within the family. Elder sons are occasionally singled out for training in certain tasks; however, this is the exception rather than the rule. Minturn and Hitchcock report "no consistent differences between mother's descriptions of what was expected of a good boy and what was expected of a good girl. In practice, obedience is stressed somewhat more for girls and bravery for boys; but both sexes are expected to be both obedient and brave, although in the contexts of different tasks" (1966:132).

Studies of child-rearing practices among sedentary villages throughout India indicate that a premium is placed on dependent behavioral qualities. Individualism, aggressiveness, and self-reliance are negatively sanctioned (see Taylor 1948; Murphy 1953; Carstairs 1967). Village child-rearing practices emphasize intrafamilial responsibility and interdependence, not self-reliance and independence. This pattern demonstrates a reciprocal relationship between individual behavior and social organization. Where land and the joint-family system are the primary cultural features, emphasis must be placed on cooperation and interdependence for group survival.

Indeed, the village, the basic and enduring feature of Asian civilization, provides both the individual and the family with a source of identity, "a nexus of activity, a stage for status, and an arena of conflict" (Mandelbaum 1970:421). Because of the difference in emphasis in child-rearing and lifelong socialization practices between Punjabi villagers and nomadic Qalandar as well as Kanjar, it was expected that villagers would be field-dependent relative to the nomads.

The Urban Setting

The Harappan culture, at least in the Punjab, had developed cities by the third millenium B.C. By the beginning of the Buddhist period (circa 560–327 B.C.), small towns were scattered over the Indo-Gangetic plain, and by the Mauryan period large cities were integral elements of Asian culture. Basham, quoting from a second-century Tamil poem, "The Garland of Madurai," describes an ancient Indian city:

> Streets are broad rivers of people, folk of every race, buying and selling in the market-place or singing to the music of wandering minstrels ... A drum beats, and a royal procession passes down the street, with elephants leading to the sound of conchs. A refractory beast breaks his chain, and tosses like a ship in an angry sea until he is again brought to order. Chariots follow, with prancing horses and fierce footmen ... Meanwhile stall-keepers ply their trade, selling sweet cakes, garlands of flowers, scented powder and betel quids. Old women go from house to house, selling nosegays and trinkets to the womenfolk. Noblemen drive through the streets in their chariots, their gold-sheathed swords flashing, wearing brightly-dyed garments and wreaths of flowers. From balconies and turrets the many jewels of the perfumed women who watch the festival flash in the sunlight. The people flock to the temples to worship to the sound of music, laying their flowers and honouring the holy sages. Craftsmen work in their shops—men making bangles of conch shell, goldsmiths, cloth-dealers, coppersmiths, flower-sellers, vendors of sandalwood, painters and weavers. Food-shops busily sell their wares—greens, jak-fruit, mangoes, sugar candy, cooked rice and chunks of cooked meat ... In the evening the city prostitutes entertain their patrons with dancing and singing to the sound of the lute (*yāl*), so that the streets are filled with music. Drunken villagers, up for the festival, reel in the roadways, while respectable women make evening visits to the temples with their children and friends, carrying lighted lamps as offerings. They dance in the temple courts, which are clamorous with their singing and chatter ... At last the city sleeps—all but the goblins and ghosts who haunt the dark, and the bold house-breakers, armed with rope ladders, swords and chisels, to break through walls of mud houses. But the watchmen are also vigilant, and the city passes the night in peace ... Morning comes with the sound of brāhmans intoning their sacred verses. The wandering bards renew their singing, and the shopkeepers busy themselves opening their booths. The toddy-sellers again ply their trade for thirsty morning travellers. The drunkards reel to their feet and once more shout on the streets. All over the city is heard the sound of opening doors. Women

sweep the faded flowers of the festival from their courtyard. Thus the busy life of the city is resumed. (Basham 1954:204)

During the Mughal period, urban centers consisted mostly of noble families and their service castes. During the British period, cities were primarily centers of colonial rule. Recently, with the growth of industrialization and the influx of Muslim refugees following partition, the urban population has become the most rapidly growing sector of society.[2] In addition to being traditional centers for trade and administration, the cities have evolved as cultural nuclei for the production and distribution of industrial goods. The middle, entrepreneurial, and upper classes have grown. Also, with the lack of good agricultural land, opportunities for economic survival and social mobility in the cities have attracted many from the villages.

Obviously, life in the city differs from rural life. Compared to the more intimate and personal relationships of the village, those of the city are more fragmentary and impersonal. While this is less marked for the urban middle class, it often creates stress for the recent rural immigrants. Therefore, urban residence does not de facto produce changes in birādari and family relations. With the exception of the new elite, most rural migrants in urban areas keep close ties of obligation and kinship with their natal villages. Srinivas has concluded that the urban household is often little more than "a satellite of a kin group in a village or town several hundreds of miles away" (1966:138).

Lahoria

Lahore is perhaps Pakistan's most cosmopolitan city, a historical center with a great tradition of Indo-Muslim architecture, religion, and education. Like Agra, Lahore reflects the ancient wealth and prosperity of the Mughal Empire. Monserrate stated that Lahore in 1581 was "not second to any city in Europe or Asia" (quoted in Ikram 1964:225).

Like other urban centers in South Asia, Lahore has rapidly grown in population. Following partition and the growth of industrialization, several social classes have emerged. Wilber (1964) has identified a number of relatively new, distinct classes in his study of Lahore, including: a new elite class of entrepreneurs, middle-class small businessmen, and industrial workers. The more traditional classes include the old elite families with hereditary property, the artisans and other specialists, and lower-class shopkeepers and small businessmen. This latter group, which includes a number of zats, has been described as "a lower middle class group . . . usually meticulous in observing the rituals of Islam, such as prayers, fasting during Ramadan, reading the Quran in Arabic, almsgiving, and maintaining their women in purdah. They live in crowded houses of the old sections of the cities and the men work in the varied occupations which a town or city offers" (Wilber 1964:43). In Lahore, this group lives in the *mohallas* (alleys) which specialize in particular businesses and are mixed in with the traditional occupational and artisan groups such as goldsmiths; furniture makers; salt, wheat, and sugar merchants; and similar groups. Those families which have traditionally lived within the confines of the walled city of Lahore are locally known as Lahorias and are generally recognized as a more conservative element in Lahore's predominantly Muslim society.

Among the Lahoria the social dichotomy between sexes is usually greater than in the village setting. This is expressed in more formal rules relating to the confinement, protection, and exclusion of women by means of strict purdah, as well as a more distinct division of labor by sex. Females are forbidden to work outside the household and seldom receive more than rudimentary literary training in primary school. If a woman is allowed secondary or university training, she seldom if ever has an opportunity to use this experience beyond the family domain. Women tend to live in a protected and succorant milieu composed of other women and young children. Males, on the other hand, have contact with a greater variety of individuals and settings through their work, and their relationships tend to be more impersonal and fragmentary, with an emphasis on verbal and technical abilities rather than household skills and affiliation. Among the Lahoria child-rearing practices and lifelong socialization emphasize the same general behaviors as described for the rural sample; however, because of the more strict regulations pertaining to the roles of males and females, especially purdah, it was hypothesized that males would be much more field independent relative to females than in the rural village setting.

Summary

The contrasting socioecological milieus of the four groups discussed above provide as well as demand different behavioral activities and skills from their members. Their variable patterns of experience or cultural curricula regulate individual access to and relative experience with activities and skills which amplify levels of perceptual-cognitive performance. The milieu and subsistence activities of the peripatetic Qalandar and Kanjar sharply contrast with those of the sedentary Jats and the traditional Lahoria. Qalandar, as spatially mobile entertainers, survive by utilizing a wide range of specialized, individual skills associated with the training of performing animals in addition to their activities as magicians, jugglers, acrobats, musicians, impersonators, and beggars. The peripatetic Kanjar invest their energies in the manufacture of clay toys, fishnets, and similar items, as well as dancing and prostitution. Thus, the peripatetic groups emphasize structural flexibility, small family units, and organizational fluidity. Their specialized skills and spatial mobility expose individuals to a variety of socioecological settings and institutions. Relative to sedentists, spatially mobile artisans and entertainers stress early self-reliance and individual competence in social and manipulative skills. The nature of these differential patterns of experience, related to social as well as technical activities in disparate socioecological settings and serving as cognitive amplifiers, recommends these groups for comparative analysis of the major hypotheses regarding cultural experience and patterns of psychological performance.

III

The Results in Context

8

Emics–Etics: Results and Conclusions

The Western world emphasizes individual-focused activities in most
spheres of psychological functioning, especially school or laboratory
settings, but the cross-cultural ethnographic record should serve to
remind us that in the rest of the world problem solving is usually a corporate activity. In these settings individuals are sensitive to and skilled
in the use of interpersonal resources representing diverse levels of experience and skill. Certainly, individuals in all cultures perform some
tasks independent of the physical presence of other people; however,
an individual's resources are temporarily embedded within the social
and contextual domains of previous experience. For example, in some
societies, like the United States, enculturation activities have become
increasingly relegated to peer groups, in which the social composition
of performance contexts, in terms of relative experience and skill,
tends to be relatively homogeneous. On the other hand, many settings
in other cultures are socially organized along intergenerational lines,
with markedly varied levels of experience, practice, and skill with
tasks in various contexts. These patterns of variability demand as well
as provide diverse spectrums of individual and group experience related to performance of psychological tasks.

Among the peripatetic Qalandar and Kanjar, individuals—as members of diverse and highly fluid groups—not only participate in a wide
range of performance contexts but are constantly reminded of their
activities through two processes. First, each individual's activities are
routinely, if not systematically, observed and evaluated by other group
members, who tap experience with the same or related tasks in differ-

ent contexts. Second, every individual, while socialized to be sensitive to group resources, especially those of older and more experienced members, is responsible for sharing these resources with succeeding generations. Here, the severity of socialization activities along lines such as compliance or independence is less important than the fact of intergenerational continuity, stressing flexibility of experience and skills within, as well as across, diverse performance contexts.

A comparable process obtains among the sedentary comparison groups; each individual has someone to direct attention to the salient features of the task at hand as well as the context within which it is embedded. The major differences between nomads and sedentists are those related to experience with a variety of material and social resources within and across contexts. These variable levels of experience direct attention to the task at hand, in this case traditional measures of visual, perceptual, and cognitive functioning, and are reflected in the differential patterns of performance between and within groups. As we have seen, each of these ecocultural systems provides and emphasizes experience with a range of perceptual skills, and these skills and experience, as cognitive amplifiers, are reflected in the results of this study.

General Approach and Context of Analysis

In experimental settings we may randomly assign subjects to treatment conditions in standardized or invariant performance contexts which enable us to control for previous experience and skill. The record of psychological activities in naturalistic domains of perceptual and cognitive functioning reminds us that performance contexts are protean in nature. Indeed, the ethnographic setting clearly indicates that the distribution of individual as well as group patterns of experience and skill in these diverse ecocultural contexts is anything but haphazard. So far, this study has focused on the diverse ecocultural domains which comprise the milieu of psychological activities in four distinct, yet interrelated social systems in Pakistan. Drawing on the cross-cultural psychological research record relating behavioral functioning to experience in different social and ecocultural milieus, I hypothesized that cognitive amplifiers in each of the social systems would promote particular patterns of psychological performance on three standardized tasks of perceptual-cognitive functioning, namely measures of perceptual field dependence/independence, Piagetian conservation tasks, and optical illusions.

Since this study focuses on peripatetic artisans and entertainers,

Gutherie's emphasis on the importance of practice in diverse contexts in determining patterns of psychological performance is particularly cogent: "There would be fewer lines confused in amateur theatricals if there were more dress rehearsals, since the cues from the stage and the actors are part of the situation to which the actor responds" (cited in Hilgard and Bower 1966:87). The data presented in this chapter represent variable patterns of perceptual and cognitive performance on traditional measures of psychological functioning both among and within the four ecocultural systems. Following Guthrie's (1952, 1959) lead, I have used anecdote to illustrate the likely correspondence between these patterns of psychological performance and task activities in the everyday realm of experience. Hopefully this will assist the reader in interpreting the data in terms of the behavioral ethnography presented in Part II as well as focus attention to problems associated with increased ecological validity in experimental research.

By focusing our attention on how specific ecocultural settings demand particular combinations of skill and experience, the concept of cognitive amplifiers suggests a context-relativistic orientation for the interpretation of variability in patterns of psychological functioning. Also, the results of this study are particularly useful for explicating the distinction between "emic" and "etic" interpretations of the data obtained for each of the comparison groups on the four measures of perceptual inference habits. In cross-cultural research, the emic–etic distinction is similar to traditional notions of nomothetic in contrast to idiographic parameters in the generalizability of research findings. The etic approach emphasizes those aspects of behavioral functioning which are universal or are manifested across societies, whereas emic approaches are specific to a particular social system or ecocultural setting. For excellent discussions of the emic–etic distinction, see Pike (1966), Berry (1969a, 1980), Brislin, Lonner, and Thorndike (1973), Irwin et al. (1977), and Brislin (1980).

The Etic Assumptions

In keeping with the cross-cultural research record of studies in perceptual-cognitive development, two levels of hypotheses were generated regarding the relationship between cognitive amplifiers in various ecocultural milieus and likely patterns of perceptual performance. At the first level of comparative analysis, the four groups represent two distinct modes of societal adaptation, namely nomads (Qalandar and Kanjar) and sedentists (village and urban dwellers). At the second level of analysis, the four groups are treated as separate social systems with distinct patterns of ecocultural experience. These level-one comparisons are examined in the data covered by hypotheses 1, 2, and 3. Hypothesis 1 incorporates several societal domains into a single peripatetic–sedentist comparison. Though the data clearly illustrates that nomadic artisans and entertainers perform in a perceptually field-independent manner relative to sedentists on the dependent measures of psychological functioning, they seriously underestimate the complexity of the research problem. Therefore, subsequent analyses explicate the effects of specific ecocultural activities in perceptual performance on each of the four dependent measures. Hypothesis 2 compares performance profiles between the two nomadic societies, and hypothesis 3 examines perceptual functioning in the two contrasting sedentary communities.

Within each social system, individuals and groups have variable patterns of experience with the content as well as contexts of specific cultural curricula across the total spectrum of activities. Focusing on sex and age, hypotheses 4, 5, and 6 examine patterns of perceptual performance within each setting. Hypotheses 4, 5, and 6 explicate sex and age differences within each community.

Statistical Treatment of Data

A major objective of the statistical analysis was to ensure that any differences in performance were not artificial but indicative of genuine variability in perceptual inference habits. However, in the analysis of cross-contextual data such as this, the potential for confounding between any two or more variables is common. In an effort to control for *some* of these difficulties while trying to maintain comparability with other cross-cultural studies, two common methods of analysis are utilized: the t-test for differences between two means, and the partial correlation coefficient. These statistical analyses and their accompanying interpretations are both conservative and cautious. However, based on previous studies of culture and perception, the evidence indicated a likely direction for each hypothesis. Thus, in contrast to pioneering intercultural studies of perceptual functioning, rather than impose a two-tailed significance test (which many psychologists cautiously prefer for survey-type data) on a theoretically one-tailed "alternative" hypothesis, we have chosen an equally cautious method. One-tailed alpha (hereafter abbreviated p) levels of .025 and .005 have been chosen to represent two stages of significance, rather than the conventional two-tailed levels of .01 and .05. This method affords both conservatism in presenting conclusions and methodological integrity in hypothesis testing.

In addition, the confounding effects of age (and in some cases formal education) are controlled via partial correlations. Formal education (experience) is used as a control variable only sparingly, because it correlates very highly with spatial mobility (experience). It should be kept in mind that none of the Qalandar or Kanjar had any "formal" education, whereas all but a few in the sedentary groups had some exposure to formal school or religious training. Because the results may be spuriously affected when one or more groups have no variance on a comparison variable, caution is needed when interpreting these particular partials. However, the partial correlations are presented where they modify a previous interpretation or where they are used within a sedentary sample exclusively. The sex dichotomy is also used as a control variable because the proportion of females is higher in the nomadic groups, especially the Qalandar, than in the sedentary comparison groups. In all cases the standard deviation of each dependent score for each group is indicated, which, I hope, will promote confidence in readers familiar with heteroscedastic effects on partial correlations. In most cases standard deviations are quite close, and where different, ceiling effects are usually the reason.

In each of the hypotheses analyzed below, perceptual-cognitive functioning was monitored by four measures: the Muller-Lyer illusion, the CEFT, the Sander Parallelogram, and the conservation tasks. They were coded in the following manner:

1. Muller-Lyer: coded by the number of nonillusion-supported responses out of 13 possible.
2. CEFT: coded by the number correct out of 38 possible.
3. Sander Parallelogram: coded by the number of nonillusion-supported responses out of 10 possible.
4. Conservation: trichotomously coded. 1, conserves both continuous and noncontinuous quantities; 0, not sure of conservation; and − 1, conserves neither continuous nor noncontinuous quantities. Only five cases were coded as unsure, so this is essentially a dichotomous variable.

In all of the hypothesis except 4, positive t-values and partial correlations result if the direction of the hypothesis is supported.

The original sample for this study consisted of 285 informants, about half nomadic and half sedentary (Berland 1977). However, to promote data quality, the original sample size has been reduced by removing informants whose response protocols displayed two or more Guttman errors on either the Muller-Lyer or Sander Parallelogram tasks. These were nineteen informants, primarily young children less than seven years of age. Thus, while the total corrected sample is now 266, the Guttman procedure changed the significance level (.01 to .05) on only two of the original measures. Where these assumptions are based on previous cross-cultural studies of perceptual-cognitive functioning, the Qalandar, based on their experience in diverse eco-cultural systems, also offered explanations regarding performance contexts and how each comparison group would perform on the measures of perceptual inference habits. As we shall see, the Qalandar predictions are more in keeping with the final results than my original hypothesis.

An Emic Model

In brief, the Qalandar delineate four interrelated sets of conditions which they consider essential for success in dealing with day-to-day tasks necessary for survival. First, individuals must be cognizant of the nature and distribution of *experience and skills as group resources* which are available and applicable in a given context. For example, individuals must decide whether to rely exclusively on personal resources or to the skills and experience available in an *ad hoc* group of compatriots. We saw a structural aspect of this in the discussion of factors which influence fission and fusion processes in camp composition. Second, Qalandar stress sensitivity to the content of each setting or context in which operations are performed, especially the social composition of performance contexts peripheral to their own cultural milieu. Third, they stress personal experience and skills with specific motoric, cognitive, or social activities, as well as their sensitive combination and appropriate execution in each setting. Finally, Qalandar hold a fundamental cultural assumption regarding the nature of man (as well as all other animals), which influences their perception and interpretation of diversity in human psychological functioning. Encapsulated in their oft-cited expression, "No five fingers are alike," is the belief that individual experience and skills are always manifested in social contexts.

Temporal and spatial factors produce social as well as material diversity within as well as across contexts in which individuals perform. Thus, patterns of psychological functioning are expressions of experience and skills within particular contexts rather than static, defining attributes of individuals. This is an extremely important cultural assumption because it sharply contrasts with Western, especially American, notions regarding individual or group difference in psychological performance. Thus, for Qalandar, no single individual (or group) *because of* his or her experience and skills in a particular context is expected to be as proficient as any other Qalandar in that same context. People as such are considered fundamentally equal; however, *experience and skills are always hierarchically organized and embedded in fluid social contexts*.

Thus, among the Qalandar and, I believe, the Kanjar as well, discussions of individual differences are mediated by references to experience and skills in particular contexts. At one level, their approach may be interpreted as "emic" or situation-focused. On the other hand, their peripatetic lifestyle promotes inferences about and interpretations of human behavior which are "etic" or generalized across diverse populations. The daily pattern of their lives affords, in fact demands, opportunities for testing of "etic" concepts in diverse "emic" domains. Succinctly stated, the Qalandar have an "it all depends," or elastic, model of psychological functioning.

Both the Qalandar and Kanjar approached the testing situation with a set of interrelated assumptions regarding the context itself and the nature of the tasks. Used to performing in diverse, frequently unfamiliar contexts, individuals were confident but cautious during the test administrations, and both groups were especially sensitive to directions and materials. During and after completion of the entire test battery, informants unanimously agreed that "success" on each of the four measures was enhanced by *rokna*—perceptual inhibitory skills or the ability to disregard unimportant or misleading features in each task. In contrast, the sedentary comparison groups tended to react to each measure as a discrete task and displayed little interest in analyzing the tests or the kinds of experience and/or skills which would promote performance. It should be kept in mind that I did not have as good a rapport with the sedentary samples; however, although impressionable, each individual seemed resigned to his or her pattern of performance, while the peripatetics tried consciously to draw on previous experience, as well as on new insights gained from one test item to the next, to understand the demands of successive tasks.

The Qalandar, extremely proud of their individual observational skills and confident of their adroitness in predicting psychological behavior, were quick to speculate about how the comparison groups would perform on the perceptual tasks. For example, they decided that both villagers and urban dwellers would have a difficult time with the tasks but that educated, "schooled" individuals would perform as well if not better than themselves. The Qalandar suspected that the test materials would be more familiar to schoolchildren. They had observed that schoolchildren are less frequently "fooled" by their simple magical performances, arguing that "something" in the school experience enhanced rokna abilities. Within groups, Qalandar argued that females would consistently do better than males. When asked specifically about urban females who observe purdah, they would smile and comment along such lines as, "A fox behind a bush is still a fox."

As we shall see, their predictions were more in keeping with the results than were my initial hypotheses. Certainly, the Qalandar sensitivity and insight into comparative psychological performance constantly served as a personal reminder for greater humility and caution in my subsequent research endeavors. More important, their explanations for variability in psychological performance, when viewed from the total context of Qalandar adaptation, provides a framework for interpreting the quantitative results. Also their observations regarding psychological functioning serve to highlight the role of cognitive amplifiers in determining particular patterns of perceptual-cognitive performance. With these preliminary assumptions in mind, let us examine how patterns of performance and the quantitative results correspond with both the original etic and emic hypotheses.

Hypothesis 1

The first hypothesis tests the broadest prediction, that all nomads (Qalandar and Kanjar) would perform in a field-independent manner relative to sedentists (village and urban dwellers). Table 4 compares the mean scores on the four dependent measures for both groups and provides a t-value and associated significance level (p) for each comparison. As the table shows, peripatetic artisans and entertainers performed significantly better than sedentists on all tasks except the CEFT, which favored the sedentists slightly. Even with this exception, the data support the hypothesis. However, the data in Table 4 do not take into account two characteristics of the comparison groups. First, the nomadic sample (average age 19.55 years) was older than the sedentary sample (average age 15.69 years). One might expect that age would account for some of the nomadic sample's superiority on these measures. Conversely, however, the sedentists had more formal education (average 2.54 years). An extremely high correlation between education and CEFT scores within the entire sample (.38) and within the sedentists (.58) calls for further examination.

To gain a better understanding of this situation, a dummy-coded "mobility" variable (nomads coded 1, sedentists coded 0) was correlated with the four dependent measures using age and formal education as control variables. Table 5 shows the resulting partial correla-

Table 4. Mean scores on tests of perceptual inference habits by nomadic and sedentary groups.

Group	Muller-Lyer	CEFT	Sander	Conservation
Nomads (n = 132)				
x (mean)	11.97	26.17	8.88	.80
s.d.	1.16	5.96	1.07	.57
Sedentists (n = 134)				
x (mean)	10.79	26.92	7.89	.50
s.d.	1.23	5.59	1.32	.87
t	8.03	− 1.05	6.77	3.37
p	.005	ns[1]	.005	.005

1. In tables 4–17, ns indicates a score that is not significant.

tions and their respective one-tailed significance levels. These results are wholly consistent with the t-test results presented earlier with one exception—the CEFT measure. As illustrated in Table 5, when education is partialed out the sign and significance of the correlation change, as might be expected. Together, the results presented in these two tables indicate that the peripatetic's lifestyle tends to encourage relatively field-independent patterns of perceptual performance. Formal education, a different kind of cognitive amplifier, tends to reverse this trend on one dependent measure, the CEFT.

Table 6 demonstrates that field-independent perceptual inference habits are utilized by nomads at an early age relative to the sedentists.

Table 5. Partial correlation coefficients and associated significance levels between mobility (dummy-coded) and the four dependent measures (n = 226).

Control Variables	Muller-Lyer	CEFT	Sander	Conservation
Age	.43	−.13	.36	.16
	p = .005	ns	p = .005	p = .005
Sex	.44	−.06	.39	.20
	p = .005	ns	p = .005	p = .005
Formal education	.35	.14	.35	.26
	p = .005	p = .025	p = .005	p = .005
Age, sex, and formal education	.31	.08	.32	.20
	p = .005	ns	p = .005	p = .005

The data indicate that the superior performance of the more mobile sample is achieved at a relatively early age, except on the CEFT, where nomads do not demonstrate advantage until about age nine. Considering the content of the nomads' cultural curricula, their encouragement of active participation in subsistence activities, and the resultant opportunities for early experience in diverse environments, the results indicate the importance of infant and early childhood activities in the ontogeny of perceptual performance skills. Although peripatetic artisans and entertainers remain field-independent relative to sedentists, the differences tend to become less marked with increasing age. The exception to this is the CEFT; here nomads become increasingly field-independent relative to sedentists as age increases. With increasing age, nomads acquire more experience and skill in performing in diverse public contexts, which demand both field-dependent and field-independent modes of psychological functioning. Conversely, sedentists, while having greater experience with materials comparable to the CEFT task (such as picture books, magazines, and other printed stimuli), tend to operate in a narrower range of private or familiar kin-based community contexts, where interpersonal sensitivity and cooperation place a premium on field-dependent psychological skills. This is particularly the case among schooled sedentists, for whom field-independent activities associated with individual psychological performance are limited to highly structured classroom settings. Also, field-independent patterns of performing in school contexts are frequently negatively sanctioned in the larger social community of family and/or neighborhood.

Table 6. Partial correlation coefficients and associated significance levels between nomadism and task performance (controlling for age, sex, and formal education).

Age group	Muller-Lyer	CEFT	Sander	Conservation
4–8 (n = 68)	.36	.02	.41	.33
	$p = .005$	ns	$p = .005$	$p = .005$
9–12 (n = 58)	.22	.27	.56	.23
	ns	$p = .025$	$p = .005$	ns
13–20 (n = 67)	.45	.24	.26	.04
	$p = .005$	$p = .025$	$p = .025$	ns
21–80 (n = 73)	.44	.22	.03	.00
	$p = .005$	ns	ns	ns

Hypothesis 2

This hypothesis predicts a significant difference between Kanjar and Qalandar on the four perceptual tasks: Qalandar perceptually field-independent relative to Kanjar. Compared to the entertainers, the Kanjar's more specialized skills and constrained spatial mobility were expected to correspond with more field-dependent patterns of perceptual functioning. Several general characteristics of the two peripatetic groups have a bearing on this hypothesis. The peripatetic entertainers are skilled in a wide variety of training and entertainment skills. Throughout a Qalandar's lifetime, both men and women have considerable active experience with such multifarious strategies as begging, training animals, magic acts, and dancing in diverse contexts. The diversity of these activities, and the basic parity in Qalandar sex-roles in general, are adjuncts to their more flexible and mobile lifestyle relative to the Kanjar. While Kanjar also dance and perform music, the range of individual activities is less than for the Qalandar.

To test hypothesis 2, the Qalandar were compared with the relatively constrained Kanjar on the four measures of perceptual style. The group means are presented in Table 7, which includes the t-statistic for the difference between the group means and the corresponding one-tailed probability. The results are consistent with the hypothesis. The more spatially mobile Qalandar are clearly superior to Kanjar on two of the four dependent measures and marginally, though not significantly, superior on the Sander Parallelogram task. The lack of a significant difference between the two groups on the conservation task is not surprising when we recall that the Kanjar work daily with

Table 7. Mean scores on tests of perceptual inference habits by Qalandar and Kanjar.

Group	Muller-Lyer	CEFT	Sander	Conservation
Qalandar (n = 95)				
x (mean)	12.26	26.89	8.99	.82
s.d.	.89	5.67	.98	.57
Kanjar (n = 37)				
x (mean)	11.24	24.32	8.62	.76
s.d.	1.42	6.34	1.23	.60
t	4.02	2.26	1.79	.58
p	.005	.025	ns	ns

clay, water, reeds, and other continuous and noncontinuous sub-
stances.

Two sources of confounding that emerged in the analysis altered
the acceptance of this hypothesis. The Qalandar sample was, on the
average, 21.80 years old, compared to an average of 13.78 among the
Kanjar. Also recall the Qalandar sample contained a disproportionately
high number of females. Table 8 presents the first-order partial correlations between the dummy variable "Qalandarism" (coded 1 if the
subject was a Qalandar, 0 if a Kanjar) and the four measures of field
independence, using age and sex as control variables. When the age
and sex are controlled in a partial correlation, the intepretation
changes somewhat. As indicated by Table 8, the Qalandar are shown
to be field-independent relative to the Kanjar on only one measure, the
Muller-Lyer illusion. The other measures tend to favor the Qalandar
as well, but not significantly. Hence one cannot readily conclude that
Qalandar are field-independent relative to Kanjar.

With the benefit of analytical hindsight, parity between the two
peripatetic groups would have been the more ethnographically sensitive prediction. However, the group differences in age are not a simple
sampling function. Instead, the sex and age composition of Kanjar
camps is truly different from that of the Qalandar. The more "talented" or skilled Kanjar children, especially females, are sold out of
the society to groups of professional dancers, musicians, and prostitutes, and this cultural selection factor contributes to the age discrepancy between the two groups. While the Qalandar utilize markedly diverse subsistence skills and tend to be more spatially mobile than the
Kanjar, both groups employ cognitive socialization activities which
promote field-independent perceptual functioning in a wide range of
performance contexts. I suspect the Qalandar tendency toward per-

Table 8. Partial correlation coefficients and associated significance
levels between mobility (dummy-coded) and the four dependent
measures (n = 132).

Control variables	Muller-Lyer	CEFT	Sander	Conservation
Age	.35	.11	.12	−.01
	$p = .005$	ns	ns	ns
Sex	.39	.19	.15	.05
	$p = .005$	$p = .025$	ns	ns
Age, sex	.35	.10	.11	−.01
	$p = .005$	ns	ns	ns

ceptual field independence is attributable to the fact that they have more experience utilizing a greater variety of psychological skills in a wider and more diverse range of performance contexts than the Kanjar. However, the fact of my greater rapport with Qalandar represents an "interpersonal" confounding factor.

Hypothesis 3

The third hypothesis asserts that sedentary agriculturalists, by virtue of their greater active experience with two diverse experience milieus (village social organization and crop production) would be more field-independent than the urban dwellers of Lahore. The mean task scores for the two groups are given in Table 9, along with the t-values and associated significance levels. Contrary to the expected results, the t-values are significant on only one dependent measure—the Muller-Lyer illusion. In fact, the mean scores on the CEFT task favor the urban dwellers. However, the two groups are not equivalent in age or education. Villagers average 14.53 years of age and have 1.21 years of education; the urban group averages 16.80 years of age with 3.92 years of formal education. Because both age and formal education correlate with the dependent measures, it was expected that partial correlations controlling for these variables might alter the conclusions.

The partial correlations between a dummy-coded "ruralism" variable (villagers coded 1, urban dwellers 0) and the dependent measures are given in Table 10. Controlling for age and education allows modification of the previous interpretation, showing that urban dwellers are not superior in CEFT task performance. It was seen be-

Table 9. Mean scores on tests of perceptual inference habits by sedentary villagers and urban dwellers.

Group	Muller-Lyer	CEFT	Sander	Conservation
Villagers (n = 68)				
x (mean)	11.22	25.77	7.90	.47
s.d.	1.13	5.29	1.49	.89
Urban (n = 66)				
x (mean)	10.34	28.10	7.89	.53
s.d.	1.18	5.68	1.14	.85
t	4.36	−2.47	.08	−.40
p	.005	ns	ns	ns

Table 10. Partial correlation coefficients and associated significance levels between "ruralism" (dummy-coded) and the four dependent measures (n = 134).

Control variables	Muller-Lyer	CEFT	Sander	Conservation
Age	.37	−.19	.06	.02
	$p = .005$	ns	ns	ns
Formal education	.30	.03	.01	.05
	$p = .005$	ns	ns	ns
Age and formal education	.31	.04	.04	.08
	$p = .005$	ns	ns	ns

fore that within the sedentary sample education and performance on the CEFT task correlate highly ($r = .58$, favoring urban dwellers), and this correlation probably accounts for the reversal on this measure. Thus the data presented only tenuously support hypothesis 3. On one measure, the Muller-Lyer illusion, the villagers were superior. The other measures tend to support the hypothesis only weakly by their consistent directionality. It will be recalled that sedentary groups in Pakistan emphasize socialization experiences and skills which promote family–community continuity and solidarity, necessary for their subsistence base, which is small commercial shops and fields. Given the relatively permanent nature of these subsistence resources and the degree of their embeddedness in a particular historical community, it appears that field-dependent functioning is consistent with the social and ecocultural contexts of performance for both groups.

Collectively, the results of hypotheses 1, 2, and 3 are consistent with the evidence from other studies of perceptual functioning comparing psychological performance across diverse social systems. Where ecocultural demands are associated with interdependent patterns of social organization as well as temporal continuity in experience and skills within an ecological niche, cognitive socialization activities stressing field-dependent perceptual functioning are emphasized. On the other hand, where ecocultural diversity and individual as well as group flexibility are important, patterns of perceptual performance are more field-independent.

Societal constellations of experience are associated with particular styles of psychological functioning, but it was expected that differential access to and experience with sociocultural activities across a variety of performance contexts within each social system would correspond with variable patterns of individual performance on the same measures of perceptual functioning. Examination of sex differences in the four groups illustrates these parameters.

Hypothesis 4

This hypothesis states that there should be no marked difference on measures of perceptual performance between Qalandar males and females, based on the ethnographic finding that Qalandar sex-role fluidity and flexibility regulate access to and experience with the important amplifying skills more or less equally by both sexes. Hypothesis 4 is literally one of "no difference" between groups, that is, that there should be no difference between Qalandar males and females on the dependent measures. Thus, an ordinary testing procedure (one that seeks a sample statistic in one or both tails of the density function) is not appropriate. Instead, we need to test for the existence of a sample statistic near the center of the density function.

It is intuitively clear and mathematically provable that hypotheses of no difference are best supported by the sample statistic $t = 0$, or in the case of correlation coefficients, $r = 0$. Thus, a t-value between -0.032 and 0.032 defines the critical region that supports hypothesis 4 to a significance level of .025. (Note that we are compelled to revert to a two-tailed procedure; the difference is that the confidence region in this case comprises the central area of the density function about the sample statistic $t = 0$.) The analogous critical region for the correlation coefficients (either zero-ordered or partial) is between $r = -0.013$ and $r = 0.013$. This defines the region where there would tend to be no association between the dummy-coded sex variable and

Table 11. Mean scores on tests of perceptual inference habits by Qalandar males and females.

Group	Muller-Lyer	CEFT	Sander	Conservation
Males (n = 37)				
x (mean)	12.24	26.78	9.03	.81
s.d.	.96	5.88	.83	.58
Females (n = 58)				
x (mean)	12.26	26.97	8.97	.84
s.d.	.87	5.59	1.08	.55
t	.08	.15	−.30	−.16
p	ns	ns	ns	ns

Table 12. Partial correlations and associated significance levels between sex (dummy-coded) and the four dependent measures for all Qalandars (n = 95).

Control variable	Muller-Lyer	CEFT	Sander	Conservation
Age	−.05	−.11	−.01	−.04
	ns	ns	ns	ns

one of the dependent measures (again to the $p = .025$ level). The data and t-values for hypothesis 4 are presented in Table 11. None of the t-values are significant in the strict sense discussed before. However, they are quite small and stand in marked contrast to the much larger values obtained in the other hypotheses (which asserted a difference) tested so far; this should lend some support to hypothesis 4.

Partial correlations were also computed using age as a control variable. In the correlations presented in Table 12 Qalandar males are coded 1, and females are coded 0. Thus, positive correlations favor males, and negative correlation values indicate superior female performance on the dependent measure. Because of the strong correlation between age and sex among the Qalandar ($r = .21$, with males older than females), the partial correlations tend to favor the females on all four of the measures.

The data in Table 13 indicate that this slight difference does not appear until Qalandar adulthood, when it becomes pronounced. These results indicate that compared to males, Qalandar females improve on perceptual tasks throughout their lifetime, except on the conservation task. This makes it difficult to substantiate conclusions regarding hypothesis 4. It could be argued that the relatively small t-values and partial correlations as a whole verify the hypothesis. Certainly no consistent sex difference appears, in contrast to the results of the other

Table 13. Partial correlations and associated significance levels between sex and task performance (controlling for age) for Qalandar.

Age group	Muller-Lyer	CEFT	Sander	Conservation
4–12 (n = 36)	.11	.05	.26	−.03
	ns	ns	ns	ns
13–20 (n = 21)	.27	−.39	−.19	.15
	ns	ns	ns	ns
21–80 (n = 38)	−.37	−.09	−.10	.00
	ns	ns	ns	ns

hypotheses and compared to other societies with rigid sex roles. Although it is not sharply marked, one phenomenon consistently underlies hypothesis 4; male Qalandar tend to perform in a relatively field-independent manner early in life, with females becoming more field-independent by adulthood. This is probably related to a somewhat differential emphasis on activities performed by male and female children between the ages of two and six. Relative to females, male children are often encouraged to engage actively in activities related to particular entertainment skills such as magic, juggling, or dancing. Although they are exposed to these activities, many girls of the same ages are encouraged instead to beg actively in the marketplace, either alone or with other females. As they grow older, and especially as adults with their own children, females engage more actively in entertainment activities in order to teach their children. The ethnographic record supports the importance of practice and experience in determining levels of performance on measures of psychological differentiation. It is therefore quite possible that practice and experience with entertainment-related skills enhance performance on the four measures of perceptual functioning.

The data of this hypothesis are consistent with a "no-difference" prediction based on previous studies of sex-role activities and perceptual style, and the outcome supports the emic performance that was universally expected by the Qalandar themselves. All Qalandar informants predicted that females would be field-independent relative to males except among young children, for at that age both sexes have less real authority in activities related to camp organization, food distribution, and movement patterns. Both sexes, noting that females are more "clever" and have greater ability to perceive details while keeping in mind the total social context, predicted that this rokna ability would favor females. Interestingly enough, their observation may be more culturally valid than the test data indicate. Although there is basic parity between the sexes, in actual practice with psychological experience related to their subsistence skills, males have slightly more experience performing these activities, such as juggling, magic, and other entertainment routines, in less familiar or more diverse public contexts. Females, on the other hand, tend to perform these activities in the more familiar contexts of processes related to intergenerational training or practice sessions within the camp milieu. My totally subjective impression was that Qalandar females were slightly more comfortable in the actual testing situation than males. It will be recalled that in the public domain as entertainers, Qalandar males behave in a very aggressive and confident manner. Within the camp context, they are more cooperative, almost submissive relative to females. Females tend to have more relative authority as well as training experience in the private domain, as opposed to the more public performance domain for males. Thus, the females were tested in a more familiar performance context. How these contextually diverse patterns of experience and action influence psychological performance remains to be investigated. However, we gain some insight into the role of performance contexts and differential sex-role experiences within the social milieu of the peripatetic Kanjar.

Hypothesis 5

Among the Kanjar it is the women and young girls who manufacture and sell the gugu ghoray and other toys, beg, and sell their sexual services in the larger sedentary community. The males primarily care for the infants, tents, and donkeys, and prepare food. If it is true that cultural fluidity and experience with amplifying skills impart field-independent functioning, then the Kanjar women should be superior to Kanjar men on the four tests of perceptual style. This is illustrated in Table 14.

Although age was partialed in the statistical analysis of these data, it did not materially alter the conclusions that can be drawn from Table 14, that Kanjar females are superior to males on only one measure, the Sander Parallelogram. The data also favor females on the other three measures, but not significantly. After well over a year's experience with these groups, I was frankly surprised that the sex difference in favor of females was not more dramatic. Among the Kanjar it is commonly believed and openly expressed that females are more intelligent, perceptive, independent, and aggressive than males. Even though the group sizes are small and the measures themselves are not

Table 14. Mean scores on tests of perceptual inference habits by Kanjar males and females.

Group	Muller-Lyer	CEFT	Sander	Conservation
Females (n = 21)				
x (mean)	11.52	24.29	8.95	.81
s.d.	1.47	6.33	1.12	.51
Males (n = 16)				
x (mean)	10.88	24.38	8.19	.69
s.d.	1.31	6.56	1.28	.70
t	1.39	−.02	1.94	.61
p	ns	ns	ns	ns

highly sensitive, there is a definite trend toward female superiority on the dependent measures, despite the fact that many of the most talented females are not included in the peripatetic groups of Kanjar. Interestingly, although the Kanjar males (unlike the Qalandar males) were tested in a context that was more familiar, that is, camp, the females were much more confident and comfortable in the testing situation.

Through the nomadic Kanjar I established contact with numerous females and males performing or undergoing training in the sedentary communities of professional entertainers and prostitutes in both Lahore and Karachi. Their quasi-legal social and political milieu prohibited any kind of systematic interviewing or psychological assessment. However, from my visits and observations of their professional skills, I am confident their performance on the measures of perceptual functioning would be markedly field-independent relative to Kanjar males.

Hypothesis 6

This last hypothesis examines sex differences within the sedentary sample, predicting that males would perform in a field-independent manner relative to females. Because the two sedentary milieus displayed a significant difference on only one measure (see hypothesis 3), and for the sake of an adequate sample size, village and urban dwellers are combined in this analysis. This combination is justifiable, for the village and urban groups did not display sex differences that were borne out in the combined analysis.

Sedentist females have a relatively limited role in the total environment, especially in the urban setting. Hence it was expected that they would perform in a relatively field-dependent manner. The mean scores on the four dependent measures for both males and females are displayed in Table 15, along with t-values and associated significance levels. Again, contrary to expectations, males performed significantly better on only one measure, the Sander Parallelogram; this result is not strong enough to verify hypothesis 6. When age and education are controlled via partialing, males become marginally superior on the CEFT task as well ($r = .14$, $p = .06$ one-tailed).

To pinpoint reasons for the lack of a marked difference between sedentist males and females, I analyzed the data by age group. Table 16 presents the partial correlations between the dummy-coded sex variables (males coded 1, females 0) and the dependent measures for four different age groups, controlling for both age and formal education. Also shown are the one-tailed significance levels. As can be seen, males tend to be relatively field-independent at an early age on three of the four perceptual tasks. Females tend to be superior to males on

Table 15. Mean scores on tests of perceptual inference habits by sedentary males and females.

Group	Muller-Lyer	CEFT	Sander	Conservation
Males (n = 65)				
x (mean)	10.91	27.31	8.25	.38
s.d.	1.33	5.26	1.28	.93
Females (n = 69)				
x (mean)	10.68	26.55	7.55	.61
s.d.	1.13	5.90	1.29	.79
t	1.06	.78	3.14	−1.51
p	ns	ns	.005	ns

the conservation tasks, though this trend becomes negligible with increasing age. This pattern is not particularly remarkable when we recall that it is the females who have almost exclusive experience, especially early in life, with the measurement and manipulation of both continuous and discontinuous quantities such as rice, beans, flour, dung patties, and the like, associated with harvesting, marketing, and food preparation. However, contrary to expectations, the data indicate that there is no consistent sex difference on the four dependent measures. Males tend to perform in a field-independent manner earlier than females and to maintain this pattern throughout the lifespan, though differences tend to diminish with increasing experience.

Table 16. Partial correlation coefficients and associated significance levels between sex (dummy-coded) and the four dependent measures, controlling for age and formal education.

Age group	Muller-Lyer	CEFT	Sander	Conservation
4–8 (n = 34)	.31	.22	.30	−.54
	ns	ns	ns	ns
9–12 (n = 35)	−.30	.43	.44	−.07
	ns	.005	.005	ns
13–20 (n = 35)	−.30	.00	.26	.20
	ns	ns	ns	ns
21–55 (n = 30)	.11	−.02	.06	.00
	ns	ns	ns	ns

In both sedentary groups it is difficult to differentiate between experience acquired as part of the day-to-day cultural curricula and that obtained through participation in formal educational settings. In an effort to isolate the effect of formal education from the age effect, I analyzed data for sedentists who were still attending school and those who had discontinued school activities within the last four years. Age was then partialed out of this correlation to help assess a "purer" education effect. Only the sedentist informants were included in these correlations because neither of the nomadic samples had any formal education. Further, only those with at least one year of education were included, so that the number of informants at each age level would be about equal. The correlations are presented with their one-tailed probabilities in Table 17.

I suspect that these data lend partial support to the carpentered-world hypothesis (Segall et al., 1958) by reflecting the influence of training in literacy skills and perceptual inference experience by exposure to two-dimensional representations of three-dimensional forms in texts and other illustrative educational material. These same perceptual inhibitory habits correspond with enhanced field-independent performance on the CEFT and Sander tasks. However, without further study among the sedentary groups, explanations of this pattern would be spurious and indefensible, because detailed ethnographic observations of perceptual performance in natural as well as formal contexts of learning are not available.

While a slight overall trend indicates that males perform in a consistently field-independent manner relative to females, the results are not significant for many of the measures, and hypothesis 6 must be rejected. The patterns of perceptual performance by males and females appear to be related to varying degrees of experience with social

Table 17. Zero-order and partial correlations between education (in years) and performance on the dependent measures (n = 72).

Correlation with education partialing out	Dependent variables			
	Muller-Lyer	CEFT	Sander	Conservation
Zero-order	.39	−.68	−.07	.42
	ns	$p<.01$	ns	$p<.01$
Age	.32	−.66	.16	.22
	ns	$p<.01$	ns	$p<.05$

and cultural activities. This is indicated in the sex differences in the performance of the youngest age group of sedentists as well as of females on the conservation tasks.

The data from the sedentary comparison groups may also reflect several sources of confounding which are infrequently examined in the cross-cultural record dealing with sex differences in psychological performance. These relate to the *social composition of the performance context*, especially formal psychological assessment settings. Among the sedentists in this study, cultural values regarding performance in same-sex groups differ from those considered desirable in mixed-sex groups. The intergenerational composition of groups also operates in a similar manner. For example, in the presence of adult males, especially contemporaries or senior members, females are expected to, and in fact do, act in a manner which should promote superior performance by males. In same-sex groups, seniority traditionally demands deference in performance by junior members. In my previous experience in South Asia, I've frequently encountered individuals in an inferior status who have played dumb or intentionally performed inaccurately to preserve contextual continuity in keeping with cultural expectations, and these kinds of constraints were probably operating in the testing contexts among the sedentary groups. Although all individuals were tested separately, I was always accompanied by my female assistant. Although the composition of the testing context was the same for all informants, the cultural values affecting actual patterns of performance were slightly different for males and females. Again, with analytical hindsight, it appears that males were more comfortable and open in the testing situation, though the presence of my female assistant appeared to promote "serious and careful" examination of the test materials. We both noted that males were inclined to answer even when it was obvious that the tasks were becoming too difficult. On the other hand, females were quite conscious of my assistant and nervous about my presence. Females appeared confused about how to respond because of the difference in contextual expectations generated by the mixed-sex setting. In dealing with the more familiar conservation tasks, females were obviously more relaxed and confident, whereas males became extremely conscious of their manipulations and performance vis-à-vis my assistant. These sorts of social factors must be investigated systematically; however, in this study the data indicate that contextual factors serve as cognitive amplifiers as well as individual experiences with a variety of social and cultural elements.

An Emic–Etic Interpretation

Perhaps the most significant finding in this study is the marked contrast in perceptual-cognitive performance between nomads and sedentists. Differential patterns of experience and skills (age, formal education, and sex for sedentists, and age, spatial mobility, and sex for nomads) correspond with disparate results in psychological performance. For example, among the nomads, age and spatial mobility (education) correspond with field-independent perceptual habits on all four measures of intellective operations. Interestingly, among the peripatetic artisans and entertainers, the dependent measures of perceptual-cognitive operations are highly intercorrelated. Conversely, in both sedentary communities, education, age, and sex effects are more ambiguously linked to psychological performance. For example, where education and age appear to promote field-independent performance on CEFT items, they enhance field-dependent operations on the other measures; in other words, formal education corresponds with an increase in perceptual inference errors on the Muller-Lyer illusion. Not surprisingly, the four dependent measures among sedentists are minimally correlated. This distinction between patterns of performance on each of the measures is clearly indicated in the correlation matrices in Appendix 2. Pertinent figures are presented in Table 18.

In the sedentary sample, with the exception of the high correlation between CEFT and conservation tasks ($r = 0.24$), the measures of field independence appear to be minimally related. Among nomads, however, each of the measures is significantly correlated. As noted earlier, the meaning of this relationship was pointed out by the nomads themselves in discussions of the tasks. Both Qalandar and Kanjar adamantly argued that each of the tests was of the same nature. By using an analogy with food, the separate tests were argued to

Table 18. Correlation matrices of measures of perceptual field independence for nomads (n = 139, upper right triangle) and sedentists (n = 146, lower left triangle).

	Muller-Lyer	CEFT	Sander	Conservation
Muller-Lyer	—	0.54	0.23	0.30
CEFT	0.08	—	0.33	0.57
Sander	0.05	0.20	—	0.26
Conservation	0.10	0.24	0.18	—

have the same "flavor" or "taste" and hence were comparable in nature. Consequently, relative success depended on an individual's skill and experience (*aqlmandip*) in discounting or inhibiting unimportant as well as misleading elements in each task. Rokna is a general term in Qalandari, Kanjari, and Urdu, designating the ability to disregard unimportant information while focusing on the essential demands of each context or task. As discussed in Chapter 5, rokna is a vital skill for the successful magician. In this sense, the child learning sleight-of-hand skills must learn verbal as well as motor skills to distract the attention of observers so that they cannot inhibit false or misleading cues in the performance. Both Qalandar and Kanjar also use the term rokna to refer to deceptive social interaction with sedentists in which a "disturbance" is generated to draw attention away from some other, often covert, activity.

Thus, among the Qalandar, the notion of rokna represents a range of perceptual skills which, in contexts which demand perceptual inhibitory and/or disembedding activities, appear to represent a sort of "contextual style." However, it should be kept in mind that these same individuals utilize field-dependent skills in contexts where global sensitivity is called for. This sort of contextually sensitive "perceptual inhibitory style" is clearly an important perceptual-cognitive activity involving disembedding skills in performing CEFT and to a certain extent the visual illusions; however, peripatetics generalized their notions of rokna to explain conservation tasks as well.

Cognitive Amplifiers in Conservation Tasks

Relative to the sedentary groups, significantly more Kanjar and Qalandar performed in a manner indicative of concrete-operational thought at very early ages. It will be recalled that several cross-cultural studies of conservation have shown that familiarity and/or experience with the testing materials appear to facilitate concrete-operational performance on traditional Piagetian tasks (Price-Williams 1961, 1962; Price-Williams, Gordon, and Ramirez 1969; Adjei 1977). In keeping with these studies, the results of this investigation indicate that manipulative experience with the testing materials is important; however, the ethnography of behavioral activities indicates that the *context* in which they are manifested also contributes to actual patterns of perceptual-cognitive performance.

The likely importance of actual manipulative experience and skill with continuous and discontinuous quantities related to day-to-day subsistence activities is illustrated in the results for each of the four comparison groups. In both the sedentary as well as peripatetic cultural milieus, patterns of familiarity, actual manipulative experience, and skill with the conservation materials corresponds with operational performance in perceptual-cognitive functioning. The nature of the relationship between experience and performance on Piagetian tasks is illustrated among the Qalandar and Kanjar.

As peripatetic artisans and entertainers, the nomads were very aware of variations in numerous social milieus and seem to be particularly sensitive to a distinction between perceived and actual properties of stimuli. This was especially the case among the Qalandar, for whom such distinctions are vital to their performance as entertainers. Consequently, the Qalandar presented some special testing problems which indicate the importance of context, previous experience, and skills in determining perceptual-cognitive processes related to levels of psychological performance. These people are very sensitive to the perceptual, as opposed to actual, properties of materials and actions. In the testing situation, it was common for subjects, even those as young as six years of age, to do the following:

1. When the actions were performed by the researcher, they would decline to make a conservation judgment, saying, "You might have done something we didn't see."
2. When they performed the conservation tasks themselves, a few drops of water often remained in the transfer beaker or splashed out, or a grain of rice spilled out. In this case they always judged the A_1 beaker (see Appendix 3) as having "more" (which, in fact, was the case, although by a *very* small amount).

Often when *roti* (dough) or *meti* (mud) were used, when breaking the large ball into two equal amounts, informants would surreptitiously pinch off a small portion and hide it. The subject would then respond that equality had been maintained. After the response had been recorded, the "stolen" portion would be brought out—with long, humorous admonitions to the researcher that the way things look is not always how they are. Many children and most adults would spend more than an hour "teaching" the investigators to conserve. Frequently, the testing situation was reversed, with Qalandar informants making any number of objects from dough or mud (snakes, other animals, pots) and querying the investigators as to relative size and quantity.

After I introduced the conservation tasks, the Qalandar felt obliged to use every opportunity to further my education about important ele-

ments in perceptual inference skills. Actually, they were deeply concerned and a bit embarrassed that a Qalandar, albeit adopted and obviously from a distant group, would go about asking such absurd
questions as those related to the conservation tasks. I might add that
they didn't hesitate to use my naiveté to amuse visiting Qalandar as
well as other peripatetic groups encountered during our travels. I
would be called over to a group and asked to sit down, and one of the
Qalandar, using stones, coins, mud, or the like, would administer a
conservation battery. Throughout the process I was ridiculed, and my
friends and their guests derived great enjoyment and mirth from these
routines. In concluding these joking sessions, the Qalandar would
boast about how they had converted a rather stupid sedentist into a
functioning Qalandar.

While these joking sessions promoted my position among the Qalandar, and thus among other peripatetic groups, they were also contexts in which Qalandar would discuss the relation among experience,
context, and perceptual skills. On numerous occasions, individuals
would call my attention to contexts that stressed varying degrees of ac-
curacy in perceptual inferences regarding "apparent" equality of
measurements. The importance of context in determining conservation responses was apparent in food distribution activities, where perceived as well as actual "equality" of portions was vital for social solidarity. Qalandar frequently joked about themselves: "When there is
little food and many stomachs, our eyes, ears, and noses are more sensitive than goldsmith's scales." In calling my attention to particular
subtleties in a particular context, they would frequently whisper,
"Yousef, remember, a hungry man observes that the cook licks his fingers." Or "The jackal in the city must use all his senses." One of the
most commonly used analogies emphasizing the contextual as well as
motivational aspects of perceptual-cognitive acuity in determining
psychological performance, especially on Piaget tasks, was "Remember, the poor man robs the ant of his due."

Qalandar cultural values regarding flexible perceptual-cognitive experiences and skills are in keeping with their peripatetic lifestyle and
the diverse contexts in which they perform a wide range of psychological operations. Certainly, keen observational skills and the ability to
discriminate finely in certain contexts (food sharing, conservation
tasks) may be vital for individual or group survival. Since measuring
conservation abilities among peripatetic artisans and entertainers, I
have had reservations about the validity of other cross-cultural studies
of conservation. For example, in conservation of liquids it is likely that
many children have been scored as nonconservers because they chose

the standard beaker as having "more" (the manipulated beaker having less) and were in fact correct. In tasks involving conservation of liquids, there is almost always a drop lost during pouring, or several drops remain in the original beaker because of adhesion to the sides or lip of the vessel. Both the Qalandar and Kanjar were quick to pick up when a grain of rice or drop of water was lost during these tasks.

As an anecdotal aside, my skepticism is reinforced by observations of my three-year-old daughter's struggles to drain the final drop of juice from her glass, despite futile parental admonitions that "it's all gone." Interestingly, several grains of rice and two peas left on the plate did *not* represent "all gone" for her parents, in spite of her pleas to the contrary. Like Qalandar children—all children, for that matter—she is learning to be contextually sensitive in her psychological performance. Certainly, in one context a drop of water or millimeter difference in length, even when observed, does not alter cognitive operations or psychological performance. However, under different conditions these "negligible" variations may be very important and demand different patterns of psychological performance.

In the diverse public and private domains of the Qalandar, assessments of particular contexts of psychological functioning focus attention on variable aspects of the content as well as processes in perceptual-cognitive operations. Certainly the Qalandar would argue that familiarily with general cultural rules governing performance in particular contexts is important. For example, societal regulations establishing the parameters of sexual relations between kinsmen or culturally based rules governing the range of logical precepts in explaining conservation of continuous quantities are useful in explaining psychological functioning in numerous contexts. However, such rules may be insufficient for understanding actual patterns of psychological performance in the wide range of interpersonal as well as ecocultural contexts constituting the day-to-day activities in which individuals perform a variety of physical and intellective operations.

Thus, these results suggest that patterns of psychological performance are determined by previous experience and skills. As well, each sociocultural system demands a range of activities and skills from its members which may depend on the task demands and social context. As indicated in the contrast between sedentists and peripatetics, the same tests used cross-culturally, or even across contexts, may tap totally unrelated or variable combinations of perceptual and cognitive activities.

Obviously, a *context-based* model of psychological functioning as generated by Qalandar, as well as the expanded notion of cognitive amplifiers, has implications for the interpretation and future investigation of the role of experience and context in both Piaget and Witkin's theories of psychological development, discussed in the next chapter. First, however, a brief note on how the results of this study correspond with evidence that biological factors account for differences in perceptual-cognitive functioning.

Biological Amplifiers

The vast majority of cross-cultural studies of cognitive development have focused on experiential or social variables in psychological functioning. On the other hand, two lines of research have indicated that biological factors alone may account for variations in perceptual-cognitive operations. Much of this research has focused on biological models to explain sex differences in perceptual-cognitive functioning. For instance, Broverman and his collaborators have suggested that sex differences in perceptual-cognitive performance are related to hormone effects in adrenergic-activity and cholinergic-inhibitory processes in the central nervous system (Broverman et al. 1968, 1972). Along similar lines, investigators such as Bock and Kolakowski (1973) have attributed perceptual field independence in males relative to females to a "recessive sex-linked gene", while Goodenough et al. (1977) have tied perceptual field-dependent patterns of performance in spatial visualization processes to X-chromosome linkages between brother pairs in Italian families. Further studies of perceptual functioning, especially optical illusion susceptibility on the Muller-Lyer tasks, have led Pollack and Silvar (1967) and Pollack (1970) to conclude that illusion-supporting visual inference habits correspond with macular pigmentation. Discounting the role of experience, Pollack (1970) suggests that levels of macular pigmentation, which corresponds with skin coloration in different bioecological niches, accounts for cross-cultural variability in geometric illusion susceptibility. Both Berry (1971c) and Jahoda (1971, 1975) report that fundus oculi pigmentation corresponds more closely with performance on the Muller-Lyer than relative experience with geometric forms in the visual environment as suggested by the carpentered-world hypothesis (Segall et al. 1966). Attempts to replicate these findings have produced ambiguous results (Jahoda 1975), and the evidence suggests that both bioecological and sociocultural factors operate in optical illusion susceptibility.

One of the striking results of this study is that relative to sedentists, the nomads are field-independent as well as less susceptible to visual illusions, though skin coloration, especially macular pigmentation, is basically the same for all groups. Sexual parity in performance among all groups, especially the tendency for nomadic females to perform in a field-independent manner relative to males, suggests that among these groups the effects of sex-linked genes, X-chromosome linkages, or sex hormones are being masked by experiential factors. While biological mechanisms undoubtedly contribute to perceptual-cognitive functioning, their effect appears to be mediated through social and cultural experiences in a variety of performance contexts. Thus, single-factor explanations, at the micro-level of fundus oculi density or the macro-level of comparisons of societal wholes, are insufficient for understanding how complex interactions between an organism and its environment result in patterns of psychological performance.

9

Potpourri: Theories in Search of Context

Following Rivers' early lead regarding the role of experience in diverse environmental settings in "focusing attention" and "providing special knowledge," I used as a model for this research the ecological functionalism of Barry, Bacon, and Childe (1957, 1959) and its intercultural elaboration in comparative psychological development research by Witkin (1967), Berry (1976), and Piaget (1964, 1966) and their collaborators. By expanding their research activities across diverse social systems, students of Piaget and Witkin have begun to demonstrate that individual as well as group differences in patterns of psychological performance are best understood as attributes of variable patterns of experience and skill with the diverse environments and material and interpersonal elements of performance contexts. To a certain extent, the results of this study lend qualified support to Witkin and Berry's (1975) differentiation hypothesis and Piaget's theory of cognitive functioning by demonstrating that patterns of performance on measures of perceptual inference habits and conservation tasks correspond with experience and skill in each social and ecocultural milieu. On the other hand, the evidence from an increasing number of cross-cultural ecological investigations of human development reviewed in Chapter 1, along with the results of this study, suggest that the ontology of psychological functioning is more context-specific and flexible than indicated in either Witkin's or Piaget's theories. Before exploring some of the implications of this study, let us briefly review the context of the results.

Drawing on Berry's (1971a, 1976) ecocultural model of perceptual-cognitive functioning, Cole and Bruner's (1971) notion of "amplifying skill" and Cole, Gay, Glick, and Sharp's (1971) pioneering call for a "theory of situations" to explain group differences in patterns of psychological functioning, I was guided by three basic assumptions in this investigation. First, I hypothesized that day-to-day activities in the diverse ecocultural milieu of peripatetic artisans and entertainers would demand greater flexibility and field-independent perceptual skills relative to sedentary adaptations. Second, because sex role activities are extremely flexible among peripatetics, I expected that male–female differences in patterns of psychological performance would be less marked among nomads relative to sedentists. Third, I expected that children of peripatetic entertainers and craftsmen would have greater as well as earlier experience with tasks requiring field-independent perceptual skills than their sedentist counterparts.

The measures of psychological differentiation and cognitive skills confirmed my initial assumptions regarding group and individual differences in perceptual inference habits. It was also shown that among the nomadic artisan and entertainers, the more independent, aggressive, and active individuals are field-independent relative to the less independent and less mobile individuals. In day-to-day subsistence-related activities, these individual differences correspond with differential patterns of experience and skill associated with behavioral tasks embedded in a wide range of social and ecocultural performance contexts. The group mean scores supporting these conclusions are summarized in Table 19.

Table 19. Tabulation, grouped by sex, of mean correct scores on the four dependent measures.

Group	Muller-Lyer	CEFT	Sander	Conservation
All nomads (n = 132)	11.97	26.17	8.88	.80
Qalandar (n = 95)	12.26	26.89	8.99	.82
Females (n = 58)	12.26	26.97	8.97	.84
Males (n = 37)	12.24	26.78	9.03	.81
Kanjar (n = 37)	11.24	24.32	8.62	.76
Females (n = 21)	11.52	24.29	8.95	.81
Males (n = 16)	10.88	24.38	8.19	.69
All sedentists (n = 134)	10.79	26.92	7.89	.50
Females (n = 69)	10.68	26.55	7.55	.61
Males (n = 65)	10.91	27.31	8.25	.38

Formal Education as Experience

As predicted, the peripatetic artisans and entertainers performed in a field-independent manner relative to sedentary comparison groups on three of the four measures of perceptual inference habits. However, none of the nomads had any formal education experience, whereas about half of the sedentary groups had been exposed to several years of schooling. When formal education is controlled for, the peripatetic artisans and entertainers perform in a significantly field-independent manner relative to sedentists on all four measures, which may be attributed to the fact that nomadic artisans and entertainers have greater flexibility and individual experience with a wider range of materials and social elements. The contrasting ecocultural systems of nomads and sedentists represent different milieus within which perceptual experience and skills are acquired and utilized. For example, relative to the sedentary villagers and urban dwellers, the Kanjar and the Qalandar are characterized by the following:

1. Display emotion and affection openly and freely
2. Behave more independently, particularly in choices of residence and affiliation
3. Are more direct in interpersonal relationships
4. Display and reinforce for independence of action and self-sufficiency
5. Emphasize individual accomplishment, autonomy, and disembedding skills
6. Include children at a very early age in the social, economic, and political world of adults, emphasizing diverse experiences and skills through lifelong socialization activities
7. Are more spatially mobile, with more contact with diverse social and environmental elements
8. Have high levels of fluidity (fusion and fission) in social organization
9. Compete for more variable resources
10. Have much greater flexibility in sex roles

Among the Qalandar and the Kanjar, specialized training, formal instruction, and other socialization processes are integral parts of day-to-day activities. The most striking difference between the curriculum of nomads in this study and that of formally schooled sedentists is the nature and context of learning. Nomadic artisans and entertainers stress learning skills based on independent thought, restructuring, interpretation, and analysis of information, which is in marked contrast with the instructional mode and learning skills expected of children in the sedentary setting. Primary schools in Pakistan, especially in the villages, emphasize rote learning; most early literacy training is memorization of the Koran. Independent thought, analysis, and interpretation are negatively reinforced in the home as well as in the school. Basic primary education always takes place in the classroom rather than the household and general community.

Along these same lines, the contexts of psychological performance are importantly different for each group. In the sedentary world, contexts such as school, household, field, or shop tend to be viewed as discrete domains where adults and children play out prescribed roles. Sedentary children are expected to perform in a "child's" world which is often separate from that of adults. Qalandar and Kanjar children, on the other hand, are integral parts of the entire social system. They are evaluated in terms of their individual experience and skills and not in a general category of "children." Compared to sedentist children, the peripatetic child performs psychological activities in more diverse *interpersonal* as well as ecocultural contexts. Not surprisingly, the results indicate that these children perform in a field-independent manner earlier than sedentary children.

These findings are important because they suggest that formal education per se, as a macro-independent variable, may not account for individual differences in perceptual or cognitive functioning. Instead, the specific content and/or contexts of a school curriculum may promote certain patterns of psychological performance, depending on their correspondence with the demands of perceptual or cognitive operations in other contexts of intellective functioning.

Contextual Experience in Conservation Performance

The importance of social and ecocultural contexts as well as experience and skills in determining perceptual inference habits was illustrated in the results of performance on the conservation tasks, which showed that Qalandar and Kanjar children conserve at a much earlier age than sedentary children. Within the Kanjar sample there is a marked tendency for females to conserve earlier than males. Because the Kanjar females make clay figurines, they are more familiar with and aware of the physical properties involved in the conservation of continuous quantities. It was also shown that Kanjar females have greater experience in a variety of social and cultural settings related to

their peddling, dancing, and prostitution activities. Because Kanjar females have direct control over their capital resources, they have
greater social status and authority than males. This combination of experiential, social, and ecocultural activities, as cognitive amplifiers,
produces their patterns of psychological performance.

Although less marked among the Qalandar, a comparable pattern of
psychological performance on measures of perceptual field-depen-
dence/independence supports the role of cognitive amplifiers. Like
the Kanjar, the peripatetic entertainers are markedly field-independent relative to sedentists and score well on the conservation tasks.
This finding is particularly significant in that it impugns an explana-
tion of precocity in perceptual-cognitive performance based exclusively on "test material experience" or specific techno-manipulative
activities related to subsistence strategies, as suggested by Price-Williams, Gordon, and Ramirez (1969). Qalandar do not manufacture
clay or other products and have little actual manipulative experience
with physical material and objects. Their craft of human social interpretation and manipulation, and their skills as magicians, jugglers,
acrobats, and trainers of performing animals promote perceptual inhibition and disembedding skills, which correspond with the psychological performance patterns found among Kanjar. Qalandar females also
tend to perform in a field-independent manner relative to males. While
the results are not statistically significant, this tendency may be related to patterns of specific techno-manipulative and interpersonal-
manupulative experience in diverse performance contexts.

There is a definite tendency in the sedentary samples for females to
conserve earlier than males, using continuous quantities such as rice,
water, dough, or mud. In both the village and urban settings, females
receive early practice in food preparation, which includes manipulation and estimation of quantities. Certainly, these data support Piaget
and Witkin and Price-Williams (1975) by demonstrating that experience and skills on certain tasks influence levels of performance.
Equally important, however, is the demonstration that the social composition of *performance contexts* may influence levels of psychological
performance, as emphasized by Cole and his collaborators (1971). It
was my impression that the peripatetic samples were more comfortable or relaxed during the testing sessions, either because they had
greater rapport and familiarity with the investigator and/or because of
their experience performing for an audience. Among the sedentists,
females were more comfortable and confident with the more familiar
conservation tasks; however, both sexes were sensitive to the social
composition of the testing situation, which always included my female

assistant. It was our impression that the investigator's presence promoted diligence on the tasks among sedentary males and appeared to inhibit performance by the females. As noted earlier, among the sedentary communities actual performance behavior is mediated by an individual's social status and/or perception of appropriate level of functioning vis-à-vis others, depending on other factors such as age and sex.

These types of *social demand characteristics* were not systematically controlled for in this study and are likely sources of confounding in the results from the sedentary samples. Overall, these findings also suggest that while such factors as settlement patterns and formal education may have an effect on the development of analytic thinking, the nature of learning experience, its social and ecocultural context, and the mode of assessment must be specified. The variety, amount, and nature of individual experience (familiarity and practice) with a particular activity seem to be crucial in determining the manifestation of perceptual inference habits and cognitive skills.

One of the most striking contrasts between the peripatetic groups and the sedentists was in socialization and child-rearing practices. Relative to sedentists, especially in formal instruction contexts, Qalandar and Kanjar were extremely supportive and indulgent in their child-rearing activities. Harsh treatment of children among peripatetics was extremely rare, and children were actively encouraged to be creative and to have personal autonomy. Each child received guidance, encouragement, and support in his skills from parents, siblings, and other camp members. In their phrase, each individual has someone to "point out" the salient features of his behavioral context. It is the interpersonal processes associated with the experience and skills of their subsistence curriculum rather than a draconian or permissive context of socialization processes which contribute to particular patterns of perceptual-cognitive performance. Recent ethnographic and developmental research reported for hunting groups supports an emphasis on the interpersonal nature of experience and skills in socialization to subsistence activities (Konner 1977a; Draper 1975, 1976). Other factors related to subsistence strategies, such as greater handling and verticality of infants through variegated socioecological environments, have been shown to amplify or push increased levels of sensorimotor and perceptual-cognitive experience (White and Castel 1964; Ayres 1973; Konner 1977a,b).

A number of factors have been discussed in this study that appear to account for sex differences or parity on measures of perceptual field independence and dependence. Sex differences have been shown to be related to the differential value, socialization process, and participation of women in basic subsistence strategies relative to males. In peripatetic societies, as in gathering-hunting adaptations, it has been demonstrated that this differentiation is less pronounced. Contrary to previous studies in sedentary communities outside South Asia, indicating marked sex differences (males more field-independent in both rural and urban settings), the results of this study are ambiguous. Although males tend to perform in a field-independent manner relative to females, the sex differences in both the urban and village settings are not conclusive. This is particularly surprising for the Lahoria sample, where women are strictly confined within a neighborhood and keep purdah restrictions. Without firsthand behavioral ethnographic experience, it is difficult to account for this finding. Based on limited experience I would suggest that females' social-contextual experiences dramatically influence their perceptual inference habits. In contexts where global or less articulated functioning is appropriate (as in the presence of Pakistani males), they perform in a field-dependent manner. Interestingly, these findings are consistent with studies conducted in India, where sex differences in traditional measures of perceptual functioning tend to favor males only slightly (Pande and Kothari 1968; Pande 1970a,b).

The "no difference" hypothesis in this study is significant in that the data supported the original assumption that Qalandar males and females are similar in their levels of psychological performance on measures of perceptual inference. The emphasis on flexibility in experiences and skills contributes to sexual parity in perceptual-cognitive development. Although all individuals do not perform the same activities equally, each Qalandar is familiar with the basic skills necessary for successful performance of a particular routine. This sort of flexibility, as a cognitive amplifier, is necessary for peripatetic individuals or group survival within the larger socioecological system.

The sexual parity among Qalandar, the lack of marked differences in the sedentary samples, and the fact that Kanjar females actually performed in a field-independent manner compared to Kanjar males lend support to experiential or ontogenetic processes rather than strict biophysiotic explanations of sex differences in perceptual inference habits or cognitive operations. The results suggest that the traditional notion that the biological role of females predisposes them to be cognitively and perceptually less differentiated than males is an overgeneralization. To the contrary, partial support is indicated for Berry's (1976:206) argument that "those who are maintained, in dependent positions, with little value attached to their roles, will attain lower levels of psychological differentiation." Also, these cultural values may regulate individual experience, with the total range of experience and skills making up a particular performance context. Thus, at the level of ordinary, day-to-day activities across numerous spheres of psychological experience, this evidence suggests that perceptual inference habits or cognitive operations are sensitive to the interpersonal composition and task-specific content of specific ecocultural contexts.

Contextual Relativism and Perceptual Field Interdependence

The findings reported above and the previously cited studies indicate that psychological performance indicative of perceptual field dependence corresponds with socioecological settings which emphasize extended kinship and family organization in a sedentary setting and socialization and child-rearing practices stressing conformity, obedience, and respect for authority. Those ecocultural systems with high mobility, fluid social organization, small family units, and permissive child-rearing practices emphasize self-reliance, independence and greater sexual parity in psychological differentiation. As Triandis (1972, 1973) has pointed out, the field-independent cognitive style is most adaptive in a culture that seeks to achieve physical, materialistic objectives in impersonal manners, whereas the field-dependent cognitive style is most adaptive where the maintenance of fusive and harmonious relationships are important. These contrasting notions of cultural milieus are similar to Tönnies (1957) conception of *Gemeinschaft* and *Gesellschaft*. At one end of the continuum we find an ecological press toward disembedding, fluidity in social organization, socialization emphasizing personal autonomy, and high levels of psychological differentiation. At the other end we find an ecological press for tight social organization, hierarchy, socialization to conformity, and relatively low levels of psychological differentiation. The adaptive significance of varying degrees of psychological differentiation has been demonstrated in the contrasting sociocultural milieus of peripatetic artisans and entertainers and sedentary populations.

Thus, when comparing ecocultural domains as entities embedded within larger social and ecological systems containing numerous societal adaptations, Witkin's notion of psychological differentiation fits Berry's ecocultural model. On the other hand, it should be kept in mind that variable patterns of psychological performance indicative of a particular schema in Piaget's theory or level of psychological differentiation in Witkin's system correspond with individual experience and skills in diverse social and cultural contexts within the same ecocultural niche. As we saw in the Qalandar ethnography, certain contexts demand field-dependent habits, and other settings stress a more articulated approach in psychological functioning.

In fact, among the peripatetic entertainers several context-specific activities would appear to demand perceptual skills which are simultaneously global and articulate. For example, when the bandarwālā performs before a mixed, unfamiliar audience, he must be sensitive to the general tone of the entire context, alert to cues from individuals regarding his routine, and sensitive to the location of his equipment and any accompanying dogs or goats. Certainly the Qalandar, with their "it all depends" model of psychological performance, would argue that field-dependent or field-independent perceptual inference habits, while based on previous experience and training, are individual skills to be utilized depending on the demands of a particular performance context.

From this perspective, perceptual inference habits such as field independence/dependence are not manifestations of global phenomena or organismic mechanisms which regulate underlying processes of intellective functioning. Rather, perceptual or cognitive styles may more profitably be viewed as psychological skills or activities—manifestations of individual experience and training which vary within as well as across the social and temporal parameters in diverse ecocultural domains of psychological performance, that is, cognitive amplifiers. Emphasizing psychological skills associated with activities in the day-to-day settings of psychological functioning, cognitive amplifiers focus attention on the importance of *contextual relativism* for interpreting individual or group differences in perceptual-cognitive performance. As well, recognition that experience and skill are contextually embedded may help in explaining variable (or flexible) patterns of individual performances across the social and ecocultural domains of psychological functioning. By focusing attention on the importance of domain-specific skills and experience as well as the interpersonal composition of performance contexts, my usage of the cognitive amplifier construct draws some support from Serpell's (1976) perceptual skills theory and the functional systems approach of Cole and his collaborators (1971) in experimental anthropology at the Laboratory of Comparative Human Cognition (LCHC 1978, 1979, 1981).

Serpell's discussion of the perceptual skills hypothesis emphasizes that patterns of psychological functioning are embedded within specific activity domains within ecocultural systems. Similar in many respects to Berry and Witkin's ecocultural model, this hypothesis concentrates on how specific activities within particular contexts promote individual patterns of perceptual performance. For example:

> The upbringing of a forest hunter will promote skills of discrim-
> ination (in vision, hearing and smell) which are quite different
> from those instilled in a Western classroom. For instance, the
> ability to separate an item from its perceptual context in EFT or
> RFT may be, in some abstract sense, conceptually equivalent
> to the ability which the hunter has acquired to spot an animal
> camouflaged in a thicket, but the perceptual skills involved are
> not the same. Hence Western architects will need protection in
> the African forest and African hunters will need assistance at
> the Western drawing-board. (Serpell 1976:45)

While most cross-cultural studies of perceptual-cognitive function-ing have assumed that patterns of performance on traditional mea-sures of cognitive development reflect general intellective processes, Cole and his collaborators have stressed that perceptual-cognitive op-erations are mediated by the content as well as context of intellectual activities. The original thrust of their argument is summed up in their observation that "cultural differences in cognition reside more in the situations to which particular cognitive processes are applied than in the existence of a process in one cultural group and its absence in an-other" (Cole et al. 1971:233). Cole and Scribner have further elabo-rated the research implications of a "situation-specific" orientation:

> To be sure, present day psychological investigations are show-
> ing that for many intellectual tasks there is a relationship be-
> tween the nature of the task materials and the operations that
> are brought to bear on it . . . In *practice*, however, most psy-
> chologists still tend to interpret performance within a given set
> of materials as revealing some fixed set of "context-free" pro-
> cesses . . . This is what they mean when they talk about cul-
> tural variations in cognition. (Cole and Scribner 1975:255)

By focusing on psychological skills in a number of naturally occur-ring behavioral contexts within the same ecocultural domain, one may interpret patterns of perceptual-cognitive performance characteristic of Piaget's schemas or Witkin's notions of a perceptual style as little more than examples of individual experience and skill with task-specific demands of a particular setting. In keeping with the Qalandar "it all depends" model, patterns of psychological performance on measures of perceptual inference habits might be better characterized as context-specific or *field-interdependent activities*. Perceptual field interdependence stresses that perceptual skills or habits are mediated through individual training and experiences, which are sensitive to the contextual demands within which task-specific activities are performed. This is nicely illustrated in Lee's (1979) extensively detailed ethnography of subsistence strategies among the !Kung San, showing how hunting and gathering activities promote perceptual inhibitory and disembedding skills characteristic of relatively high levels of psychological articulation. On the other hand, organizing activities within and between bands stresses interpersonal skills which depend on a more global orientation. And in some hunting activities, constant interpersonal awareness is as important as individual perceptual skills.

Cultural Amplifiers and Ecocultural Validity

While cross-cultural comparative studies of cognitive development have had to come to grips with cultural relativism, the notion of cultural amplifiers focuses attention on *contextual relativism* in interpreting variable patterns of psychological performance within ecocultural systems. In keeping with Serpell's (1976) perceptual skills hypothesis and the situational determinism of Cole and colleagues, the ethnography of psychological experience and skills suggests that individual patterns of perceptual-cognitive performance reflect contextually embedded and temporally mediated task-specific skills, rather than organism-wide propensities to performance independent of social and ecocultural domains. Initially formulated by Rivers nearly a century ago, the question of interpreting the complex relationship among ecocultural, social, and training variables in determining psychological performance remains a challenge today. In a remarkably astute and ethnographically sensitive overview of cross-cultural developmental psychology, Cole and his associates (LCHC 1980) have captured the essence of an observation that plagued me almost daily as I observed psychological skills and experiences in day-to-day Qalandar life and tried to relate these activities to individual performance on the measures of perceptual inference habits. Notable was the fact that *"no context of observation, despite the care taken in its construction, is culturally neutral. Settings for behavior are socially organized, and they are embedded in larger systems of social organization which influence them."* (LCHC 1980:5, emphasis in original). While it is personally gratifying to discover support for my own thesis on cognitive amplifiers, it is particularly exciting to find a practically perfect correspondence between Cole and associates' conclusions and the centuries-old Qalandar "it all depends" model of psychological performance. Cole and colleagues' ethnographic psychology stresses situational determinism and draws attention to the fact that "behavioral contexts are socially organized . . . and . . . embedded in larger systems of social organization which influence them," but one should also keep in mind that "systems of social organization" are in turn embedded in wider socioecological systems.

The nomadic artisans and entertainers exploit a complex socioecological system containing a number of distinct but related ecocultural groups, including pastoral nomads, rural villagers, and urban dwellers. Thus, at a contextual-relativistic level of analysis, cognitive amplifiers, are manifested in the day-to-day activities of individuals or groups embedded in numerous behavioral domains within each ecocultural system. In turn, each of these ecocultural systems are interrelated elements in the larger socioecological spheres within Southwest Asia. Consequently, group differences, based on samples from distinctive ecocultural niches, should be interpreted in terms of their manifestation vis-à-vis the wider social, cultural, and ecological systems within which they are embedded. Thus, ecocultural groups may be treated as reflecting a particular "psychological style" in contrast to other cultural groups occupying different but interrelated ecocultural niches within the same system. Each ecocultural system provides a curriculum of task- and context-specific experiences which promote variable patterns of individual performance within as well as across generations. As such, these individual-group-environment interactions correspond with variable spheres of experience which promote patterns of continuity as well as distribution of psychological skills within groups through time. At the level of cross-cultural comparison, the evidence supports Witkin and Berry's ecocultural model of psychological differentiation:

> The cluster of characteristics found in field-dependent people and the cluster found in field-independent people each has components that are helpful in dealing with particular situations. The field-dependent and field-independent cognitive styles are thus not inherently good or bad. Their value can only be judged with reference to their adaptiveness in particular life circumstances. (Witkin and Goodenough 1977:682)

However, at the level of individual functioning, patterns of psychological performance appear to be contextually interdependent. Thus, an individual may utilize field-dependent or field-independent perceptual skills depending on his experience and the demands of a particular setting.

Intercultural studies of psychological functioning have made us aware that diverse ecocultural adaptations promote variable patterns of psychological performance. At the same time, detailed intracultural studies indicate variable patterns in group or even individual performance which are contextually sensitive. Consequently, it would seem that variability *within* as well as across groups on measures of perceptual or cognitive functioning should be the rule rather than the exception. If we accept this thesis, what does it tell us about the value of cross-cultural (contextual) psychological research where the emphasis is on the generality or "ecocultural validity" of knowledge claims based on Western theories derived from methods and data in the Western world? Serpell has captured the thrust of this argument in his particularly cogent questions regarding the primary goals of cross-cultural comparative research:

> Is it to vindicate (with a variety of provisos) a conceptual model developed in the West by showing that it yields results in a variety of different cultures? Or is it to explore, with whatever instruments and models are available, the relation between culture and human behavior? If the latter is a more important goal, there is a danger in relying too heavily on the theories and more especially on tests established in one cultural context. For it leads too easily to a focus on: 'how do *they* resemble, or differ from, *us*? rather than the more general question: 'how do different peoples become the way they are? . . . If theories originally formulated to explain the behaviour of Western populations are to be productive in cross-cultural research they will need to be prised free of particular standardized tests, and new instruments devised appropriate for measuring the same psychological constructs in different cultural settings. (Serpell 1976:54)

Concurrently, we must keep in mind that extensions of Western theories, their attending methods, and material may be insensitive to the role of diversity or variable patterns of psychological performance as integral elements of flexibility associated with disparate ecocultural adaptations.

Cognitive Amplifiers:
The Contexts of Psychological Activities

For the peripatetic artisans and entertainers in this study, the testing situation was little more than another context within which they were asked to perform a particular set of psychological operations. I imagine that their approach to this situation is somewhat similar to that of university students who participate in psychological experiments; the laboratory is but one of many performance contexts in their college experience. Like Rivers' "special knowledge and the direction of attention," Bateson's (1958) notion of *eidos* and the ethnographic psychology of Cole and his associates, the notion of cognitive amplifiers stresses that individual pattens of psychological performance are contextually embedded and mediated by previous experience and training. Rather than emphasizing the differences in approach between ethnographers and psychologists, the cognitive amplifier construct is offered as a conceptual link between the experimentalist and ethnologist where our common concern is psychological activities in ecoculturally embedded contexts. To a degree, the experimental psychologists' concern with demand characteristics and Rosenthal (Pygmalion) Effects are the cross-cultural investigators' concerns writ large.

In human groups we have seen that access to and actual experience with basic interpersonal as well as technical skills are embedded in patterns of social organization, particularly in the division of labor by sex and age. It is the intergenerational (socialization) or historical nature of these skills and activities, the social-contextual as well as interpersonal processes by which they are learned and within which they are utilized that I have termed "cognitive amplifiers." The influence of these interrelated experiences, activities, and skills, as *cognitive amplifiers*, in individual perceptual-cognitive functioning is the key to understanding group variability in patterns of psychological performance.

In addition to an emphasis on detailed analysis of subsistence or task-specific activities and skills, the concept of cognitive amplifiers stresses the interdependent or interpersonal domain as much as the ecocultural contexts of psychological performance. Perhaps as a function of methodological convenience rather than of the ethnocentrism inherent in "individual-focused" Western psychological theory, traditional anthropological and psychological approaches tend to treat the "perceiver" as a separate, closed system, independent of social as well as environmental context. The concept of cognitive amplifiers demands that we interpret individual or group activities and skills as integral elements in larger social and ecological systems. It is no longer sufficient to point to general cultural (Greenfield and Child, 1974) or environmental (Serpell et al. 1966) influences in perceptual-cognitive development. Instead, we must concentrate on understanding how these skills are behaviorally manifested throughout the entire range of social-environmental domains within a culture. As Cole stated, "if there is a simple, central lesson to be derived from years of research on learning sets, it is that animals (including man) learn generalized problem-solving skills through repeated experience with different problems of the same type" (1975:157–175).

Before concluding with a few recommendations for future research, I must add a cautionary methodological note. Anthropologists have often criticized cross-cultural studies of group or individual differences in levels of psychological performance as "ethnocentric" or "cultural-relativistic." While these criticisms are not without considerable merit, taking into account the anthropologists' emphasis on long-term participant observation, their studies offer little methodological or ethnographic insight into the nature of the relationship among specific ecocultural activities, settings, and patterns of psychological performance in what cognitive psychologists call "the context of natural purposeful activities" (Neisser 1976). Cross-cultural psychologists, on the other hand, while sensitive to the call for "culturally relevant and meaningful" systematic assessment strategies, continue to administer tests and interpret results without first-hand, long-term observations of psychological activities, such as perceptual inference habits, in the normal course of "natural purposeful activities." This sort of quasi-experimental or "Land Rover psychometry" frequently generates ethnographically spurious data and interpretations. More often, results are often ethnocentrically limited by the investigator's perceptual inference habits in descriptions of unfamiliar ecocultural settings. For example, in a description of the influence of visual ecologies it is still common to find perceptual fields described as homogeneous, uniform, or highly variegated. To whom, one has to wonder? These sorts of ethnographic inference errors will be reduced when cross-cultural psychological assessment strategies include first-hand descriptions of psychological activities in naturalistic social and environmental systems where informants "point out" the nature of the sensory field.

Notable among recent studies in cross-cultural research has been the "experimental anthropology" or "ethnographic psychology of cognition" of Cole and his collaborators (Cole et al. 1971; Cole and

Scribner 1974, Scribner 1976, LCHC 1979, 1980). While largely confined to quasi-experimental contexts within naturalistic settings, their
methodological emphasis is on ecocultural settings and task validity by
"situating the experiment" within naturally occurring skill and experience contexts. By "experimenting with the experiment" these investigators are able to "identify certain distinctive features of the experimental situation as a context for cognitive behavior, and to fit it
into the range of situations in the culture in which this behavior is
manifested" (Scribner 1976:312).

The situationally specific or "functional systems" approach posited
by Cole and his collaborators is important because of their emphasis
on meticulous attention to diverse elements (social as well as material) making up performance contexts and how these contribute to
perceptual inference habits and cognitive operations. From the perspective of day-to-day activities within naturally occurring domains of
psychological functioning, an ethnographic psychology of perceptual
or cognitive socialization and performance contexts demands methodological ingenuity and a tenacious commitment to naturalistic observations—requirements which are staggering but challenging. The
nature of this challenge has been nicely explicated in Jahoda's remarkably perspicuous overview of experimental anthropology and his
reservations regarding the effectiveness of Cole and colleagues' functional systems approach to cross-cultural comparative studies:

> It appears to require extremely exhaustive, and in practice al-
> most endless, explorations of quite specific pieces of behavior,
> with no guarantee of a decisive outcome. This might not be
> necessary if there were a workable "theory of situations" at our
> disposal, but as Cole admits there is none. What is lacking in
> Cole's approach are global theoretical constructs relating to
> cognitive processes of the kind Piaget provides, and which save
> the researcher from becoming submerged in a mass of unman-
> ageable material. It may be that the concept of "functional sys-
> tems" may become a more suitable tool for this purpose; but at
> present it appears to be insufficiently specific. Thus there is no
> guidance provided as to what constitutes such a system, or the
> operations whereby it is capable of being assessed. (Jahoda
> 1980:126–127)

Having lived for more than two years with peripatetic artisans and
entertainers while gathering data across their diverse ecocultural milieu, I feel tremendous empathy for Jahoda's concerns. Indeed, I did

collect a "mass of unmanageable material"—doubly so in that it had
to be transported by donkey, then organized and analyzed in a totally
different as well as distant context. During this process, especially in
the daily round of naturally occurring activities, I became increasingly
sensitized to exactly what Cole and his collaborators are arguing: patterns of psychological functioning (performance) are situationally
sensitive and much more flexible than either Piaget's or Witkin's
theories would suggest. Current research along these lines by Price-
Williams and Ciborowski (Ciborowski 1980) in Hawaii illustrates
how contextual and experiential factors correspond with specific perceptual and inferential cognitive skills. In an intensive ethnographic-
psychological investigation of Hawaiian families, these investigators
are attempting to "isolate and analyze" the particular cognitive (perceptual) skills that children utilize in daily contexts and how these
skills transfer to other ecocultural domains such as formal school
settings. For example, Price-Williams and Ciborowski have observed
that:

> Many of the older children are already accomplished boatmen
> and fishermen. They are accustomed to going considerable dis-
> tances (perhaps five miles) out to sea in what seem to be dis-
> tressingly small outrigger canoes. Many times these older chil-
> dren must contend with waves and swells that are far larger
> than the canoe itself. More than simple brawn and daring are
> involved in not only staying afloat, but also fishing. It is likely
> that a number of specific perceptual and inferential cognitive
> skills are involved in this activity.
>
> Once out at sea, these older children must be able to detect
> and cope with strong currents in order to fish successfully.
> They must know, for example, how and when to throw out the
> correct chum (fish bait) in a particular current, and how to
> stay within that current and ahead of the fish, in order to catch
> a load of fish. Obviously, they must be able to estimate accu-
> rately the speed of the current, and the location (and speed) of
> the fish they hope to catch. This ability calls for specific com-
> plex perceptual and inferential cognitive skills. Because of
> space limitations the many other skills that are associated with
> fishing are not mentioned; for example: using nets; estimating
> how far down to drop a baited hook; how to land a 300–400-
> pound marlin or ahi (tuna) that is practically the same size as
> the canoe, etc. (Ciborowski 1980:291–292)

Such studies as this, along with a growing number of situationally specific investigations of skills associated with weaving, tailoring, and other specialized activities illustrate the complex nature of the relationship between spheres of experience in naturally occurring contexts and patterns of psychological performance (see, for example, Greenfield and Child 1974; Serpell 1977a,b; Super, Harkness, and Baldwin 1977; Lave 1977a; Scribner and Cole 1978; Reed and Lave 1979; and Cole, Hood, and McDermott 1980).

Further investigations of cognitive socialization will draw our attention to the fact that experience and skills are acquired and manifested in socially organized contexts where interpersonal processes influence patterns of perceptual and cognitive performance (Adjei 1977; Kirk 1977). By stressing context, experience, and interpersonal processes within diverse ecocultural settings both within and across social systems, these lines of investigation have focused attention on the interrelationship between dependent and independent variables in most naturally occurring contexts of psychological functioning. At the same time, cross-cultural ethnographic psychological approaches should draw our attention to a cognitive amplifier in Western behavior and social science which must be monitored in our comparative analyses of intercultural data—namely, individual-focused psychology, where psychological functioning is investigated and interpreted as if independent of the ecocultural or interpersonal contexts in which it is inextricably embedded. Our Western values, expressed in practically every behavioral sphere, from home through school and work settings, stresses "independent" individual functioning. In the day-to-day contexts of task performance in much of the non-Western world, especially Asia and the Pacific, tasks are frequently corporate activities where skills and experience are organized *inter*individually, and the interpersonal processes related to a task are frequently more important than completion of the task itself.

This study is submitted as another exploratory effort toward combining intensive ethnographic description of perceptual-cognitive experiences and skills in naturalistic domains with the experimental performance context approach. Because it expands earlier notions of cultural aids and amplifying skills, the notion of cognitive amplifiers is recommended as a global theoretical construct for bridging specific ecocultural contexts of psychological experience and skills to patterns of perceptual and cognitive performance in cross-cultural comparative theories of behavioral functioning and development.

Certainly, future intensive ethnographies of perceptual and cognitive activities will complement the experimental anthropological approaches now in fashion by increasing the social and ecocultural validity of our research efforts. Such behavioral ethnography will require a tenacious commitment to intensive naturalistic observation more characteristic of ethology than the "Land Rover psychometry" techniques popular in both psychology and social anthropology today. New leads along these lines are available in Leiderman et al. (1977), von Cranach et al. (1979), Bochner (1980), and Longabaugh (1980), Altmann (1980), and Rogoff (1978, 1981).

If the Qalandar I lived with during this study were able to read the conclusions presented above, they would quietly smile and tolerantly praise me for demonstrating the obvious: patterns of psychological performance depend on the social context and the experience and skill of the entertainer. My adoptive Qalandar father would apologize for my naiveté, then caution others that one should not expect too much from a man who could not perceive that a drop of water or grain of rice spilled during his tasks actually diminished the amount in comparison beakers during the conservation of continuous quantities. In their presence I would be admonished that for them survival depends on *learning to pay attention*. Privately the Qalandar would chuckle to themselves, renewed in their confidence that the humans who are their subsistence resources remain ripe for the picking. When I returned with my new family for a reunion with the Qalandar, in the fall of 1979, we discussed my description of their social system and the general pattern of results. They agreed with my conclusions but were suspicious that I had "improved" the male scores on the measures of the dependent variable. They were still convinced that Qalandar as well as other females are more articulate in their perceptual skills than males.

During one of the festive moments celebrating my return to Pakistan, my three-year-old daughter must have dropped a few crumbs of a biscuit on the dust floor of a Qalandar tent. Ignorant of this but seeing her poking in the dust and weeds beside a baby monkey, I called out a caution to get her nose out of the dust, just as she recovered a few crumbs stuck to the end of her finger. Seeing this, my adoptive Qalandar uncle called to me, "Yousef, you see, Kelsay is already a Qalandar. Her sharp eye deprives the monkey and the ant of their due." Whereupon he gathered her up, placed her astride a 150-kilo black bear, and led them out of camp, leaving me to "point out" to my wife that she would be safe and knowledgeable about dangerous bears when returned—which indeed she was.

Appendixes
Notes
References
Index

Appendix 1

Correlation Matrices

The following correlation matrices are intended to aid the reader in interpreting the six hypotheses and investigating relationships not explained in the main body of this study. The variable names have been shortened as follows to permit inclusion of the matrices in a single format:

MYLER—number correct on the Muller-Lyer Illusion

CEFT—number correct on the Children's Embedded Figures Test

SANDER—number correct on the Sander Parallelogram Illusion

CONSERV—behavior coded: −1, does not conserve; 0, unsure; 1, conserves using continuous and discontinuous quantities

AGE and EDUCATION are reported in years.

Entire sample (n=266)

	MYLER	CEFT	SANDER	CONSERV	AGE	SEX	EDUC
MYLER	—						
CEFT	.21	—					
SANDER	.23	.21	—				
CONSERV	.14	.34	.27	—			
AGE	.22	.36	.29	.35	—		
SEX	−.03	.03	.07	−.10	.11	—	
EDUC	−.33	.38	−.07	.06	.03	.02	—

All Nomads (n=132, lower left) and all sedentists (n=134, upper right)

	MYLER	CEFT	SANDER	CONSERV	AGE	SEX	EDUC
MYLER	—	.01	−.04	−.10	−.06	.09	−.21
CEFT	.54	—	.20	.26	.31	.07	.58
SANDER	.23	.33	—	.18	.41	.26	.02
CONSERV	.30	.57	.26	—	.46	.13	.21
AGE	.26	.42	.17	.27	—	.07	.21
SEX	−.10	−.02	−.09	.02	.16	—	.10
EDUC	—	—	—	—	—	—	—

Village (n=68, lower left) and urban (n=66, upper right)

	MYLER	CEFT	SANDER	CONSERV	AGE	SEX	EDUC
MYLER	—	.06	−.05	−.23	.05	.04	−.09
CEFT	.13	—	.22	.28	.31	.01	.73
SANDER	−.05	.20	—	.12	.29	.34	−.01
CONSERV	.06	.20	.23	—	.47	−.07	.31
AGE	.18	.27	.53	.46	—	.09	.24
SEX	.11	.17	.21	−.18	.07	—	−.16
EDUC	−.11	.24	.09	.06	.02	.10	—

Qalandar (n=95, lower left) and Kanjar (n=37, upper right)

	MYLER	CEFT	SANDER	CONSERV	AGE	SEX	EDUC
MYLER	—	.60	−.03	.46	.25	−.23	—
CEFT	.47	—	.06	.62	.47	.01	—
SANDER	.34	.45	—	.14	−.08	−.31	—
CONSERV	.22	.54	.32	—	.26	−.10	—
AGE	.21	.41	.21	.28	—	.07	—
SEX	−.01	−.02	.03	.02	.21	—	—
EDUC	—	—	—	—	—	—	—

Appendix 2

Analysis of Experiments

This appendix contains the results of three "experimental" analyses (loosely interpreted, as no manipulation of variables took place). Based on the original sample (Berland 1977), each experiment is briefly summarized below.

Experiment One incorporates four variables—age, sex, education, and nomadism, dummy-coded 1 if the informant is nomadic, 0 if sedentary. All 285 informants are included in this analysis.

Experiment Two includes only the sedentary sample (n=146). The variables analyzed are age, sex, education, and ruralism, dummy-coded 1 if the informant is a rural dweller, 0 if an urban dweller.

Experiment Three includes only the nomadic sample (n=139). The variables analyzed include age, sex, and mobility, dummy-coded 1 if the informant is a Qalandar, 0 if a Kanjar. Each experiment was analyzed in an "analysis of variance" style with the four dependent measures in each; hence there are twelve analyses. However, the analysis of variance used here is not a classical analysis of variance; instead, a multiple regression technique is employed. Each effect (either a main effect or an interaction effect) is assessed only *after* all the other effects have been assessed. Thus the SS of an effect E on dependent variable Y would be:

$$Y = SS_E = SS_{all\ other\ effects} - SS_{all\ effects\ except\ E}$$

This represents a very conservative approach to assessing the various effects. So in all twelve cases below:

$$SS_{TOT} > SS_{residual} + SS_{effects}$$

Also notice that higher-order interactions have been pooled into $SS_{residual}$. This again represents a cautious approach to these analyses. Higher-order interactions were assumed to be theoretically problematic.

Experiment One: Analysis of Variance, Including Age, Sex, Education, and Relative Spatial Mobility for Sedentists and Peripatetics

Dependent variable: Muller-Lyer

Source of variation	S.S.	d.f.	M.S.	F	sig. of F
Main effects					
Age	27.01	1	27.01	15.76	.00
Education	4.64	1	4.64	2.71	.10
Mobility	25.99	1	25.99	15.16	.00
Sex	.62	1	.62	.36	.55
Interactions					
Age by education	14.59	1	14.59	8.51	.00
Age by mobility	1.13	1	1.13	.66	.42
Age by sex	1.46	1	1.46	.85	.36
Education by mobility					
(zero variance, not an effect)					
Education by sex	5.00	1	5.00	2.92	.09
Nomadism by sex	6.51	1	6.51	3.80	.05
Within and residual	471.39	275	1.71	—	—

Dependent variable: CEFT

Source of variation	S.S.	d.f.	M.S.	F	sig. of F
Main effects					
Age	1371.24	1	1371.24	56.37	.00
Education	928.10	1	928.10	38.16	.00
Mobility	105.22	1	105.22	4.33	.04
Sex	80.52	1	80.52	3.31	.07
Interactions					
Age by education	357.40	1	357.40	14.69	.00
Age by mobility	45.64	1	45.64	1.88	.17
Age by sex	128.27	1	128.27	5.27	.02

Source of variation	S.S.	d.f.	M.S.	F	sig. of F
Education by mobility					
(zero variance, not an effect)					
Education by sex	1.64	1	1.64	.07	.80
Mobility by sex	48.47	1	48.47	1.99	.16
Within and residual	6689.14	275	24.36	—	—

Dependent variable: Sander Parallelogram

Source of variation	S.S.	d.f.	M.S.	F	sig. of F
Main effects					
Age	31.03	1	31.03	21.26	.00
Education	.88	1	.88	.61	.44
Nomadism	42.92	1	42.92	29.41	.00
Sex	8.32	1	8.32	5.70	.02
Interactions					
Age by education	1.69	1	1.69	1.16	.28
Age by nomadism	8.41	1	8.41	5.76	.02
Age by sex	3.68	1	3.68	2.52	.11
Education by nomadism					
(zero variance, not an effect)					
Education by sex	3.97	1	3.97	2.72	.10
Nomadism by sex	8.63	1	8.63	5.91	.02
Within and residual	401.39	275	1.46	—	—

Dependent variable: Conservation

Source of variation	S.S.	d.f.	M.S.	F	sig. of F
Main effects					
Age	23.58	1	23.58	51.76	.00
Education	2.96	1	2.96	6.50	.01
Nomadism	15.48	1	15.48	33.98	.00
Sex	1.17	1	1.17	2.56	.11
Interactions					
Age by education	1.79	1	1.79	3.93	.05
Age by nomadism	9.31	1	9.31	20.43	.00
Age by sex	.00	1	.00	.00	.95
Education by nomadism					
(zero variance, not an effect)					
Education by sex	.72	1	.72	1.59	.21
Nomadism by sex	.54	1	.54	1.18	.28
Within and residual	125.30	275	.46	—	—

Experiment Two: Analysis of Variance Including Age, Education, Ruralism, and Sex for Sedentists and Peripatetics

Dependent variable: Muller-Lyer

Source of variation	S.S.	d.f.	M.S.	F	sig. of F
Main effects					
Age	10.10	1	10.10	5.52	.02
Education	6.00	1	6.00	3.28	.07
Ruralism	4.02	1	4.02	2.20	.14
Sex	.86	1	.86	.47	.49
Interactions					
Age by education	10.09	1	10.09	5.52	.02
Age by ruralism	.12	1	.12	.07	.79
Age by sex	.11	1	.11	.06	.81
Education by ruralism	.06	1	.06	.03	.86
Education by sex	7.85	1	7.85	4.29	.04
Ruralism by sex	.56	1	.56	.30	.58
Within and residual	246.92	135	246.92	1.83	—

Dependent variable: CEFT

Source of variation	S.S.	d.f.	M.S.	F	sig. of F
Main effects					
Age	573.64	1	573.64	29.55	.00
Education	742.55	1	742.55	38.25	.00
Ruralism	.19	1	.19	.01	.92
Sex	90.21	1	90.21	4.65	.03
Interactions					
Age by education	295.80	1	295.80	15.24	.00
Age by ruralism	3.32	1	3.32	.17	.68
Age by sex	52.07	1	52.07	2.68	.10
Education by ruralism	2.85	1	2.85	.15	.70
Education by sex	2.72	1	2.72	.14	.71
Ruralism by sex	.43	1	.43	.02	.88
Within and residual	2621.07	135	19.42	—	—

Dependent variable: Sander Parallelogram

Source of variation	S.S.	d.f.	M.S.	F	sig. of F
Main effects					
Age	18.42	1	18.42	11.15	.00
Education	1.01	1	1.01	.61	.44
Ruralism	3.62	1	3.62	2.19	.14
Sex	20.59	1	20.59	12.46	.00
Interactions					
Age by education	.09	1	.09	.05	.82
Age by ruralism	6.06	1	6.06	3.67	.06
Age by sex	5.44	1	5.44	3.29	.07
Education by ruralism	2.17	1	2.17	1.31	.25
Education by sex	7.68	1	7.68	4.65	.03
Ruralism by sex	7.22	1	7.22	4.37	.04
Within and residual	223.08	135	1.65	—	—

Dependent variable: Conservation

Source of variation	S.S.	d.f.	M.S.	F	sig. of F
Main effects					
Age	18.93	1	18.93	31.54	.00
Education	3.20	1	3.20	5.33	.02
Ruralism	1.21	1	1.21	2.02	.16
Sex	1.51	1	1.51	2.51	.12
Interactions					
Age by education	1.92	1	1.92	3.19	.08
Age by ruralism	.32	1	.32	.53	.47
Age by sex	.15	1	.15	.25	.62
Education by ruralism	.02	1	.02	.04	.84
Education by sex	.29	1	.29	.48	.49
Ruralism by sex	.12	1	.12	.19	.66
Within and residual	81.02	135	.60	—	—

Experiment Three: Analysis of Variance, Including Age, Sex, and Relative Spatial Mobility for Peripatetics

Dependent variable: Muller-Lyer

Source of variation	S.S.	d.f.	M.S.	F	sig. of F
Main effects					
Age	8.13	1	8.13	5.85	.02
Mobility	10.19	1	10.19	7.33	.01
Sex	.07	1	.07	.05	.82
Interactions					
Age by mobility	1.56	1	1.56	1.12	.29
Age by sex	3.16	1	3.16	2.27	.13
Mobility by sex	1.74	1	1.74	1.25	.27
Within and residual	183.39	132	1.39	—	—

Dependent variable: CEFT

Source of variation	S.S.	d.f.	M.S.	F	sig. of F
Main effects					
Age	574.63	1	574.63	19.22	.00
Mobility	103.73	1	103.73	3.47	.06
Sex	4.54	1	4.54	.15	.70
Interactions					
Age by mobility	93.09	1	93.09	3.11	.08
Age by sex	54.53	1	54.53	1.82	.18
Mobility by sex	.61	1	.61	.02	.89
Within and residual	3946.91	132	29.90	—	—

Dependent variable: Sander Parallelogram

Source of Variation	S.S.	d.f.	M.S.	F	sig. of F
Main effects					
Age	.02	1	.02	.02	.90
Mobility	.06	1	.06	.05	.82
Sex	.02	1	.02	.02	.90
Interactions					
Age by mobility	1.58	1	1.58	1.35	.25
Age by sex	3.05	1	3.05	2.61	.11
Mobility by sex	5.44	1	5.44	4.65	.03
Within and residual	154.40	132	1.17	—	—

Dependent Variable: Conservation

Source of variation	S.S.	d.f.	M.S.	F	sig. of F
Main effects					
Age	1.97	1	1.97	6.19	.01
Mobility	.08	1	.08	.24	.62
Sex	.14	1	.14	.45	.50
Interactions					
Age by mobility	.19	1	.19	.60	.44
Age by sex	.01	1	.01	.03	.87
Mobility by sex	.02	1	.02	.07	.79
Within and residual	42.06	132	.32	—	—

Appendix 3

Test Descriptions and Directions

Except for the measures of conservation of continuous and discontinuous quantities, the tests used to measure perceptual inference have been extensively described in test manuals and the research literature. For a description of the Children's Embedded Figures Test, see Witkin et al. (1971). For a description of the Visual Illusion Battery, see Segall et al. (1966).

The tests have standardized directions to be given to each subject, but because of the cross-cultural nature of the testing situations, the directions were slightly modified from those given in the sources cited above. These modifications are summarized below, and examples of the two forms of CEFT items are shown.

Illusion Battery (Muller-Lyer and Sander Parallelogram)

"I'm going to show you some lines drawn on paper and ask you some questions about them. What is the color of this line? This line? Which line is longer, the red or the black one? Which of these two red lines is longer? Which line is longer, the red one or the black one? Which of the two red lines is longer, the one on this side or the one on that side? Which of the two red lines is longer, the one on the top or the one on the bottom?

H8

T₇

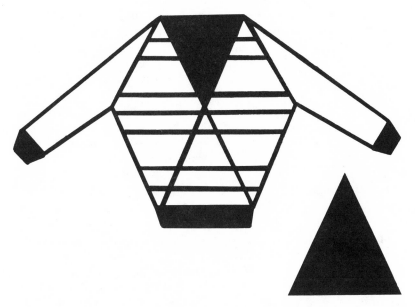

Figures T-7 and H-8 from the CEFT. (From *The Children's Embedded Figures Test* by Stephen Karp and Norma Konstadt, copyright 1971, Consulting Psychologists Press, Palo Alto, Calif. Reprinted by permission of the publisher.)

Children's Embedded Figures Test

"This looks something like a tent, doesn't it? This black line at the bottom shows where the tent rests on the ground. See if you can find another tent that looks exactly like this one on this paper. Good. Find the tent here . . . A tent like this one is hidden somewhere in this picture. Find the hidden tent. Show me where the tent is. What does this look like to you? House? Tent? Mosque? Good. Now find it just the way you did before."

Conservation Tasks

Piaget's (1952) techniques were followed as closely as possible.

Conservation of Continuous Quantities

To assure familiarization with the conservation stimuli, we used materials which were known to the informant (see Price-Williams 1961:297–305). In the pilot testing situation, Qalandar children and adults were "suspicious" of the properties of plasticine (clay). Therefore, the following familiar materials were used: *chawal* (dry rice), *dal* (split dried peas), *pani* (water), *meti* (mud), and *roti* (bread dough).

The informant was given two glass beakers of equal dimensions (A_1 and A_2) and asked to fill them three-quarters full with one of the continuous quantities. Water was used first, followed by dal or rice. The informant was then asked to make sure that both beakers contained exactly the same amount. Once equality was determined, the informant was asked to pour the contents of A_2 into two smaller beakers of equal dimensions (B_1 and B_2), such that the level was identical in both. The informant was then asked whether the amount that had been in A_2 and was now in B_1 and B_2 was *more than, less than,* or *the same* as the amount in A_1. Once equality or inequality was established, the informant was asked to pour the contents of B_1 and B_2 back into A_2. He was then asked to pour the contents of A_1 into C, a long, thin measuring cylinder. The same questioning procedure as before was employed.

"Here I have some rice. Here I have some glasses [two standard beakers, two short beakers, and a tall measuring beaker]. Now, you take the rice and pour equal amounts into these two glasses [A_1 and A_2]. Do they have the same amount in them? Good. Now pour this glass [A_2] into these two glasses [B_1 and B_2]. Good. Now, do these two glasses contain the same amount of rice as this glass [A_1]? Yes? Why? No? Why? Now pour these [B_1 and B_2] back into this glass [A_2]. Does this glass [A_2] have the same amount as this glass [A_1]? Yes? No? Why? Good. Now pour this glass [A_1] into this glass [C, tall beaker]. Does this glass [C] have the same amount as this glass [A_2]? Yes? No? Why?"

With bread dough and mud the process was similar. Directions: "Here I have some *atta* [whole wheat flour] or *meti* [dust or dirt]. Put the atta in this pan and add enough water to make roti. Mix them up good so the roti will be good. Now, break the ball of roti into two equal balls [A_1 and A_2]. Good. Are the two balls equal in amount? Good, now take the roti [A_2] and pat it out into a *chapati* [flat, round cake]. Good. Now, does this roti [A_2] have the same amount as this roti [A_1]? Yes? No? Why?" The dough was then recombined and the informant asked to shape one ball into a rope or snake. The same questions were asked.

Conservation of Discontinuous Quantities

The same procedure was used with discontinuous quantities. Marbles or stones were put into two glasses one at a time so that the informant agreed each glass had equal numbers, and the above tests were given. Then an additional test was performed. Marbles or stones from one glass were laid out in a line 24 inches long. Another row, containing the same number of marbles, was set out in a line 12 inches long (see Price-Williams 1961). Informants were then asked if the longer line had *more, fewer,* or *the same* number of objects as the shorter line.

In this study, conservation or nonconservation is treated as an indication of perceptual field dependence or independence. Therefore, the conservation data is recorded as "yes," "no," or "don't know." In addition, the reasoning behind the informant's answers was requested and recorded for each task situation in terms of the major stimuli utilized in making each conservation judgment.

Notes

1. Theoretical Setting

1. Excellent reviews of the history of research on culture and perception are available in Boring (1950), Segall, Campbell, and Herskovits (1966), Cole et al. (1971), Cole and Scribner (1974), Berry (1976), and Deregowski (1980).

2. See Honigmann (1954), Singer (1961), Wallace (1970), Hsu (1972), Barnouw (1973), Spindler (1978), Bourguignon (1979), and Tapp (1981) for reviews of culture and personality approaches in cultural anthropology.

3. Compare Pascual-Leone (1976), Neisser (1977), and Reed and Jones (1979) on the theoretical and methodological contrast between contemporary "constructivist" models of cognitive activities and ecological, organism–context interaction approaches to psychological functioning. Cole and his collaborators (Laboratory of Comparative Human Cognition 1981) have provided one of the more succinct discussions of this issue, including a review of recent Soviet research in this area in terms of competing theories in cognitive development research.

4. For excellent reviews of Piaget's theory of cognitive development, see Ginsberg and Opper (1968), and Elkind and Flavell (1969). Several reviews of cross-cultural Piagetian research are available from Goodnow (1969a,b), Furby (1971), Dasen (1972a, 1977a,b,c), Cole and Scribner (1977), Dasen, Berry, and Witkin (1979), Laboratory of Comparative Human Cognition (1979), Jahoda (1980), and Dasen and Heron (1981). For excellent recent summaries of Witkin's theory of psychological differentiation see Witkin and Berry (1975), Goodenough and Witkin (1977), Witkin, Goodenough, and Oltman (1977), Jahoda (1980), and Berry (1981).

5. See Elkind (1967) and Furby (1971) for excellent discussions of Piagetian conservation tasks.

6. In measures of field dependence/independence, the basic ability is perceptual disembedding of a part from the whole. The importance of this skill is

its relationship to greater differentiation; when developed, it is characteristic of an analytical way of articulating experience. The field-dependent/independent perceptual dimension represents—at its extremes—contrasting ways of approaching a field, whether the field is immediately present or represented symbolically. It has been designated a global versus analytical dimension of cognitive functioning (Witkin et al. 1971). In support of the global-articulated dimension, Witkin et al. (1963) conclude:

> The tendency to adhere to the structure of the prevailing field in the EFT shows itself in another way with stimulus material that lacks internal organization, e.g., the ink-blots of the Rorschach. Characteristically, the field-dependent persons tend to leave such material "as is," rather than imposing structure on it. The result is percepts which are vague and indefinite. In contrast, persons who are field independent in the EFT are likely to impose structure on inkblots which lack it, with the result that their percepts are organized and definite.

The tests of perceptual field dependence/independence are described in detail in Witkin et al. (1961). For studies showing self-consistency in the perceptual domain, see Vernon (1965a,b), Berry (1966), Dawson (1967a,b, 1977), Okonji (1969), Siann (1972), Amir (1972), Vigeland (1973), MacArthur (1973a), and Witkin, Price-Williams et al. (1974).

7. The anthropological study of socialization (the intergenerational transmission of culture) has always shared a domain with developmental psychology. Recent studies in socialization strongly reflect developments in ethology and social anthropology, such as adaptation, ecology, social complexity, and evolution. See Poirier (1972), Blurton-Jones (1972), Williams (1972, 1975), Konner (1977a, 1981), Leiderman, Tulkin, and Rosenfeld (1977), Heimstra and McFarling (1978), Werner (1979), Whiting (1981), and Super (1981a,b) for excellent perspectives on this literature.

8. Accounts of sex differences indicate two major task areas in cognitive development on which males and females consistently differ in performance: (1) simple perceptual-motor associations and (2) inhibitory perceptual restructuring. A number of traditional studies have demonstrated that females are superior to males in tasks (the digit symbol subtests from the WISC and WAIS) requiring relatively simple, perceptual-motor association. See Staples (1932), Stroop (1935), Gesell and Halverson (1940), McNemar (1942), Paterson and Andrew (1946), Tiffin and Asher (1948), Norman (1953), Miele (1958), Gainer (1962), and Frankenburg and Dodds (1967). On the other hand, it has consistently been found that males are superior to females on inhibitory perceptual restructuring tasks (that is, the RFT and EFT). These tasks require suppression of responses to the immediately obvious stimulus attributes in favor of delayed responses to other, less immediately obvious stimulus attributes. See Porteus (1918, 1950), Kohs (1926), Newbigging (1952, 1964), Andrieux (1955), Gardner, Jackson, and Messick (1960), Spence and Spence (1966), Franks (1967), and Witkin (1969). See Stewart-Van Leeuwen (1978) for a review of cross-cultural studies of sex differences in psychological differentiation.

3. *Research Setting and Methods*

1. For excellent ethnographic accounts of nomad cultural ecology, see, for hunters and gatherers, Lee and DeVore (1968), Bicchieri (1972), and Lee (1979). For pastoral nomads see Evans-Pritchard (1940), Barth (1961), Nelson (1973), Edgerton (1971), Elam (1973), Spooner (1973) and D. Cole (1975). Beginning with the Aryans, pastoral nomadism has been an integral part of Asian civilization. See Leshnik and Sontheimer (1975) for an excellent review of pastoral nomadism in South Asia. See N. K. Bose (1956), Misra (1969, 1970, 1978), and Berland (1979a, 1980) for reviews of peripatetic groups such as spatially mobile artisans and entertainers in South Asia.

2. For further discussion relating visual illusion susceptibility to psychological experience and perceptual skills see Gardner and Long (1961), Immergluck (1966), Mercado, Ribes, and Barrera (1967), Davis (1970), Davis and Carlson (1970), Robinson (1972), and Berland (1979b, 1981).

7. *Peripatetic and Sedentist Comparison Groups*

1. For descriptions of village administration, see Lewis (1958), Egler (1960), Mayer (1960), Mathur (1964), Minturn and Hitchcock (1966), Mandelbaum (1970), and Ahmad (1974). Villages in the northern Punjab, especially around Lahore and Rawalpindi, are very old settlements. Beginning in the 1860s many new villages were founded along the massive networks of irrigation canals, particularly in the more arid districts of Sargodhā, Lyāllpur, and Sahiwal. According to the 1960 Pakistan Census of Agriculture, there were a total of 4.8 million farms in the country; one half were 5 acres or less in size. Only 2 percent were as large as 50 acres and less than 14,000 has as much as 150 acres. The land supply available for redistribution is therefore extremely limited. See Lewis (1958), Barth (1959), Egler (1960) and Minturn and Hitchcock (1966) for excellent descriptions of daily and seasonal rounds of village activities.

2. See Wilber (1964) for an excellent analysis of the urban setting in Pakistan, especially Lahore. See also Nazeer (1966), Singer (1961), Gould (1965), Bose (1965), and Singer and Cohn (1968).

References

Adjei, K. 1977. Influence of specific maternal occupation and behavior on Piagetian cognitive development. In *Piagetian Psychology: Cross-cultural contributions*, ed. P. Dasen. New York: Garden Press.

Ahmad, K. S. 1969. *A geography of Pakistan*. Karachi: Oxford University Press.

Ahmad, S. 1970. Social stratification in a Punjabi village. *Contributions to Indian Sociology* 4:105–125.

———— 1974. A village in Pakistani Punjab: Jalpānā. In *South Asia: seven community profiles*, ed. Clarence Maloney. New York: Holt, Rinehart and Winston.

Alavi, H. 1971. The politics of dependence: A village in West Punjab. *South Asian Review* 4 (2):120–137.

———— 1972. Kinship in West Punjab villages. *Contributions to Indian Sociology* 6:1–27.

Allport, G. W., and T. F. Pettigrew. 1957. Cultural influence on the perception of movement: The trapezoidal illusion among Zulu. *Journal of Abnormal and Social Psychology* 55:104–113.

Altmann, J. 1980. *Baboon mothers and infants*. Cambridge, Mass.: Harvard University Press.

Amir, Y. 1975. Perceptual articulation in three Middle Eastern cultures. *Journal of Cross-Cultural Psychology* 6:406–416.

Andrieux, C. 1955. Contribution à l'étude des différences entre hommes et femmes dans la perception spatiale. *L'Année Psychologique* 55:41–60.

Ayres, B. 1973. Effects of infant carrying practices on rhythm in music. *Ethos* 4:387–403.

Barker, R. G. 1968. *Ecological psychology*. Stanford: Stanford University Press.

Barnouw, V. 1973. *Culture and personality*, rev. ed. Homewood, Ill.: Dorsey.

Barry, H., M. Bacon, and I. Child. 1957. A cross-cultural survey of some sex differences in socialization. *Journal of Abnormal and Social Psychology* 55:327–332.

Barry, H., I. Child, and M. Bacon. 1959. Relation of child-training to subsistence economy. *American Anthropologist* 61:51–63.

Barry, H., and L. Paxon. 1971. Infancy and early childhood: cross-cultural codes 2. *Ethnology* 10:466–508.

Barth, F. 1959. *Political leadership among the Swat Pathans.* London: Athlone Press.

———— 1961. *Nomads of South Persia: the Basseri tribe of the Khamseh Confederacy.* Boston: Little, Brown.

Basham, A. L. 1954. *The wonder that was India.* London: Sidgwick and Jackson.

Bateson, G. 1958. *Naven: a study of the problems suggested by a composite picture of the culture of a New Guinea tribe drawn from three points of view,* 2nd ed. Stanford: Stanford University Press.

Bean, L. L. 1974. The population of Pakistan: an evaluation of recent statistical data. *Middle East Journal* 28:177–184.

Benedict, R. 1934. *Patterns of culture.* Boston: Houghton Mifflin.

———— 1938. Continuities and discontinuities in cultural conditioning. *Psychiatry* 1:161–167.

Berland, J. 1977. Cultural amplifiers and psychological differentiation among khānābādōsh in Pakistan. Ph.D. dissertation, University of Hawaii.

———— 1978. Paryatan: peripatetic adaptations in Pakistan. Paper presented at the American Association for Asian Studies Conference, October, 1978, Tucson.

———— 1979a. Peripatetic, pastoralist, and sedentist interactions in complex societies. *Newsletter of the Commission on Nomadic Peoples, IUAES* 4:6–8.

———— 1979b. Cultural activities and visual illusions: rethinking the carpentered-world hypothesis. Paper presented at the Educational Testing Service, May, 1968, Princeton.

———— 1980. Nomads and gypsies on the Afghan-Pakistan frontier. Paper presented at the School of Social and Economic Development, University of the South Pacific. Summarized in *Information Bulletin* (University of the South Pacific) 13 (21):6–8.

———— 1981. Dress rehearsals for psychological performances: context, practice and skill in perceptual-cognitive functioning. Paper presented at the NATO Conference on Human Assessment and Cultural Factors, August, 1981, Queens University, Kingston, Ontario.

Berry, J. W. 1966. Temne and Eskimo perceptual skills. *International Journal of Psychology* 1:207–229.

———— 1967. Independence and conformity in subsistence-level societies. *Journal of Personality and Psychology* 7:415–418.

———— 1968. Ecology, perceptual development and the Muller-Lyer illusion. *British Journal of Psychology* 59:205–210.

———— 1969a. On cross-cultural comparability. *International Journal of Psychology* 4:119–128.

———— 1969b. Ecology and socialization as factors in figural assimilation and the resolution of binocular rivalry. *International Journal of Psychology* 4:271-280.

———— 1970. Marginality, stress and ethnic identification in an acculturated aboriginal community. *Journal of Cross-Cultural Psychology* 1:239–252.

———— 1971a. Ecological and cultural factors in spatial perceptual development. *Canadian Journal of Behavioral Science* 3:324–336.

———— 1971b. Psychological research in the north. *Anthropologica* 13:143–157.

———— 1971c. Muller-Lyer susceptibility: culture, ecology or race? *International Journal of Psychology* 6:193–197.

———— 1974. Acculturative stress: the role of ecology, culture and differentiation. *Journal of Cross-Cultural Psychology* 5:382–406.

———— 1975. Ecology, cultural adaptation, and psychological differentiation: traditional patterning and acculturative stress. In *Cross-cultural perspectives on learning*, eds. Richard W. Brislin et al. New York: John Wiley and Sons.

———— 1976. *Human ecology and cognitive style.* New York: John Wiley and Sons.

———— 1980. Introduction to methodology. In *Handbook of cross-cultural psychology*, vol. 2, *Methodology*, eds. H. C. Triandis and J. W. Berry. Boston: Allyn and Bacon.

———— 1981. Developmental issues in the comparative study of psychological differentiation. In *Handbook of cross-cultural human development*, eds. R. Monroe, and B. Whiting. New York: Garland.

Berry, J. W., and R. C. Annis. 1974. Ecology, culture and psychological differentiation. *International Journal of Psychology* 9:173–197.

Berry, J. W., and P. R. Dasen, eds. 1974. *Culture and cognition: readings in cross-cultural psychology.* London: Methuen.

Bicchieri, M., ed. 1972. *Hunters and gatherers today.* New York: Holt, Rinehart and Winston.

Blunt, E. A. H. 1931. *The caste system of northern India.* London: Oxford University Press.

Blurton-Jones, N. G., ed. 1972. *Ethological studies of child behavior.* Cambridge: Cambridge University Press.

Boas, F. 1911. *The mind of primitive man.* New York: Macmillan.

Bochner, S. 1980. Unobtrusive methods in cross-cultural experimentation. In *Handbook of cross-cultural psychology*, vol. 2, *Methodology,* eds. H. C. Triandis and J. W. Berry. Boston: Allyn and Bacon.

Bock, D. and D. Kolakowski. 1973. Further evidence of sex-linked major-gene influence on human spatial visualizing ability. *American Journal of Human Genetics* 1:1–14.

Boonsong, S. 1968. *The development of conservation of mass, weight and volume in Thai children.* Unpublished M. Ed. thesis, Bangkok College of Education.

Boring, E. G. 1950. *A history of experimental psychology.* New York: Appleton-Century-Crofts.

Bornstein, M. 1975. The influence of visual perception on culture. *American Anthropologist* 77:778–798.

Bose, A. B. 1975. Pastoral nomadism in India: nature, problems and prospects. In *Pastoralists and nomads in South Asia*, eds. L. Leshnik and G. Sontheimer. Wiesbaden: Otto Harrassowitz.

Bose, N. K. 1956. Some observations on nomadic castes in India. *Man in India* 36:1–6.

———— 1965. Change in tribal cultures before and after independence. *Man in India* 4:23–41.

Bourguignon, E. 1979. *Psychological anthropology: an introduction to human nature and cultural differences.* New York: Holt, Rinehart and Winston.

Bovet, M. C. 1968. Etudes interculturelles de developpement intellectuel et processus d'apprentissage. *Revue Suisse de Psychologie Pure et Appliquée* 27:190–199.

———— 1973. Cognitive processes among illiterate children and adults. In *Culture and cognition: readings in cross-cultural psychology,* eds. J. W. Berry and P. R. Dasen. London: Methuen.

Brislin, R. W. 1980. Translation and content analysis of oral and written materials. In *Handbook of cross-cultural psychology,* vol. 2, *Methodology,* eds. H. C. Triandis and J. W. Berry. Boston: Allyn and Bacon.

Brislin, R., W. Lonner, and R. Thorndyke. 1973. *Cross-cultural research methods.* New York: Wiley.

Bronfenbrenner, U. 1977. Toward an experimental ecology of human development. *American Psychologist* 32:513–531.

Broverman, D. M., F. E. Clarkson, E. L. Klaiber, and W. Vogel. 1972. The ability to automize: a function basic to learning and performance. In *Learning disabilities: multidisciplinary approaches to identification, diagnosis, and remedial education,* ed. C. Kris. New York: Macmillan.

Broverman, D. M., E. L. Klaiber, V. Kobayshi, and W. Vogel. 1968. Roles of activation and inhibition in sex differences in cognitive abilities. *Psychological Review* 75:23–50.

Bruner, J. S. 1964. The course of cognitive growth. *American Psychologist* 19:1–15.

———— 1966. On cognitive growth. In *Studies in cognitive growth,* eds. J. S. Bruner, R. Olver, and P. Greenfield. New York: John Wiley.

Bruner, J. S., R. Olver, and P. Greenfield, eds. 1966. *Studies in cognitive growth.* New York: JohnWiley.

Brunswik, E. 1943. Organismic achievement and environmental probability. *Psychological Review* 51 (3):255–272.

———— 1955. Representative design and probabilistic theory. *Psychological Review* 1955 (62):193–217.

———— 1956. *Perception and the representative design of experiments.* Berkeley: University of California Press.

Burton, R. G. 1934. *The thousand nights and a night.* New York: Heritage Press.

Carstairs, G. M. 1967. *The twice-born: a study of a community of high-caste Hindus.* Bloomington: Indiana University Press.

Chevalier-Skolnikoff, S. 1977. A Piagetian model for describing and comparing socialization in monkey, ape, and human infants. In *Primate biosocial development: biological, social, and ecological determinants,* eds. S. Chevalier-Skolnikoff and F. Poirer. New York: Garland.

Ciborowski, T. 1980. The role of context, skill, and transfer in cross-cultural experimentation. In *Handbook of cross-cultural psychology,* vol. 2,

Methodology, eds. H. C. Triandis and J. W. Berry. Boston: Allyn and Bacon.

Cole, D. P. 1975. *Nomads of the nomads: the Āl Murrah Bedouin of the Empty Quarter*. Chicago: Aldine.

Cole, M. 1975. An ethnographic psychology of cognition. In *Cross-cultural perspectives on learning*, eds. R. W. Brislin et al. New York: John Wiley.

Cole, M., and J. S. Bruner. 1971. Cultural differences and inference about psychological processes. *American Psychologist* 26:867–876.

Cole, M., J. Gay, J. Glick, and D. W. Sharp. 1971. *The cultural context of learning and thinking*. New York: Basic Books.

Cole, M., L. Hood, and R. McDermott. 1978. Concepts of ecological validity: their differing implications for comparative cognitive research. *Quarterly Newsletter of the Institute for Comparative Human Development* 2:34–37

———— 1980. *Ecological invalidity as an axiom of experimental cognitive psychology*. Cambridge, Mass.: Harvard University Press.

Cole, M., and S. Scribner. 1974. *Culture and thought: a psychological introduction*. New York: John Wiley.

———— 1975. Theorizing about socialization of cognition. *Ethos* 3:250–268.

———— 1977. Developmental theories applied to cross-cultural cognitive research. *Annals of the N. Y. Academy of Sciences* 385:366–373.

Comalli, P. E. 1965. Life span developmental studies in perception: theoretical and methodological issues. Paper presented at a symposium on research on the cognitive process of elderly people, Eastern Psychological Association meetings, Atlantic City.

Corah, N. L. 1965. Differentiation in children and their parents. *Journal of Personality* 33:300–308.

Count, E. 1958. The biological basis of human sociality. *American Anthropologist* 60:1049–1085.

Cowley, J. J., and M. M. Murray. 1962. Some aspects of the development of spatial concepts in Zulu children. *Journal of Social Research* 13:1–18.

Cox, P. W., and H. Witkin. 1978. *Field dependence-independence and psychological differentiation: bibliography with index*. R-B-78-8. Princeton: Educational Testing Service.

Croft, R. 1977. The relationship of maternal teaching style and socio-economic status to four year old children's locus of control orientation. Ph.D. dissertation, University of Rochester.

Crooke, W. 1896. *The tribes and castes of the Northwestern Province and Oudh*. Calcutta: Government of India Central Printing Office.

———— 1907. *The native races of the British Empire: natives of northern India*. London: Archibald Constable.

Damas, D. 1969. *Ecological essays*. National Museum of Canada Bulletin no. 230.

Dart, F. E., and P. L. Pradhan. 1967. Cross-cultural teaching of science. *Science* 155:649–656.

Dasen, P. R. 1970. Cognitive development in Aborigines of central Australia: concrete operations and perceptual activities. Unpublished Ph.D. thesis, Australian National University, Canberra.

———— 1972a. Cross-cultural Piagetian research: a summary. *Journal of Cross-Cultural Psychology* 3:23–39.

———— 1972b. The development of conservation in Aboriginal children: a replication study. *International Journal of Psychology* 7:75–85.

———— 1973. Biologie ou culture? La psychologie interethnique d'un point de vue Piagetian. *Psychologie Canadienne* 14(2):149–166.

———— 1974. The influence of ecology, culture and European contact on cognitive development in Australian Aborigines. In *Culture and cognition: readings in cross-cultural psychology*, eds. J. W. Berry and P. R. Dasen. London: Methuen.

———— 1975. Concrete operational development in three cultures. *Journal of Cross-Cultural Psychology* 6(2):156–172.

———— 1977a. Cross-cultural cognitive development: the cultural aspects of Piaget's theory. *Annals of the N. Y. Academy of Sciences* 285:332–337.

———— 1977b. Are cognitive processes universal? A contribution to cross-cultural Piagetian psychology. In *Studies in cross-cultural psychology*, vol. 1 ed. N. Warren. London: Academic Press.

Dasen, P. R., ed. 1977c. *Piagetian psychology*. New York: Gardner Press.

Dasen, P. R., J. W. Berry, and H. A. Witkin. 1979. The use of developmental theories cross-culturally. In *Cross-cultural contributions to psychology*, eds. L. Eckensberger, Y. Poortinga and W. Lonner. Amsterdam: Swets and Zeitlinger.

Dasen, P., and A. Heron. 1981. Cross-cultural tests of Piaget's theory. In *Handbook of cross-cultural psychology*, vol. 4, *Developmental psychology*, eds. H. C. Triandis and A. Heron. Boston: Allyn and Bacon.

Dashiell, J. P. 1931. *An experimental manual in psychology*. Cambridge, Mass.: Riverside Press.

Davis, C. M. 1970. Education and susceptibility to the Muller-Lyer illusion among the Baynankole. *Journal of Social Psychology* 85:25–34.

Davis, C. M., and J. A. Carlson. 1970. A cross-cultural study of the strength of the Muller-Lyer illusion as a function of attentional factors. *Journal of Personality and Social Psychology* 16(3):403–410.

Dawson, J. L. M. 1967a. Cultural and physiological influences upon spatial-perceptual processes in West Africa. Pt. 1. *International Journal of Psychology* 2:115–128.

———— 1967b. Cultural and physiological influences upon spatial-perceptual processes in West Africa. Pt. 2. *International Journal of Psychology* 3:171–185.

———— 1977. Theory and method in biosocial psychology: a new approach to cross-cultural psychology. *Annals of the N. Y. Academy of Sciences* 285:46–65.

Dawson, J. L. M., B. M. Young, and P. P. C. Choi. 1974. Developmental influences in pictorial depth perception among Hong Kong Chinese children. *Journal of Cross-Cultural Psychology* 5:3–22.

DeLacey, P. R. 1970. A cross-cultural study of classificatory ability in Australia. *Journal of Cross-Cultural Psychology* 1:293–304.

———— 1971. Verbal intelligence, operational thinking and environment in part-Aboriginal children. *Australian Journal of Psychology* 23:145–149.

DeLemos, M. M. 1974. The development of spatial concepts in Zulu children.

In *Culture and Cognition: Readings in Cross-Cultural Psychology*, eds. J. W. Berry and P. R. Dasen. London: Methuen.

Deregowski, J. B. 1968. On perception of depicted orientation. *International Journey of Psychology* 3:149–156.

——— 1971. Orientation and perception of pictorial depth. *International Journal of Psychology* 6:111–114.

——— 1972a. Reproduction of orientation of Kohs-type figures: a cross-cultural study. *British Journal of Psychology* 63:283–296.

——— 1972b. Pictorial perception and culture. *Scientific American* 227:82–88.

——— 1980. Perception. In *Handbook of cross-cultural psychology,* vol. 3, *Basic processes,* ed. H. C. Triandis et al. Boston: Allyn and Bacon.

Dershowitz, Z. 1971. Jewish subcultural patterns and psychological differentiation. *International Journal of Psychology* 6:223–231.

De Vore, I., and M. Konner. 1974. Infancy in hunter-gatherer life, an ethological perspective. In *Ethology and psychiatry.* ed. N. White. Toronto: University of Toronto Press.

Draper, P. 1975. Cultural pressure on sex differences. *American Ethnologist* 2(4):602–616.

——— 1976. Social and economic constraints on child life among the !Kung. In *Kalahari Hunter-Gatherers: Studies of the !Kung San and Their Neighbors,* eds. R. M. Lee and I. De Vore. Cambridge, Mass.: Harvard University Press.

Dubois, C. 1944. *People of Alor.* Minnesota: University of Minnesota Press.

Dyk, R. B. 1969. An exploratory study of mother-child interaction in infancy as related to the development of differentiation. *Journal of the American Academy of Child Psychiatry* 8:657–691.

Dyk, R. B., and H. A. Witkin. 1965. Family experiences related to the development of differentiation in children. *Child Development* 30:21–55.

Edgerton, R. E. 1971. *The individual in cultural adaptation: a study of four East African peoples.* Berkeley: University of California Press.

Egler, Z. 1960. *A Punjabi village in Pakistan.* New York: Columbia University Press.

Elam, Y. 1973. *The social and sexual roles of Hima women: a study of nomadic cattle breeders in Nyabushozi County, Ankole, Uganda.* Manchester: Manchester University Press.

Elkind, D. 1967. Piaget's conservation problems. *Child Development* 38:15–27.

Elkind, D. and J. H. Flavell. 1969.*Studies in cognitive development: essays in honor of Jean Piaget.* New York: Oxford University Press.

Etienne, G. 1968. *Studies in Indian agriculture: the art of the possible.* Berkeley: University of California Press.

Evans-Pritchard, E. E. 1940. *The Nuer: a description of the modes of livelihood and political institutions of a Nilotic people.* Oxford: Clarendon Press.

Fantz, R. L., J. F. Fagan, and S. B. Miranda. 1975. Early visual selectivity. In *Infant perception: from sensation to cognition,* vol. I, *Basic visual processes,* eds. L. B. Cohen and P. Salapatek. New York: Academic Press.

Faterson, H. F., and H. A. Witkin. 1970. Longitudinal study of development of the body concept. *Developmental Psychology* 2:429–438.

Feldman, C. F. 1971. Cognitive development in Eskimos. Paper presented at the meeting of the Society for Research in Child Development, Minneapolis, April, 1971.

Finley, G. E., J. Kagan, and O. Layne. 1972. Development of young children's attention to normal and distorted stimuli: a cross-cultural study. *Developmental Psychology* 6:288–292.

Firth, C. R. 1951. *Elements of social organization.* London: Watts.

Forsius, H. 1973. The Finnish Skolt Lapp children. *Acta Paediatrica Scandinavica Supplement* 239:1–74.

Fortes, M. 1938. Education in Taleland. *Africa* 11 (4).

Frankenburg, W. K., and J. B. Dodds. 1967. The Denver developmental screening test. *Journal of Pediatrics* 71:181–191.

Franks, C. M. 1967. Differences determinés par le personalité dans la perception visuelle de la verticalité. *Revue de Psychologie Appliqué* 6:235–246.

Furby, L. 1971. A theoretical analysis of cross-cultural research in cognitive development: Piaget's conservation tasks. *Journal of Cross-Cultural Psychology* 2:241–255.

Gainer, W. L. 1962. The ability of the WISC subtests to discriminate between boys and girls of average intelligence. *California Journal of Educational Research* 13:9–16.

Gaines, R. 1975. Developmental perception and cognitive styles: From young children to master artists. *Perceptual and Motor Skills* 40:983–988.

Galt, E. A. 1913. *Census of India, 1911, report.* Calcutta: Central Government Printing Office.

Galton, F. 1869. *Hereditary genius.* London: Clay and Sons.

———— 1883. *Inquiries into human faculty and its development.* London: Macmillan.

———— 1887. *English men of science: their nature and nurture.* London: Macmillan.

Gardner, R. W. 1957. Field-dependence as a determinant of susceptibility to certain illusions. *American Psychologist* 12:397.

———— 1961. Cognitive controls of attention deployment as determinants of visual illusions. *Journal of Abnormal and Social Psychology* 62:120–127.

Gardner, R. W., D. N. Jackson, and S. J. Messick. 1960. Personality organization in cognitive controls and intellectual ability. *Psychological Issues* 2 (8):1–148.

Gardner, R. W., and R. I. Long. 1961. Selective attention and the Muller-Lyer illusion. *Psychological Record* 11:317–320.

Gesell, A., and H. M. Halverson. 1940. *The first five years of life.* New York: Harper.

Ghuman, P. 1978. Nature of intellectual development of Punjabi children. *International Journal of Psychology* 13 (4):281–294.

Gibson, E. J. 1969. *Principles of perceptual learning and development.* New York: Appleton-Century-Crofts.

Gibson, E. and V. Olum. 1960. Experimental methods of studying perception in children. In *Handbook of research methods in child development,* ed. P. H. Mussen. New York: John Wiley.

Gibson, J. J. 1966. *The senses considered as perceptual system.* Boston: Houghton Mifflin.

———— 1979. *The ecological approach to visual perception*. Boston: Houghton Mifflin.

Gibson, K. R. 1977. Brain structure and intelligence in macaques and human infants from a Piagetian perspective. In *Primate biosocial development: biological, social and ecological determinants*, eds. S. Chevalier-Skolnikoff and F. E. Poirer. New York: Garland.

Ginsburg, H., and S. Opper. 1968. *Piaget's theory of intellectual development: an introduction*. Englewood Cliffs, N. J.: Prentice-Hall.

Gladwin, T. 1970. *East is a big bird*. Cambridge, Mass.: Belknap Press.

Goldberg, S. 1977. Infant development and mother-infant interaction in urban Zambia. In *Culture and infancy: variations in the human experience*, eds. P. H. Leiderman, S. R. Tulkin, and A. Rosenfeld. New York: Academic Press.

Goodenough, D. R., and C. Eagle. 1976. A modification of the embedded figures test for use with young children. *Journal of Genetic Psychology* 103:67–74.

Goodenough, D. R., E. Gandini, I. Olkin, L. Pizzamiglio, D. Thayer, and H. A. Witkin. 1977. A Study of X-chromosome linkage with field dependence and spatial visualization. *Behavior Genetics* 7(5):373–387.

Goodenough, D. R., and S. A. Karp. 1961. Field dependence and intellectual functioning. *Journal of Abnormal and Social Psychology* 63:241–246

Goodenough, D. R., and H. A. Witkin. 1977. *Origins of the field-dependent and field-independent cognitive styles*. RM-77-9. Princeton: Educational Testing Service.

Goodnow, J. J. 1962. A test of milieu effects with some of Piaget's tasks. *Psychological Monographs* 76(36) (whole no. 555).

———— 1969a. Cultural variations in cognitive skills. In *Cross-cultural studies*, ed. D. R. Price-Williams. Harmondsworth: Penguin Books.

———— 1969b. Problems in research on culture and thought. In *Studies in cognitive development*, eds. D. Elkind and J. H. Flavell. New York: Oxford University Press.

Goodnow, J. J., and G. Bethon. 1966. Piaget's tasks: the effects of schooling and intelligence. *Child Development* 37:573–582.

Goodnow, J. J., B. M. Young, and E. Kvan. 1976. Orientation errors in copying by children in Hong Kong. *Journal of Cross-Cultural Psychology* 7:101–110.

Gore, M. 1977. *Indian youth: processes of socialization*. New Delhi: Vishwa Savak Kedra.

Gould, H. A. 1965. Lucknow rickshawallas: the social organization of an occupational category. *International Journal of Comparative Sociology* 6:24–47.

Graves, P. 1978. Infant behavior and maternal attitudes: early sex differences in West Bengal, India. *Journal of Cross-Cultural Psychology* 9(1):45–60.

Greenfield, P. M. 1976. Cross-cultural research and Piagetian theory: paradox and progress. in *The developing individual in a changing world*, eds. K. F. Riegel and J. A. Meacham. The Hague: Mouton.

Greenfield, P. M., and J. S. Bruner. 1966. Culture and cognitive growth. *International Journal of Psychology* 1:89–107.

Greenfield, P. M., and C. Child. 1974. Weaving, color terms and pattern representation: cultural influences and cognitive development among the Zinacantecos of southern Mexico. In *Readings in cross-cultural psychology*, eds. J. Dawson and W. Lonner. Hong Kong: University of Hong Kong Press.

Grierson, G. 1922. *Linguistic survey of India: gipsy languages.* Calcutta: Central Government Printing Office.

Gutherie, E. R. 1952. *The psychology of learning*, rev. ed. New York: Harper and Row,.

———— 1959. Association by contiguity. In *Psychology: a study of a science*, vol. 2., ed. S. Koch. New York: McGraw-Hill.

Hallowell, A. I. 1951. Cultural factors in the structuralization of perception. In *Social Psychology at the Crossroads*, eds. J. H. Rohrer and M. Sherif. New York: Harper.

Harlow, H., and C. Mears. 1979. *The human model: primate perspectives.* New York: John Wiley.

Harris, S. 1977. Milingimbi Aboriginal learning contexts. Ph.D. thesis, University of New Mexico, Albuquerque.

Heimstra, N., and L. H. McFarling. 1978. *Environmental psychology.* Monterey, Calif.: Brooks/Cole.

Heron, A. 1971. Concrete operations, "g" and achievement in Zambian children. *Journal of Cross-Cultural Psychology* 2:325–336.

Heron, A., and M. Simonsson. 1969. Weight conservation in Zambian children: a non-verbal approach. *International Journal of Psychology* 4:281–292.

Hilgard, E. R., and G. H. Bower. 1966. *Theories of learning*, 3rd. ed. New York: Appleton-Century-Crofts.

Honigmann, J. J. 1954. *Culture and personality.* New York: Harper and Row.

Hsu, Francis L. K. 1972. *Psychological anthropology.* Cambridge, Schenkman.

Hudson, W. 1967. The study of the problem of pictorial perception among unacculturated groups. *International Journal of Psychology* 2:90–107.

Ibbetson, D. 1911. *A glossary of the tribes and castes of the Punjab and Northwest Frontier Province.* Lahore: Civil and Military Gazette Press.

———— 1916. *Punjab castes.* Lahore: Superintendent Government Printing.

Ikram, S. M. 1964. *Muslim civilization in India.* New York: Columbia University Press.

Immergluck, L. 1966. Resistance to an optical illusion, figural after effects, and field dependence. *Psychonomic Science* 6(6):281–282.

Irwin, M., R. Klein, P. Engle, C. Yarbrough, and S. Nerlove. 1977. The problem of establishing validity in cross-cultural measurements. *Annals of the N. Y. Academy of Sciences* 285:308–325.

Jackson, D. N. 1958. Independence and resistance to perceptual field forces. *Journal of Abnormal and Social Psychology* 56:279–281.

Jahoda, G. 1971. Retinal pigmentation, illusion susceptibility and space perception. *International Journal of Psychology* 6:199–208.

———— 1975. Retinal pigmentation and space perception: a failure to replicate. *Journal of Social Psychology* 97:133–134.

———— 1980. Theoretical and systematic approaches in cross-cultural psychology. In *Handbook of cross-cultural psychology*, vol. 1, *Perspectives*, eds. H. C. Triandis and W. W. Lambert. Boston: Allyn and Bacon.

Jahoda, G., and H. McGurk. 1974. Pictorial depth perception in Scottish and Ghanaian children. *International Journal of Psychology* 9:255–267.

Kagan, J. 1970. The determinants of attention in the infant. *American Scientist* 58:298–306.

——— 1979. Family experience and the child's development. *American Psychologist* 34 (10):886–891.

Kakar, S. 1979. *Indian childhood: cultural ideals and social reality.* Oxford: Oxford University Press.

Kane, J. R. 1973. Perceptual differentiation in Ojibway and white populations. Bachelor's thesis, Queen's University.

Kardiner, A. 1939. *The individual and his society.* New York: Columbia University Press.

Karp, S. A. 1963. Field dependence and overcoming embeddedness. *Journal of Consulting Psychology* 27:294–302.

Karp, S. A., L. Silberman, and S. Winters. 1969. Psychological differentiation and socioeconomic status. *Perceptual and Motor Skills* 28:55–60.

Kato, N. 1965. A fundamental study of rod frame test. *Japanese Psychological Research* 7:61–68.

Kelly, M. R. 1971. Some aspects of conservation of quantity and length in Papua and New Guinea in relation to language, sex and years at school. *Territory of Papua and New Guinea Journal of Education* 7:55–60.

——— 1977. New Guinea and Piaget—an eight-year study. In *Piagetian psychology: cross-cultural contributions,* ed. P. Dasen. New York: Garden Press.

Kirk, L. 1977. Maternal and subcultural correlates of cognitive growth rate: the GA pattern. In *Piagetian psychology: cross-cultural contributions,* ed. P. Dasen. New York: Garden Press.

Klein, R. E. 1972. Cross-cultural evaluation of human intelligence. In *Lipids, malnutrition and developing brain* (symposium), pp. 249–265. Amsterdam: Associated Scientific Publishers.

Klein, R. E., B. M. Lester, C. Yarbrough, and J. P. Habicht. 1975. On malnutrition and mental development. In *Proceedings of Ninth International Congress on Nutrition, Mexico,* vol. 2. Basel: Karger.

Kluckhohn, C. K. 1962. *Culture and behavior.* New York: Free Press.

Kohlberg, L., and G. Gilligan. 1971. The adolescent as a philosopher: the discovery of self in a post-conventional world. *Daedalus* 100:1051–1086.

Kohs, S. C. 1926. *Intelligence measurement.* New York: Macmillan.

Konner, M. 1976. Maternal care, infant behavior and development among the !Kung. In *Kalahari hunter-gatherers: studies of the !Kung San and their neighbors,* eds. R. Lee and I. De Vore. Cambridge, Mass.: Harvard University Press.

——— 1977a. Evolution of human behavior development. In *Culture and infancy: variations in the human experience,* eds. P. H. Leiderman, S. R. Tulkin, and A. Rosenfeld. New York: Academic Press.

——— 1977b. Infancy among the Kalahari Desert San. In *Culture and infancy: variations in the human experience,* eds. P. H. Leiderman, S. R. Tulkin, and A. Rosenfeld. New York: Academic Press.

——— 1981. Evolution of human behavior development. In *Handbook of cross-cultural human development*, eds. R. Monroe, R. Monroe, and B. Whiting. New York: Garland.

Kopp, C. B., E. W. Khokha, and M. A. Sigman. 1977. A comparison of sensori-motor development in India and the United States. *Journal of Cross-Cultural Psychology* 8:435–452.

Korner, A., and E. Thoman. 1970. Visual alertness in neonates as evoked by maternal care. *Journal of Experimental Child Psychology* 10:67–78.

Laboratory of Comparative Human Cognition. 1978. Cognition as a residual category in anthropology. *Annual Review of Anthropology* 7:51–69.

———— 1979. What's cultural about cross-cultural cognitive psychology? *Annual Review of Psychology* 30:145–172.

———— 1980. Cross-cultural psychology's challenges to our ideas of children and development. *American Psychologist* 34:827–833.

———— 1981. Culture and intelligence. Unpublished manuscript. La Jolla: University of California, San Diego.

Lave, J. 1977a. Tailor-made experiments and evaluating the intellectual consequences of apprenticeship training. *Quarterly Newsletter of the Institute for Comparative Human Development* 1:1–3.

———— 1977b. Cognitive consequences of traditional apprenticeship training in West Africa. *Anthropology and Education Quarterly* 8:177–180.

Lee, R. B. 1979. *The !Kung San: men, women, and work in a foraging society.* Cambridge: Cambridge University Press.

Lee, R. B., and I. De Vore, eds. 1968. *Man the hunter.* Chicago: Aldine.

———— 1976. *Kalahari hunter-gatherers: studies of the !Kung San and their neighbors.* Cambridge, Mass.: Harvard University Press.

Leiderman, P. H., S. R. Tulkin, and A. Rosenfeld, eds. 1977. *Culture and infancy: variations in the human experience.* New York: Academic Press.

Leshnik, L. S., and G. D. Sontheimer, eds. 1975. *Pastoralists and nomads in South Asia.* Wiesbaden: Otto Harrassowitz.

Lewin, K. 1943, Defining the "field at a given time." *Psychological Review* 50(3):292–310.

Lewis, O. 1958. *Village life in northern India.* New York: Random House.

Levi-Strauss, C. 1963. *Structural Anthropology.* New York: Basic Books.

Loasa, L. 1978a. Maternal teaching strategies and field-dependent-independent cognitive styles in Chicano families. Research Bulletin 78–12, Educational Testing Service, Princeton, N.J.

———— 1978b. Maternal teaching strategies in Chicano families of varied educational and socioeconomic levels. Child Development 49:1129–1135.

Longabaugh, R. 1980. The systematic observation of behavior in naturalistic settings. In *Handbook of cross-cultural psychology*, vol. 2, *Methodology*, eds. H. C. Triandis and J. W. Berry. Boston: Allyn and Bacon.

Lovell, K. 1961. *The growth of basic mathematical and scientific concepts in children.* London: University of London Press.

MacArthur, R. S. 1967. Sex differences in field dependence for the Eskimo: A replication of Berry's findings. *International Journal of Psychology* 2:139–140.

———— 1969. Some cognitive abilities of Eskimo, white and Indian—Metis pupils aged 9 to 12 years. *Canadian Journal of Behavioral Science* 1:50–59.

———— 1971. Mental abilities and psychological environments: Igcolik Eskimos. Paper presented at Mid-Project Review, International Biological Programme, March, 1971, Toronto.

———— 1973a. Some ability patterns: Central Eskimos and Nsenga Africans. *International Journal of Psychology* 8:239–247

———— 1973b. Cognitive strengths of Central Canadian and Northwest Greenland Eskimo adolescents. Paper presented at the Western Psychological Association meeting, April, 1973, Anaheim, California.

———— 1974. Differential ability patterns: Inuit, Nsenga and Canadian whites. Paper presented at the second international conference of the International Association for Cross-Cultural Psychology, April, 1974, Kingston, Jamaica.

MacKinnon, A. A. 1972. Eskimo and Caucasian: a discordant note on cognitive-perceptual abilities. *Proceedings of the Annual Convention of the American Psychological Association* 9:303–304.

McNemar, Q. 1942. *The revision of the Stanford-Binet scale: an analysis of the standardization data.* Boston: Houghton Mifflin.

Mandelbaum, D. G. 1970. *Society in India.* vol. II, *Change and continuity.* Berkeley: University of California Press.

Mathur, K. S. 1964. *Caste and ritual in a Malwa village.* Bombay: Asia Publishing House.

Mayer, A. C. 1960. *Caste and kinship in central India: a village and its region.* Berkeley: University of California Press.

Mead, M. 1932. An investigation of the thought of primitive children, with special reference to animism. *Journal of the Royal Anthropological Institute* 62:173–190.

Meek, F., and V. Skubie. 1971. Spatial perception of highly skilled and poorly skilled females. *Perceptual and Motor Skills* 33:1309–1310.

Mercado, S. J., I. E. Ribes, and R. F. Barrera. 1967. Depth cues effect in the perception of visual illusions. *Revista Interamericana de Psicologia* 1:137–142.

Mermelstein, E., and L. S. Shulman. 1967. Lack of formal schooling and the acquisition of conservation. *Child Development* 38:39–52.

Miele, J. A. 1958. Sex differences in intelligence: the relationship of sex to intelligence as measured by the Wechsler Intelligence Scale for Children. *Dissertation Abstracts* 18:2213.

Minturn, L. 1963. The Rajputs of Khalapur, Pt. II, Child training. In *Six cultures: studies of child rearing,* ed. B. B. Whiting. New York: John Wiley.

Minturn, L., and J. T. Hitchcock. 1966. *The Rajputs of Khalapur, India.* New York: John Wiley.

Minturn, L., and W. W. Lambert. 1961. Pancultural factor analysis of reported socialization practices. *Journal of Abnormal and Social Psychology* 62:631–639.

———— 1964. *Mothers of six cultures: antecedents of child rearing.* New York: John Wiley.

Misra, P. K. 1969. Nomadism in India. *Journal of the Indian Anthropological Society* 4:79–87.

———— 1970. Study of nomads. In *Research programmes in cultural anthro-*

pology and allied disciplines, ed. S. Sinha. Calcutta: Anthropological Survey of India.

———— 1975. The Gadulia Lohars. In *Pastoralists and nomads in South Asia*, eds. L. S. Leshnik and G. Sontheimer. Weisbaden: Otto Harrassowitz.

———— 1978. National symposium on Indian nomads: resumé. *Newsletter of the Commission on Nomadic Peoples, IUAES* 2:2–6.

Mohseni, N. 1966. La comparaison des reactions aux epreuves d'intelligence en Iran et en Europe. In *Culture and cognition: readings in cross-cultural psychology*, eds. J. W. Berry and P. R. Dasen. London: Methuen.

Mugny, G., and W. Doise. 1978. Socio-cognitive conflict and structure of individual and collective performances. *European Journal of Psychology* 8:181–192.

Murphy, L. 1953. Roots of tolerance and tensions in Indian child development. In *The minds of men*. New York: Basic Books.

Murray, M. M. 1961. The development of spatial concepts in African and European children. Unpublished MSc thesis, University of Natal.

Nazeer, M. 1966. Urban growth in Pakistan. *Asian Survey* 6(1):1–39.

Nedd, A. N., and L. W. Gruenfeld. 1976. Field dependence-independence and social traditionalism: a comparison of ethnic subcultures of Trinidad. *International Journal of Psychology* 11:23–41.

Neisser, U. 1976. *Cognition and reality: principles and implications of cognitive psychology*. San Francisco: W. H. Freeman.

———— 1977. Gibson's ecological optics: consequences of a different stimulus description. *Journal for the Theory of Social Behavior* 7(1):17–28.

———— 1979. The limits of cognition. In *On the nature of thought: essays in honor of D. O. Hebb*, eds. P. W. Jusczyk and R. M. Klein. Hilldale, N. J.: Lawrence Erlbaum Associates.

Nelson, C., ed. 1973. *The desert and the sown*. Berkeley: Institute of International Studies.

Newbigging, P. L. 1952. Individual differences in the effects of subjective and objective organizing factors on perception. Unpublished doctoral dissertation, University College, University of London.

Nimkoff, M. F., and R. Middleton. 1960. Types of family and types of economy. *American Journal of Sociology* 66:215–225.

Norman, R. D. 1953. Sex differences and other aspects of young superior adult performance on the Wechsler Bellevue. *Journal of Consulting Psychology* 17:411–418.

Okonji, O. M. 1969. The differential effects of rural and urban upbringing on the development of cognitive style. *International Journal of Psychology* 4:293–305.

———— 1971. Culture and children's understanding of geometry. *International Journal of Psychology* 6:121–128.

Pande, C. G. 1970a. Performance of a sample of Indian students on a test of field-dependence. *Indian Journal of Experimental Psychology* 4:46–50.

———— 1970b. Sex differences in field-dependence: confirmation with Indian sample. *Perceptual and Motor Skills* 31:70.

Pande, C. G., and S. Kothari. 1969. Field-dependence and the raven's progressive matrices. *Psychologia* 12:49–51.

Parente, J. A., and J. J. O'Malley. 1975. Training in musical rhythm and field-dependence of children. *Perceptual and Motor Skills* 40:392–394.

Park, J. Y., and R. Gallimore. 1975. Cognitive style in urban and rural Korea. *Journal of Cross-Cultural Psychology* 6:227–237.

Parker, S. T. 1977. Piaget's sensorimotor series in an infant macaque: a model for comparing unstereotyped behavior and intelligence in human and nonhuman primates. In *Primate Biosocial Development: Biological, Social, and Ecological Determinants*, eds. S. Chevalier-Skolnikoff and F. Poirer. New York: Garland.

Pascual-Leone, J. 1976. The forms of knowing in the psychological organisms. *Philosophy of the Social Sciences* 6:175–181.

Paterson, D. G., and D. M. Andrew. 1946. *Manual for the Minnesota vocational test for clerical workers*. New York: Psychological Corporation.

Pelto, P. J. 1968. The difference between "tight" and "loose" societies. *Transaction* 4:37–40.

Peluffo, N. 1962. Les notions de conservation et de causalité chez les enfants provenant de différents milieux physiques et socio-culturels. *Archives de Psychologie* 38:275–291.

——— 1967. Culture and cognitive problems. *International Journal of Psychology* 2:187–198.

Perret-Clermont, A. N. 1980. *Social interaction and cognitive development in children*. London: Academic Press.

Piaget, J. 1950. *The psychology of intelligence*. London: Routledge and Kegan Paul.

——— 1951. *Play, drama and imitation in childhood*. New York: Norton.

——— 1952. *The child's conception of number*. London: Routledge and Kegan Paul.

——— 1964. Development and learning. In *Piaget rediscovered*, eds. E. R. Ripple and V. N. Rockcastle. Ithaca, N. Y.: Cornell University Press.

——— 1966. Need and significance of cross-cultural studies on genetic psychology. *International Journal of Psychology* 2:3–13.

——— 1967. Problems of genetic psychology. In *Six psychological studies*, ed. D. Elkind. New York: Random House.

——— 1969. *The mechanisms of perception*. New York: Basic Books.

——— 1970. Piaget's theory. In *Carmichael's manual of child psychology*, vol. 1, 3rd ed., ed. P. Mussen. New York: John Wiley.

——— 1972. Intellectual evolution from adolescence to adulthood. *Human Development* 15:1–12.

Piaget, J., Vinh-Bang, and B. Matalon. 1958. Note on the law of the temporal maximum of some optico-geometric illusions. *American Journal of Psychology* 71:277–282.

Piaget, J., and B. von Albertini. 1950. L'illusion de Muller-Lyer. *Archives de Psychologie* 33:1–48.

Pike, K. L. 1966. *Language in relation to a unified theory of the structure of human behavior*. The Hague: Mouton.

Platts, J. T. 1977. *A dictionary of Urdū, classical Hindī and English*. New Delhi: Oriental Books Reprint Corp.

Poirer, F. E. 1972. *Primate socialization*. New York: Random House.

Pollack, R. H. 1970. Muller-Lyer illusion: effect of age, lightness, contrast and hue. *Science* 170:93–95.

Pollack, R. H., and D. S. Silvar. 1967. Magnitude of the Muller-Lyer illusion in children as a function of the pigmentation of the fundus oculi. *Psychonomic Science* 8:83–84.

Porteus, S. D. 1918. The measurement of intelligence. *Journal of Educational Psychology* 9:13–31.

———— 1950. *The Porteus maze test and intelligence.* Palo Alto: Pacific Books.

Preale, I., Y. Amir, and S. Sharan. 1970. Perceptual articulation and task effectiveness in several Israeli subcultures. *Journal of Personality and Social Psychology* 15:190–195.

Price-Williams, D. R. 1961. A study concerning concepts of conservation of quantities among primitive children. *Acta Psychologica* 18:297–305.

———— 1962. Abstract and concrete modes of classification in a primitive society. *British Journal of Educational Psychology* 32:50–61.

———— 1969. *Cross-cultural studies.* Harmondsworth, England: Penguin Books.

———— 1974. Psychological experiment and anthropology: the problem of categories. *Ethos* 2:95–114.

———— 1975. *Explorations in cross-cultural psychology.* San Francisco: Chandler and Sharp.

———— 1981. Concrete and formal operations. In *Handbook of cross-cultural human development,* eds. R. Monroe, R. Monroe, and B. Whiting. New York: Garland.

Price-Williams, D. R., W. Gordon, and M. Ramirez. 1969. Skill and conservation: a study of pottery-making children. *Developmental Psychology* 1:769.

Prince, J. R. 1968. The effect of western education on science conceptualization in New Guinea. *British Journal of Educational Psychology* 68:64–74.

———— 1969. *Science concepts in a Pacific culture.* Sydney: Angus and Robertson.

Ramirez, M., and D. R. Price-Williams. 1974. Cognitive styles in children: two Mexican communities. *Inter-American Journal of Psychology* 8(1–2):93–101.

Reed, E. S., and R. K. Jones. 1977. Towards a definition of living systems: a theory of ecological support for behavior. *Acta Biotheoretica* 26:153–163.

———— 1979. James Gibson's ecological revolution in psychology. *Philosophy of Social Sciences* 9:189–204.

Reed, H. J., and J. Lave. 1979. Arithmetic as a tool for investigating relations between culture and cognition. *American Ethnologist* 6(3):568–582.

Rehfish, R., ed. 1975. *Gypsies, tinkers and other travellers.* London: Academic Press.

Reuning, H., and W. Wortley. 1973. Psychological studies of the Bushman. *Psychologia Africana Monograph Supplement* 7:1–113.

Rivers, W. H. R. 1901. Introduction and vision. In *Reports of the Cambridge anthropological expedition to the Torres Straits,* ed. A. C. Haddon. vol. II, Pt. I. Cambridge: The University Press.

———— 1905. Observations of the sense of the Todas. *British Journal of Psychology* 1:321–396.

Robinson, J. 1972. *The psychology of visual illusions.* London: Hutchinson University Press.

Rogoff, B. 1978. Spot observation: an introduction and examination. *Quarterly Newsletter of the Institute for Comparative Human Development* 2:21–26.

———— 1981. Adults and peers as agents of socialization: a highland Guatemala profile. *Ethos* 9(1):18–36.

Ruhela, S. P. 1968. *The Gaduliya Lohars of Rajasthan: a study in the sociology of nomadism.* New Delhi: Impex India.

Salkind, N. J. 1977. Cognitive tempo in Japanese and American children. Paper presented at meeting of the Society for Research in Child Development, March, 1977, New Orleans.

Samuels, H. 1980. The effect of an older sibling on infant locomotor exploration of a new environment. *Child Development* 51:607–609.

Schimek, J. G. 1968. Cognitive style and defenses: a longitudinal study of intellectualization and field-independence. *Journal of Abnormal Psychology* 73:575–580.

Schwartz, D. W., and S. A. Karp. 1967. Field-dependence in a geriatric population. *Perceptual and Motor Skills* 24:495–504.

Scribner, S. 1976. Situating the experiment in cross-cultural research. In *The developing individual in a changing world*, eds. K. Riegel and J. Meacham. Chicago: Aldine.

Scribner, S., and M. Cole. 1978. Literacy without schooling: testing for intellectual effects. *Harvard Educational Review* 48(4):448–461.

Seder, J. A. 1957. The origin of differences in extent of independence in children: developmental factors in perceptual field-dependence. Unpublished Bachelor's thesis, Radcliffe College.

Segall, M. H., D. T. Campbell, and M. J. Herskovits. 1963. Cultural differences in the perception of geometric illusions. *Science* 139:769–771.

———— 1966. *The influence of culture on visual perception.* New York: Bobbs-Merrill.

Sellers, M. J., R. Klein, J. Kagan, and C. Minton. 1972. Developmental determinants of attention: a cross-cultural replication. *Developmental Psychology* 6:185.

Serpell, R. 1971a. Discrimination of orientation by Zambians. *Journal of Comparative and Physiological Psychology* 75:312–316.

———— 1971b. Preference for specific orientation of abstract shapes among Zambian children. *Journal of Cross-Cultural Psychology* 2:225–239.

———— 1976. *Culture's influence on behavior.* London: Methuen.

———— 1977a. Strategies for investigating intelligence in its cultural context. *Quarterly Newsletter of the Institute for Comparative Human Development* 1(3):11–16.

———— 1977b. Context and connotation: the negotiation of meaning in a multiple speech repertoire. *Quarterly Newsletter of the Institute for Comparative Human Development* 1(4):10–15.

Siann, G. 1972. Measuring field-dependence in Zambia: a cross-cultural study. *International Journal of Psychology* 7:87–96.

Sigel, I., and F. Hooper. 1968. *Logical thinking in children: research based on Piaget's theory.* New York: Holt, Rinehart and Winston.

Silberbauer, G. 1972. The G/wi Bushman. In *Hunters and gatherers today*, ed. M. G. Bicchieri. New York: Holt, Rinehart and Winston.

Singer, M. 1961. A survery of culture and personality research. In *Studying personality cross-culturally*, ed. B. Kaplan. New York: Row, Peterson.

Singer, M., and B. Cohn. 1968. *Structure and change in an Indian society*. Chicago: Aldine.

Skinner, B. F. 1966. The phylogeny and ontogeny of behavior. *Science* 153:1205–1213.

Spence, K. W., and J. L. Spence. 1966. Sex and anxiety differences in eyelid conditioning. *Psychological Bulletin* 65:137–142.

Spindler, G., ed. 1978. *The making of psychological anthropology*. Berkeley: University of California Press.

Spooner, B. 1973. *The cultural ecology of pastoral nomads*. Addison-Wesley Modular Publications no. 45.

Srinivas, M. N. 1966. *Social change in modern India*. Berkeley: University of California Press.

Staples, R. 1932. The responses of infants to color. *Journal of Experimental Psychology* 15:119–141.

Stevenson, M., and M. Lamb. 1979. Effects on infant sociability and the caretaking environment on infant cognitive performance. *Child Development* 50:340–349.

Stewart, V. M. 1973. Tests of the "carpentered world" hypothesis by race and environment in America and Zambia. *International Journal of Psychology* 8:83–94.

Stewart-Van Leeuwen, M. S. 1978. A cross-cultural examination of psychological differentiation in males and females. *International Journal of Psychology* 13(2):87–122.

Stroop, J. R. 1935. Studies of interface in serial verbal learning. *Journal of Exerimental Psychology* 18:643–672.

Super, C. M. 1981. Behavioral development in infancy. In *Handbook of cross-cultural human development*, eds. R. H. Monroe, R. L. Monroe, and B. B. Whiting. New York: Garland.

Super, C. M., S. Harkness, and L. M. Baldwin. 1977. Category behavior in natural ecologies and in cognitive tests. *Quarterly Newsletter of the Institute for Comparative Development* 1(4):4–7.

Tandon, P. 1961. *Punjabi century: 1857–1947*. Berkeley: University of California Press.

Taylor, W. S. 1948. Basic personality in orthodox Hindu culture patterns. *Journal of Abnormal Social Psychology* 43:3–12.

Tiffin, J., and E. J. Asher. 1948. The Purdue pegboard: norm and studies of reliability and validity. *Journal of Applied Psychology* 32:234–247.

Tolman, E. C., and E. Brunswik. 1935. The organism and the causal texture of the environment. *Psychological Review* 42:43–47.

Tönnies, F. 1957. *Community and society*, trans. C. P. Loomis. New York: Harper Torchbooks.

Triandis, H. C. 1972. *The analysis of subjective culture*. New York: John Wiley.
——— 1973. Subjective culture and economic development. *International Journal of Psychology* 8:163–180.

Tuddenham, R. D. 1968. Psychometricizing Piaget's method clinique. Paper presented at the American Educational Research Association convention, February, 1968, Chicago.

———— 1969. A "Piagetian" test of cognitive development. Paper presented at the Symposium on Intelligence, Ontario Institute for Studies in Education, Toronto.

Underwood, B. 1957. *Psychological research*. New York: Appleton.

Vayda, A. P. 1969. *Environment and cultural behavior*. Garden City, N. Y.: Natural History Press.

Vayda, A. P., and R. A. Rappaport. 1968. Ecology, cultural and non-cultural. In *Introduction to cultural anthropology*, ed. J. Clifton. Boston: Houghton Mifflin.

Vernon, P. E. 1965a. Ability factors and environmental influences. *American Psychologist* 20:723–733.

———— 1965b. Environmental handicaps and intellectual development. *British Journal of Educational Psychology* 35:9–20, 117–126.

———— 1966. Educational and intellectual development among Canadian Indians and Eskimos. *Educational Review* 17:79–91, 186–195.

———— 1967a. Administration of group intelligence tests to East African pupils. *British Journal of Educational Psychology* 37:282–291.

———— 1967b. Abilities and educational attainments in an East African environment. *Journal of Special Education* 4:335–345.

———— 1969. *Intelligence and cultural environment*. London: Methuen.

Vigeland, K. 1973. Cognitive style among rural Norwegian children. *Scandinavian Journal of Psychology* 14:305–309.

Von Cranach, M., K. Foppa, W. Lepenies, and D. Ploog, eds. 1979. *Human ethology: claims and limits of a new discipline*. Cambridge: Cambridge University Press.

Wallace, A. F. C. 1970. *Culture and personality*, 2nd ed. New York: Random House.

Wechsler, D. 1958. *The measurement and appraisal of adult intelligence*. Baltimore: Williams and Wilkins.

Wei, T. T. O. 1966. Piaget's concept of classification: a comparative study of advantaged and disadvantaged young children. Unpublished Ph.D. thesis, University of Illinois.

Weitz, J. M. 1971. Cultural change and field dependence in two native Canadian linguistic families. Ph.D. dissertation, University of Ottawa.

Weller, L., and S. Sharan. 1971. Articulation of body concept among first-grade Israeli children. *Child Development* 42:233–250.

Werner, E. E. 1972. Infants around the world: cross-cultural studies of psychomotor development from birth to two years. *Journal of Cross-Cultural Psychology* 3:111–134.

———— 1979. *Cross-cultural child development: a view from the planet Earth*. Monterey, Calif.: Brooks/Cole.

Werner, E. E., L. Simonian, and R. Smith. 1968. Ethnic and socioeconomic status differences in abilities and achievement among preschool and school-age children in Hawaii. *Journal of Social Psychology* 75:43–59.

White, B. L., and P. W. Castel. 1964. Visual exploratory behavior following post-natal handling of human infants. *Perceptual and Motor Skills* 18:497–502.

Whiting, B., and J. Whiting. 1975. *Children of six cultures: a psychocultural analysis.* Cambridge, Mass.: Harvard University Press.

Whiting, J. W. M. 1981. Environmental constraints on infant care practices. In *Handbook of cross-cultural human development*, eds. R. H. Monroe, R. L. Monroe, and B. B. Whiting. New York: Garland.

Whiting, J. W. M., I. L. Child, and W. W. Lambert. 1966. *Field Guide for the study of socialization.* New York: John Wiley.

Wikeley, J. M. 1932. *Punjabi Musalmans.* Lahore: Book House Press.

Wilber, D. N. 1964. *Pakistan: yesterday and today.* New York: Holt, Rinehart and Winston.

Williams, T. R. 1975. *Introduction to socialization: human culture transmitted.* St. Louis: C. V. Mosby.

Williams, T. R., ed. 1975. *Socialization and communication in primary groups.* Chicago: Mouton.

Witkin, H. A. 1952. Further studies of perception of the upright when the direction of the force acting on the body is changed. *Journal of Experimental Psychology* 43:9–20.

——— 1965. Psychological differentiation and forms of pathology. *Journal of Abnormal Psychology* 70:317–336.

——— 1967. A cognitive style approach to cross-cultural research. *International Journal of Psychology* 2:233–250.

——— 1969. Social influences in the development of cognitive style. In *Handbook of socialization theory and research*, ed. D. A. Goslin. New York: Rand McNally.

Witkin, H. A., and J. W. Berry. 1975. Psychological differentiation across cultures: a theoretical and empirical integration. *Journal of Cross-Cultural Psychology* 6:5–87.

Witkin, H. A., J. Birnbaum, S. Lomonaco, S. Lehr, and J. L. Herman. 1963. *Psychological differentiation: studies of development.* New York: John Wiley.

Witkin, H. A., P. W. Cox, and F. Friedman. 1976. *Field-dependence-independence and psychological differentiation: bibliography with index.* RB-76-28. Princeton: Educational Testing Service.

Witkin, H. A., P. W. Cox, F. Friedman, A. G. Hrishikesan, and K. N. Siegel. 1974. *Supplement 1, field-dependence/independence and psychological differentiation: bibliography with index.* Research Bulletin 74–42. Princeton: Educational Testing Service.

Witkin, H., R. B. Dyke, H. F. Faterson, D. R. Goodenough, and S. A. Karp. 1962. *Psychological differentiation.* New York: Wiley.

Witkin, H. A., and D. R. Goodenough. 1977. Field dependence and interpersonal behavior. *Psychological Bulletin* 84 (4):661–689.

Witkin, H. A., D. R. Goodenough, and S. A. Karp. 1967. Stability of cognitive style from childhood to young adulthood. *Journal of Personality and Social Psychology* 7:291–300.

Witkin, H. A., D. R. Goodenough, and P. K. Oltman. 1977. *Psychological differentiation: current status.* RB-77-17. Princeton: Educational Testing Service.

Witkin, H. A., H. B. Lewis, M. Hertzman, K. Lachover, P. B. Meissner, and S. Wapner. 1954. *Personality through perception: an experimental and clinical study.* New York: Harper.

Witkin, H. A., and P. K. Oltman. 1968. Cognitive style. *International Journal of Neurology* 6:119–137.

Witkin, H. A., P. K. Oltman, P. W. Cox, E. Erlichman, R. M. Hamm, and R. W. Ringler. 1973. *Field-dependence/independence and psychological differentiation: a bibliography through 1972 with index*. Research bulletin 73–62. Princeton: Educational Testing Service.

Witkin, H. A., P. K. Oltman, E. Raskin, and S. A. Karp. 1971. *A manual for the embedded figures test*. Palo Alto: Consulting Psychologists Press.

Witkin, H. A., D. Price-Williams, M. Bertini, B. Christiansen, P. K. Oltman, M. Ramirez, and J. Van Meel. 1974. Social conformity and psychological differentiation. *International Journal of Psychology* 9:11–29.

Wober, M. 1966. Sensotypes. *Journal of Social Psychology* 70:181–189.

Wundt, W. 1916. *Elements of folk psychology*. London: Allen and Unwin.

Zadik, B. 1968. Field-dependence/independence among Oriental and Western school children. *Behavioral Science Quarterly* 16:51–58.

Index

abuse, 110–111; as skill, 112
achievement, sex differences in, 38
acrobats, 103–104
adaptivity: of cognitive style, 185; psychological differentiation and, 189
age, 199–208 passim; field independence/dependence and, 31; labor division by, 108–109; perceptual inference and, 156–171 passim, 183; of test takers, 69–70. *See also* intergenerational activities
aggressiveness: cognitive style and, 32; field independence and, 179; of Kanjar females, 127, 132
Ahmad, S., 136
alliances among Qalandar tents, 86–87, 88, 93
almsgiving, 106. *See also* begging
Altmann, J., 23
amplifiers, 45–48, 49. *See also* cognitive amplifiers
animals, 82–84; author and, 62; care of, 108–109, 129; discussions of, 3; distribution of, 80, 84; training, 95
articulation, perceptual/cognitive, 30, 40, 64–66, 186
artisans, nomadic, 1. *See also* Kanjar
Asian brown bear, 83, 94, 95, 98, 99
associations, perceptual-motor, 215n8
attention, focusing of, 178; psychological performance and, 44, 50. *See also* observation
audiences, sensitivity to, 97–98, 103, 186
autonomy, 185; in loose societies, 34–35, 37; of nomads, 180, 183. *See also* self-reliance

bacha jhamura, 101–102, 120, 122
bagpipes, 77, 78
Baluch, 63
bandarwālā, 94, 96–98, 123, 186
Barry, H., 33–34, 38, 178
Basham, A. L., 132–133, 143–144
Bateson, G., 191
bathing, 120–121
Bazigar, 58, 123
bears, 5, 94–95, 98–101, 196. *See also* Asian brown bear; Kashmiri black bear
begging, 106–107, 123; by bērūpiā, 104–105, 106–107; children and, 5, 6, 106–107, 119, 120, 123; discussions of, 3; Kanjar, 128, 129, 130, 131, 132
behavior: group and individual, 3–4; village children's, 141–142
behaviorists, 16
Benedict, Ruth, 16
Berry, J. W., 178–179, 185; on cognitive socialization, 41; on differentiation, 28; on dependency, 184–185; ecological model of, 35–40, 49, 52, 53, 186, 189; on Muller-Lyer, 176
bērūpiā, 104–106, 123
bhālūwālā, 94, 98–101
biological factors in psychology, 18, 19–20, 21, 176–177, 185
biradari, 75, 85, 128
Boas, Franz, 15
Bock, D., 176
bovar (brideprice), 89, 90, 91, 128
Bovet, M. C., 48
breast feeding, 114
brideprice, 89, 90, 91, 128
British in Pakistan, 4, 73–74, 144

Darwin, Charles, 13
Dasen, P. R., 24–25, 26, 27, 48–49
Dashiell, J. P., 16
defecation, infants', 118–119
demand characteristics, 183, 191
dependence, *see* perceptual field independence/dependence; self-reliance
determinism, situational, 188–189
development, perceptual–cognitive: socialization and, 40–41; stimulus field and, 29–30
differentiation, psychological, 27–42 passim, 178, 179, 185; adaptiveness of, 189; by Qalandar, 96; testing influences on, 66
discussions, evening (Qalandar), 3–4, 6
discontinuous quantities, 209, 213
disembedding, 66, 172, 182, 185, 214–215n6
disputes, author's neutrality in, 63
divorce among Qalandar, 85, 90, 91
dogs, 83
donkeys, 82, 83, 84
dress, Qalandar, 78
drums (dug-dug-gee), 77, 78

earnings, sharing of, 110–111
ecocultural model, *see* Berry, J. W.
ecocultural settings, psychological performance and, 8
ecoculture: sensorimotor activities and, 19–20; use of term, 9
ecological functionalism, 178
ecological model, *see* Berry, J. W.
ecological press, 36
ecology, psychological functioning and, 1–2
economy, socialization strategies and, 34
education, formal: perceptual inference habits and, 180, 181; test results and, 156–157, 158, 161–162, 169, 171, 180–181, 199–208 passim; of test takers, 69–70, 180–181
EFT, *see* Embedded Figures Test
Egler, Z., 139–141
Embedded Figures Test, 29, 38, 67–68, 215n8
"emic" interpretations, 151, 154, 155, 156, 165
emotions, nomads', 180
encouragement among Qalandar, 183
endogamy, Kanjar, 128
engagements, marital, 88–89
entertainers, 1, 122–123; perceptual inference and skills of, 165–166; popularity of, 73. *See also* acrobats; audiences;

bacha jhamura; bandarwālā; bērūpiā; bhālūwālā; dancing; jugglers; magicians
environment: cognitive amplifiers and, 191–192; experience, behavior, and, 18; perception and, 16–18
equilibration, in Piaget's theory, 21
Eskimo, 26, 38–39, 40, 48
ethnocentrism, 191, 192
ethnography: natural contexts and, 169; psychological functioning and, 1–3; role of, 7
"etic" assumptions, 151–152, 155, 156
evaluation by group (Qalandar), 149–150
evening activities, 3–4, 6
evil eye, 100, 115, 116, 119
exchange marriage, 128
experiences, 195; cognitive amplifiers and, 186, 191; conservation and, 181–185; nomads' versus sedentists', 158, 180; perception and, 44–45; perceptual skills and, 174, 175–176, 178; psychological differentiation and, 179; psychological performance and, 42, 149–150, 196; Qalandar analysis of, 3–5, 6; Qalandar versus Kanjar, 159–160; research approaches to, 195–196; varied access to, 50
experiments: analysis of, 202–208; in natural contexts, 193; success and, 3, 154

families, 185; in ecological model, 37; of sedentists, 158, 162; structure of, 53; tents and, 85
farmers: field dependence of, 41; Jat, 132–142; psychological conservation and, 48–49. *See also* villagers
farming, 55, 56. *See also* harvest
farms, size of, 216n1, ch. 7
females: Algerian, 48; dominant, 130–131; Kanjar, 126, 127, 128, 129–130, 131, 132. *See also* girls; purdah; sex roles; sexual jokes; women
field independence/dependence, *see* perceptual field independence/dependence
Firth, Raymond, 9
fishermen, 36, 194
flexibility: emphasis on, 51, 87–88, 93, 184; of experience, 180; field independence and, 162; of peripatetics versus sedentists, 179; spatial mobility and, 82
fluidity of social organization, 53, 87–88, 180
food: accumulation of, 34, 36–38; for animals, 82, 83; distribution of, 110–111,